Access your online resources

Morph Mastery: A Morphological Intervention for Reading, Spelling and Vocabulary is accompanied by a number of printable online materials, designed to ensure this resource best supports your professional needs.

Activate your online resources:

Go to www.routledge.com/cw/speechmark and click on the cover of this book
Click the "Sign in or Request Access" button and follow the instructions in order to access the resources

‘*Morph Mastery* uses recent research on the development of morphological knowledge to support structured and cumulative learning. The games are fun and adaptable, the learners are encouraged to develop independence through their “word espionage” and the materials are engaging for all ages.’

Professor Julia Carroll

Morph Mastery

Morph Mastery is an accessible, practical guide designed to support learners with specific learning difficulties (SpLD) who are struggling with spelling, reading and vocabulary. It is an effective, research-based and fun solution for when phonics-based teaching has run its course.

Understanding the morphological regularities in English helps to support both spelling and reading comprehension, yet there are few practical interventions that take a morphological approach. *Morph Mastery* combines this exciting new approach with tried-and-tested teaching methods that work. The activities in this book follow three engaging ninja-like characters, Prefa, Root and Sufa, who represent the three core components of morphology (prefixes, root words and suffixes) and use their sceptres to craft words.

Key features include:

- Exciting and engaging activities and games, designed to be used by individuals or small groups
- Detailed, curriculum-linked assessments, enabling specific target setting
- Photocopiable and downloadable activity sheets and resources

Written in a user-friendly tone, for teaching assistants, teachers and other professionals with little or no specialist knowledge, this book is a must for any school with struggling readers and writers aged 9–13.

Louise Selby is a primary trained teacher with 20 years of experience in teaching and supporting learners with Special Educational Needs in mainstream schools. After a number of years of class-based teaching, support teaching and SENCO experience in primary schools, Louise spent 11 years working for Hertfordshire Local Authority as a specialist advisory teacher for specific learning difficulties across the age ranges. She now works freelance in consulting, training and assessing for specific learning difficulties and dyslexia. For more information about Louise's work, visit her website on www.louiseselbydyslexia.com.

Morph Mastery

A Morphological Intervention for Reading, Spelling and Vocabulary

LOUISE SELBY

LONDON AND NEW YORK

First published 2022
by Routledge
2 Park Square, Milton Park, Abingdon, Oxon OX14 4RN

and by Routledge
605 Third Avenue, New York, NY 10158

Routledge is an imprint of the Taylor & Francis Group, an informa business

British Library Cataloguing-in-Publication Data
A catalogue record for this book is available from the British Library

Library of Congress Cataloging-in-Publication Data
Names: Selby, Louise, author.
Title: Morph mastery : a morphological intervention for reading, spelling and vocabulary / Louise Selby.
Description: London ; New York : Routledge, 2021. | Includes bibliographical references and index.
Identifiers: LCCN 2020057182 (print) | LCCN 2020057183 (ebook) | ISBN 9780367725761 (hardback) | ISBN 9780367420000 (paperback) | ISBN 9780367817220 (ebook)
Subjects: LCSH: English language—Remedial teaching. | English language—Study and teaching (Elementary) | English language—Morphology. | Learning disabled children—Education.
Classification: LCC LB1029.R4 S45 2021 (print) | LCC LB1029.R4 (ebook) | DDC 372.43—dc23
LC record available at https://lccn.loc.gov/2020057182
LC ebook record available at https://lccn.loc.gov/2020057183

ISBN: 978-0-367-72576-1 (hbk)
ISBN: 978-0-367-42000-0 (pbk)
ISBN: 978-0-367-81722-0 (ebk)

Typeset in Antitled
by Apex CoVantage, LLC

Access the companion website: www.routledge.com/cw/speechmark

Contents

Foreword

People often dismiss the English spelling system as irregular and opaque. In fact, many of these 'irregularities' can be explained when we understand that English is a morphophonemic system – in other words, spellings depend on more than just phonetics. They also depend upon the morphemes, or units of meaning, within the words. For example, the word 'interrupt' has two 'r's in it because it is formed of the morphemes 'inter' and 'rupt'. The word 'sign' has a silent 'g' because it shares a root with 'signature' and 'signal'.

Understanding the morphological regularities in our language help to support both spelling and reading comprehension. This is well established in academic research. It has also been shown that it is particularly helpful for those with literacy difficulties. My own research has shown that individuals with literacy difficulties have sensitivity to morphemes in words, but that they also tend to find them confusing and don't necessarily use morphological rules to support spelling. The logical conclusion is that we should teach morphological rules systematically to support reading and spelling, and that this is particularly important in struggling readers.

Whenever I present my research to educators, they always ask me to recommend a morphological teaching approach that is good quality and easy for a non-expert to use. Until now, I have found it difficult to recommend something. I believe that a successful programme would use similar principles to successful phonics-based tuition: the teaching should be structured, cumulative, and multi-sensory, the learning objectives clear and the materials should be engaging. I am now extremely pleased to be able to recommend the Morph Mastery programme, because I believe it does meet these criteria.

Teaching phonics to young children is a task that seems manageable: we have 26 letters and 44 sounds in the English language, and the task is to teach children which sounds map to which letters and letter combinations. Some of these mappings are extremely regular and common, others are less so, but still, the amount of information to be taught is quantifiable. The morphological system is much less manageable: there are hundreds of roots, prefixes and suffixes, all varying in how common, regular and productive they are. This can make the task of planning morphological teaching seem huge, even insurmountable.

Morph Mastery uses our recent research on the development of morphological knowledge to support structured and cumulative learning. However, it is also clear that the programme has been developed by an experienced teacher who understands the needs of other teachers. The programme uses the framework of the morphemes included in the UK Spelling, Punctuation and Grammar Curriculum to structure the programme, meaning that it aligns closely to the National Curriculum. Guidance on the words and morphemes to select and focus on is very clear and explicit, making it easy for teachers to use for children with a wide range of ages and abilities. The games are fun and adaptable, the learners are encouraged to develop independence through their 'word espionage' and the materials are engaging for all ages.

I commend Louise Selby for her work on *Morph Mastery*, and I am confident that it will help many teachers and learners master the morphological system for themselves.

Professor Julia Carroll

Acknowledgements

Heartfelt thanks go to Renate Manners, whose initial encouragement to push boundaries and think outside the box were the catalyst to this project. Thanks also to Julia Carroll and Hannah-Leigh Nicholls whose time and generosity with their research in the early days led me in the direction that I took with the intervention. I'm also extremely grateful to Judy Capener, without whose affirmation, time and encouragement I would probably not have continued the project.

Sincere thanks go to all staff and children involved in the pilot; especially Rosie Burlingham, Gill Carpenter, Michelle Curry, Kerri Duffy, Elizabeth Foley, Anne Langley, Gemma Rajiah, Clare Shafe, Annette Walker. Credits have been given to schools within the case studies chapter in the book. The level of commitment, teachability and sheer brilliance from these individuals far exceeded my expectations. Thanks to Anne Langley and Alison Moore for diligent proof-reading and commentary, which helped me to craft this book. Thanks also to my glamourous film stars, colleagues and friends who gave me so much support and time in so many ways, not least in filming the games: Claire Goudkoff, Anne Langley, Alison Moore, and Claire Smith. Thanks to my mum and dad, Rosemary and Alwyn Craig, for their expertise in Latin.

It takes a village to raise a book, as I have discovered this past year. I am so indebted to Clare Ashworth, Leah Burton and Cathryn Henderson for their expertise and support. I suspect that I am their author with SEN (special editing needs), and their patience and good humour with my endless questions has been really appreciated.

Finally thanks to my husband Eddy for his love, patience and support and to the superstar who is Sidney, my awesome son, who was willing to try everything and was so very generous with his mum's time, enabling me to complete this book.

Author's note

Morph Mastery was crafted with the UK English curriculum in mind. However, all of the assessments and resources are just as applicable in other English-speaking countries. The age ranges for year groups are as follows: Year 1 (5 – 6 years), Year 2 (6–7 years), Year 3 (7–8 years), Year 4 (8–9 years), Year 5 (9–10 years), Year 6 (10–11 years), Year 7 (11–12 years), Year 8 (12–13 years).

How to use this book

What do you want to do?	In other words	Where to find it
Understand the theory and application of basic morphology	Understand what morphology is and why we use it in teaching Understand key terminology involved in morphology and **Morph Mastery**	Chapter 1 Chapter 5
Understand spelling difficulties	Understand key reasons why some learners find spelling difficult	Chapter 2
Identify individual learners' gaps in spelling, reading words and language Set targets for teaching individuals and groups	Assess specific skills & knowledge Get the information you need to set SMART targets for personal and group learning plans Find out spelling gaps beyond phonics	Chapter 7 Chapter 7 Chapter 7
Understand the key skills and principles involved in delivering **Morph Mastery** in any context	Understand what **Morph Mastery** is all about Know the 3 golden rules in teaching **Morph Mastery** the intervention and how to apply them	Chapter 3 Chapter 4
Plan & Teach **Morph Mastery** the intervention	Administer Assessments Use the assessments to plan Be familiar with planning documents & word lists How to teach the lessons Games	Chapter 7 Chapter 8 Chapter 8 Chapter 9 Chapter 10
Use **Morph Mastery** in the whole class	Some ideas for use in class Adapting games for class	Chapter 11 Chapter 10
Monitor and evaluate impact of **Morph Mastery**	How **Morph Mastery** fits into the SEND Code of Practice (assess, plan, do and review) How to make sure you measure and evaluate impact What to do if it doesn't work	Chapter 6 Chapter 12 Chapter 12
See how **Morph Mastery** the intervention worked in the Hertfordshire pilot	Read the case studies View data from case studies	Case studies p. xv–xxiii Appendix 17

Case studies

The Morph Mastery pilot

Four Hertfordshire schools took part in a pilot of the Morph Mastery intervention during 2019–2020. The pilot was forced to a premature end in March 2020 due to the national lockdown in response to the coronavirus pandemic. However, much was still gained by all involved, and the experiences of practitioners, parents and children on the pilot have significantly influenced the content of this book. All the pupils involved in the pilot had been identified because of significant and persistent difficulties with literacy.

The pupils were assessed at the start and end of the pilot using the Wechsler Individual Achievement Test 3rd edition for Teachers (hereafter named WIAT 3T) and the Morph Mastery Assessments. A period of six months elapsed between entry and exit testing, as required by the WIAT 3T. The SENCOs and teaching assistants were all trained face to face prior to the intervention. Mutual feedback was offered regularly about the methods and materials, and data was collected at the end of the intervention.

The WIAT 3T measures Reading Comprehension, Word Reading, Oral Reading Fluency (the ability to read aloud both accurately and at speed) and Spelling. In the case studies, where the word "accelerated" is used to describe progress, this refers to where a pupil's progress was above what would be expected in six months (the time between entry and exit testing), and therefore what is considered to be noteworthy. For those who enjoy it, more technical information about standardised scores can be found in Appendix 17.

It's helpful to understand at this point that if expected progress has been made, standard scores and percentiles would be expected to ***stay the same***. Therefore, an increased standard score and percentile indicate accelerated progress; if they decrease, progress is less than expected. In contrast, reading and spelling ages would be expected to ***rise*** with expected progress over time. Therefore, the age equivalents for pupils in this pilot would be expected to rise by 6 months (the period between entry and exit testing). A rise of more than six months can be considered accelerated progress. In the case studies, some of the age equivalents for reading comprehension have not been cited. This is because those pupils whose reading comprehension rose to above the 50th percentile achieved extremely high reading ages which were not felt to be representative. However, all these scores are represented in Figure A17.1 in Appendix 17.

Heartfelt and extensive thanks go to the staff, parents and children at all four schools. The determination and enthusiasm that embraced the project made it not only successful, but extremely enjoyable. It was truly a privilege to work with such dedicated, humble and capable staff, as well as some tenacious, enthusiastic and remarkable pupils. In the following case studies the pupils' names have been changed.

Wilshere Dacre Junior Academy, Hitchin

Wilshere Dacre Junior Academy is a two-form entry Junior School. Anne Langley, who is employed as a Support Teacher, was trained with Gill Carpenter, the Inclusion Leader and Assistant Head. Anne taught Eve (Year 5) on a 1:1 basis, and Nathan (Year 5) and Ivan (Year 6) in a pair. All three children were identified for intervention because of their weakness in literacy and language. They all received nine weeks of intervention. Unfortunately, it was not possible to administer final assessments of Eve before lockdown, but she and her mother were interviewed over the telephone.

Anne's pupils loved the intervention, particularly the games, portals, handshake and characters. They loved to talk about words and to come up with words for themselves; there was a large amount of discussion. Anne felt that the intervention worked well in a pair, because "they worked so well together as a team and helped each other." The enthusiasm and discussion that was generated was really positive:

> ***As soon as I told them this week's root they were coming up with words. Sometimes I even had to slow them down in their word building so that we could get it right.***

Morph Mastery also helped Anne and Gill to more specifically identify the gaps in the pupils' language, in particular Ivan, who spoke English as an Additional Language:

> ***We had an idea that there were gaps in his English language development, but Morph Mastery meant that we were able to be much more specific. It isn't just a spelling difficulty for Ivan. For example, he didn't know the difference between "teachers" and "teaches". It has actually highlighted the gaps in all of the pupils' vocabulary and grammatical knowledge.***

Anne was surprised by the level of improvement her pupils made in their morphological awareness over the weeks, even Ivan, for whom this was a real challenge in the initial assessment. By the end of the intervention, she said that all the pupils were "tuning in to words much more actively". They had confidence to talk about parts of words they hadn't even been taught. She found that the change in Nathan in particular was obvious:

> ***I never expected such a clear, overt change. Just playing those games has really helped him to listen to the words and parts of words. Even when you've hit a word he doesn't know he's been able to***

think about the structure – he isn't floundering like he used to, he has a tool to think about it. I could see in the sessions how much he was really getting into words.

Anne advised any practitioners coming to Morph Mastery for the first time to not skip planning ahead of the lesson and to remember their targets:

Don't be too worried if you think it's not going to come because it really does. In a group, don't let them go off track; they really want to explore words, for example they were intrigued as to whether "recounter" could be a word and wanted to discuss it over and over again! It's a fine line between encouraging interest and staying with your targets. Be organised, especially with the games. You do need your resources, so get them ready in advance. Think about how you are going to organise them.

The pupils commented as follows:

I feel like I'm learning more. The games help. I practise at home.

(Ivan)

It's good. I seem like I am doing better in classes. I like doing prefixes and suffixes and changing words. I can recognise which suffixes to put on. The games are fun.

(Nathan)

I feel I understand it all better. I feel I can say what I mean.

(Eve)

Ivan made outstanding progress in all the areas in the WIAT 3T. His Reading Comprehension age increased by 20 months (more than three times the expected rate of progress) from 7 years 0 months to 8 years 8 months, shifting from the Well Below Average to Mid Average range. Ivan's Word Reading also improved dramatically, his reading age increasing from 6 years 8 months to 10 years 0 months (an increase of 38 months, more than six times the expected rate of progress), again a move from the Well Below Average to the Mid Average range. His Oral Reading Fluency age equivalent moved from 7 years 8 months to 8 years 8 months (double the expected rate of progress), and from the Well Below Average range to the Below Average range. Finally, his Spelling progressed from 6 years 4 months to 7 years 8 months (2.5 times the expected rate), moving from the Very Low range to the Well Below Average range. His teacher assessments also indicated good progress in reading and writing.

Nathan's progress in Reading Comprehension was also accelerated. His standard score increased by 15 points and his percentile from 34 to 73. In Word Reading, Nathan made less than expected progress, but his Oral Reading Fluency progress was accelerated, his age equivalent score increasing by 12 months

(double the expected rate of six months) from 9 years 8 months to 10 years 8 months. His teachers also reported accelerated progress in their school reading assessments. Nathan's progress in the Spelling assessment was less than expected, but it was felt by his teachers that his vocabulary had increased. His teachers also reported sound progress in writing. What was most noticeable in Nathan, and was reported by his teachers, was the change in his reading. When he started the intervention his reading speed was phenomenal, but the reading itself was full of errors. At the end, his speed was slower but with fewer errors, he had better comprehension of the text and more confidence.

Knebworth Primary and Nursery School

Knebworth Primary and Nursery School is a two to three form entry school. Two pupils and two teaching assistants were identified for 1:1 work in Morph Mastery. Rosie Burlingham, who is very experienced in delivering 1:1 interventions in Literacy, taught Elsie (Year 5), while Kerri Duffy, who was newer to 1:1 interventions, taught Mary (Year 6). Rosie and Kerri attended face to face training with the SENCO, Gemma Rajiah. Both the children selected, Elsie and Mary, were identified because of difficulties with spelling and writing. Elsie received 12 weeks of intervention, and Mary received nine weeks.

Both girls loved the games, portals, characters and handshake, and both adults commented on these, as well as the great discussion that was generated during the lessons. Rosie commented that Elsie was much more active in thinking about vocabulary by learning this way:

> ***It is really interesting and a fun way of looking at words. I've realised that we don't talk about spelling enough in school. We just give them a list of spellings. There is so much more meaning in words when you look at them this way. You aren't just learning spellings by rote but making sense of them.***

Rosie felt that the breaking up of words into parts was really helpful:

> ***I think they stick better because you are really zoning in. Elsie often struggles with reading words – she becomes tongue tied. Breaking them up into morphemes has really helped her. She loves the handshake for this as well.***

Kerri commented on how much fun she had had with Mary:

> ***She has thoroughly enjoyed it, like really enjoyed it. She's enjoyed learning new words and learning about words. She's loved putting the words together using the morpheme cards when she wasn't sure. She has enjoyed the feeling of it and seeing it in front of her. You can see she's really engaged when playing the games. It's really nice to see her confidence growing with it.***

Having used a number of phonics-based interventions before, Rosie commented on the very new way of looking at and teaching words. This was challenging to her at first, and she needed to read and plan carefully, but she enjoyed the experience and felt it was valuable:

> ***At first I was a bit frightened of it, but now I really enjoy it as well as Elsie. I am learning as well! We use the dictionary more, in looking things up, and thinking about what things mean.***

Rosie and Kerri both stressed the need to begin slowly and the importance of allocating time for planning:

> ***I would definitely try not to do too much at once. Concentrate on one game at first. Give yourself time to get your head around the terminology. Don't worry too much about the allotted time to start with – take it slowly until you get used to the lessons.***
>
> (Rosie)

> ***Do your preparation and make sure you have allocated time to do it. Otherwise the lessons will take much longer and it feels very pressurised; you'll miss bits. Get your box of resources ready first or it will take time out of your lesson.***
>
> (Kerri)

The class teachers of both girls, Kelly Reed-Peck and Grace Maynard, commented that they had noticed increased confidence and willingness to "have a go" in class. Both girls happily used their Morph Mastercard in class, and Elsie was reported to independently go and practise her Morph Mastery words in class.

Elsie was really pleased with her progress:

> ***I am better at spelling now because it has helped me to concentrate on the words. I understand my spellings better and know what to do. I understand words better now. I love the handshake. I know what the real parts of the words are. It helps me to know what the root is because I know the real bit. I read more quickly and my reading is definitely better. It's really fun.***

Mary also felt she had made progress and enjoyed herself:

> ***I like it – it's fun and enjoyable. I like the games especially the card games. I am better at spelling.***

Elsie was thrilled with her progress at the end of the intervention and she couldn't wait to tell her mum. Her Reading Comprehension improved dramatically from the Mid Average range to the Above Average range, and from the 47th percentile to the 87th percentile. Her Oral Reading Fluency showed accelerated progress; her age equivalent increased by 12 months (double the expected rate of 6 months), from 7 years 8 months to 8 years

8 months, and her score moved from the Low Average to the Mid Average range. Elsie's Word Reading Accuracy increased more than expected, as did her Spelling, with her age equivalent in both these areas increasing by eight months (two months more than the expected rate of six months), from 8 years 0 months to 8 years 8 months in both sub-tests. Her teacher assessments showed steady progress in reading and writing.

Mary also made accelerated progress in Reading Comprehension. Her percentile in this test moved from 50 to 77, from the Mid Average to the High Average range. Her Word Reading did not progress over the period, but her Oral Reading Fluency moved from the Low Average to the Mid Average range, and her age equivalent by 12 months from 8 years 4 months to 9 years 4 months. In spelling, Mary also made accelerated progress, increasing by eight months (two months more than the expected rate) from 7 years 8 months to 8 years 4 months, and from the Below Average to the Low Average range.

Ickleford Primary School, Ickleford, near Hitchin

Ickleford Primary School is a one form entry village school. Annette Walker is employed as a Special Educational Needs Teaching Assistant, whose focus is interventions. Annette is very experienced in delivering literacy interventions. Claire Shafe, the SENCO, attended training with Annette. Their Morph Mastery pupil, Matty, was identified because of increasing difficulty with spelling and writing as well as reading comprehension. Matty received 11 weeks of intervention.

Annette felt that the biggest bonus of Morph Mastery was the ability to explore words in ways that they hadn't done before, leading to increased vocabulary development:

> ***One of the things that has surprised me is that the intervention has supported Matty to develop his vocabulary, not just his spellings. It's not just about morphological awareness or spelling morphemes, I think it's also helping him to increase his vocabulary bank as well. It's bringing words to the fore that Matty wouldn't usually use.***

Like Rosie and Kerri at Knebworth, Annette also felt that it had been a joint learning curve:

> ***I haven't always considered how a word has been put together. I've learnt from it as well. I feel like it's been a joint journey. It's been really good to challenge my own thinking around words. Quite often Matty will come up with a word and I have to really think about it. So for example yesterday we had poisoner - we had to think about whether that is a word. Morph Mastery has reignited our love of the English language.***

Matty said that he loved the games, especially the Spinner Games and Happy Families. He also loved the highlighting. He said it had helped him with his work in class.

Matty also made accelerated progress in Reading Comprehension, his percentile moving from 8 to 68, from the Well Below Average range to the Mid Average Range. This is an outstanding improvement. His Word Reading progressed more than expected, as did his Oral Reading Fluency, his reading age in both cases increasing by 8 months, from 9 years 8 months to 10 years 4 months, an increase of two months more than expected. Matty's Spelling progress was accelerated, moving from the 39th to the 53rd percentile, his spelling age increasing by 12 months (double the expected six months) from 8 years 8 months to 9 years 8 months. His teacher assessment showed accelerated progress in reading and writing.

St Vincent de Paul Catholic Primary School, Stevenage

St Vincent de Paul Catholic Primary School is a two-form entry school. Two pupils were identified for 1:1 intervention; Phoebe (Year 5) and Tamsin (Year 6). The SENCO, Michelle Curry, was trained face to face in Morph Mastery, alongside Elizabeth Foley, a Teaching Assistant. Due to unforeseen circumstances beyond her and the school's control, Elizabeth was unable to continue teaching after four weeks, so I worked with Michelle to continue the programme myself. Tamsin received a total of nine weeks of intervention, and Phoebe received a total of six weeks (two of these were with the teaching assistant). Unfortunately, it was not possible to administer the final assessments for Phoebe before lockdown.

Before the intervention, Tamsin's vocabulary and language were good, but her teachers felt that her weak spelling prevented her from showing this in her writing. She lacked confidence and struggled to keep up. The Morph Mastery gave her a new spring in her step and both her reading and writing improved significantly. According to her class teacher, Simon Crump, her reading and writing in class displayed a new confidence:

> ***From a class perspective, Tamsin has absolutely flown in her writing since working with Morph Mastery. The ability to form sentences in a much more effective way has improved dramatically. Spelling of words has slightly improved and she is more willing to look back at certain words and identify what went wrong. I am very pleased with her progress.***

Tamsin was thrilled with her progress and enjoyed the lessons:

> ***I really like the games. I've learnt new things about words, especially Latin roots. It's helped me learn spelling rules. My writing is better and I can do more in class.***

Like the other pupils on the pilot, Tamsin made accelerated progress in Reading Comprehension, progressing from the 23rd percentile to the 63rd percentile and from a standard score of 89 to 105. This indicates a move from the Low Average range to the Mid Average range. She made good, but not accelerated, progress in Word Reading and Oral Reading Fluency, while her Spelling progress was accelerated, moving from the 5th percentile to the 18th percentile and the Well Below Average range to the Low Average Range, with an increase in spelling age by 20 months (more than three times the expected increase of six months) from 7 years 4 months to 9 years 0 months. She also made double the expected rate of progress in both reading and writing, according to her teacher assessment.

What emerged from the final assessments of Tamsin was that she had a specific weakness in reading speed. Because she had improved so much in her reading accuracy and comprehension, it was easier to see from the final test results that this was her specific problem, and therefore there was now a need to consider strategies to support her with speed of reading.

These case studies are purely anecdotal, and the sample small. However, inspection by eye leads to a few observations. Firstly, the level of accelerated progress was dramatic in reading comprehension. This might be surprising, given that Morph Mastery is a spelling intervention. However, given the strong focus on understanding and interpreting words and their meanings, it is understandable that comprehension is also improved. Many of the comments in the interviews referred to understanding words and appreciating their value, so it is no surprise that all pupils made very good progress in comprehension.

The second observation from the case studies is the positivity expressed about the experience of engaging actively with words, which seemed to help with confidence as well. In all the interviews, there was a strong sense of learners feeling empowered and confident with word play and investigation. This reflects the aim of Morph Mastery to enable learners to be powerful masters of words.

A third observation from the case studies is the extent to which practitioners said they enjoyed the morphological approach, finding it effective and meaningful. They all commented on the steep learning curve with a new methodology, but each practitioner commented very positively on this way of teaching spellings and vocabulary, finding it both effective and enjoyable.

In future, it would be interesting to conduct a similar pilot with a focus on a whole school approach to Morph Mastery. It would also be useful to gain statistically significant progress data from a larger sample of schools and pupils.

1. Morphology and the mastery of language

An introduction

Morphology is a key component of how English words are made up, but there are still many of us in education who have little understanding of what it is. It certainly has neither been a strong feature of mainstream literacy education nor a main feature of popular intervention programmes. However, research is increasingly showing us how important morphology is for learners of all abilities in reading and writing. More specifically, we learn through research that a morphological approach is ***particularly*** effective for struggling readers and spellers. It follows that there is a need among educators, especially those who teach students with spelling and reading difficulties, to understand and implement a morphological approach more systematically. *Morph Mastery: A Morphological Intervention for Reading, Spelling and Vocabulary* addresses this need, whilst also adopting the well-established principles of effective intervention: it is multi-sensory, cumulative, personalised and structured. Though designed as an intervention for individuals or small groups, many of its resources and games can also be used within a class for all learners.

Developed with the newcomer to morphology in mind, this manual is a step by step guide to teaching Morph Mastery. The good news to "morph newbies" is that morphology is neither difficult to understand, nor a new concept. To access and use this resource manual, you need neither prior knowledge of morphology nor a specialist qualification. In fact, all you need is access to a photocopier, children to work with, time and a willingness to learn. We'll start with the basics.

What is morphology?

Morphology is the system of language by which words can be broken up into units of meaning, called morphemes. Morphemes can be root words, prefixes or suffixes.

A ***morpheme*** is the term for any single unit of meaning. It is therefore by definition a root, prefix or suffix. A ***root*** is the purest unit of meaning within a word, once prefixes and suffixes are removed. It is the most basic form of a word. Roots can be words that we know and use in their own right (Figure 1.1). They can also derive from Greek or Latin (Figure 1.2). Due to the evolution of language, these Greek and Latin roots are not often used in our language today as words in their own right.

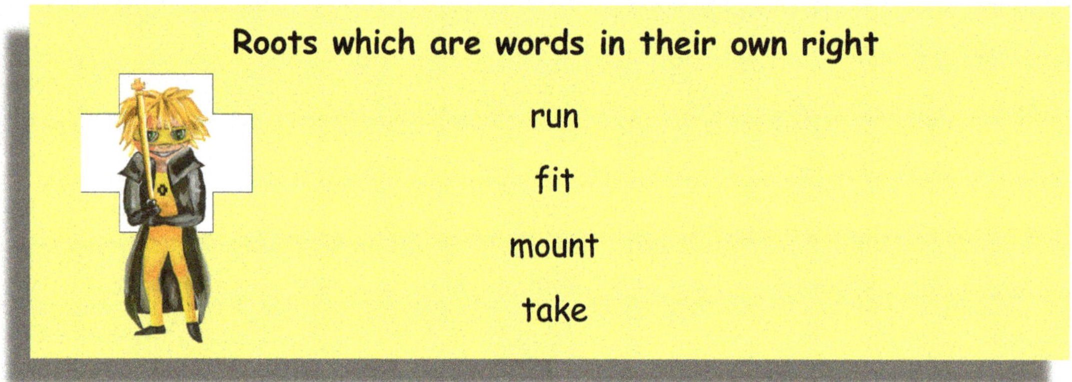

Roots which are words in their own right
run
fit
mount
take

Figure 1.1

Latin roots
port (carry)
scrib (write)
vac (empty)
Greek roots
biblio (book)
doc (teach)
dyno (power)

Figure 1.2

Prefixes are the units of meaning (morphemes) which are placed in front of a root. For example, the prefix ***re-*** can be added to the root ***take*** to create the word ***retake***. Prefixes are not words in themselves (Figure 1.3).

Figure 1.3

Suffixes, like prefixes, are not words in their own right, but units of meaning (morphemes) which are placed at the end of the word (Figure 1.4).

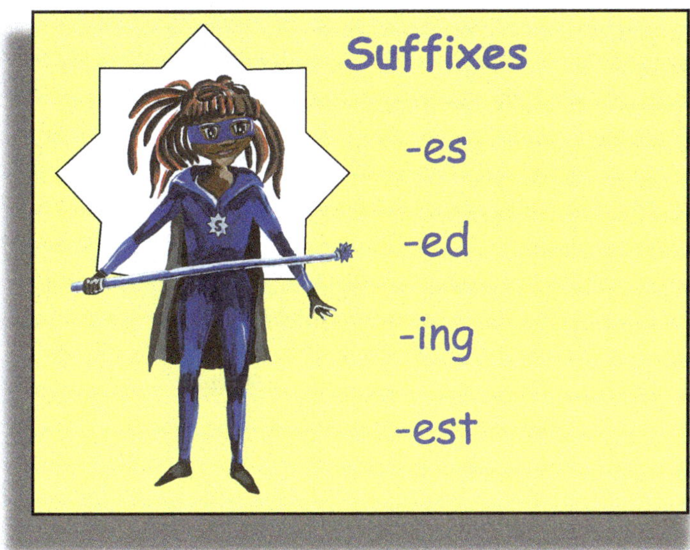

Figure 1.4

Let's piece all this together with some examples. The word ***mistaking*** has been formed from the root ***take***, with the prefix ***-mis*** and the suffix ***-ing***. ***Unkind*** has been formed from two morphemes: the prefix ***-un*** and the root ***kind. Stayed,*** also formed from two morphemes, is formed with the root ***stay*** and the suffix ***-ed***. This is morphology.

We have already mentioned Greek and Latin. This can be the point in a conversation about morphology where people become scared and feel disempowered. Don't! There are simple ways to crack these codes which can add immense value and breadth to your teaching of language and vocabulary, as well as spelling. Exciting connections between words can be made and layers of meaning added, as well as some very interesting conversations.

In general, the most basic and frequently used words in our language derive from Old English; for example **say, when, come, that, play, look, grow, child**; the list goes on. These are often words we use all the time, but they are also often tricky to spell and can be huge stumbling blocks for children with spelling difficulties. This is because the rules they follow are not phonetic and they sometimes appear bizarre to the phonetic speller.

The next layer of language usually derives from Latin; words we use regularly and with familiarity but words whose origin may not be fully understood by their users. For example, **cent** comes from the Latin word for **hundred** and is the root for many words; **centipede, century, centimetre**. **Rupt** means to tear and leads to **rupture, interrupt, erupt, bankrupt**. Knowing a few of these Latin origins can make all the difference when making sense of language and making exciting connections. Speaking as a parent, I often love being reminded that **pare** means make ready, so parent simply means getting someone ready for the world. Many more examples of these can be found in Appendix 15.

The third layer of language is Greek, which involves more sophisticated language, often words at the highest level of vocabulary, linked to education, science, maths, and culture. For example **pneu** means air and leads to words like **pneumatic** and **pneumonia**. **Micr** means small and leads to words like **microsope** and **microphone**. Again, this can be interesting when studying vocabulary. Telling a child that **tele** in **television** means afar can be a great way to ask him to move further back from the TV!

Greek and Latin morphemes usually come later on in the language curriculums, but ironically they are sometimes easier to learn to spell for learners with specific learning difficulties. They have fewer irregularities, there are fewer exceptions and they often follow phonetic rules. You don't need to know any Greek or Latin in order to teach morphology, but you will need to have an enquiring mind and know where to look for the origins of words. Appendix 15 in this book is a useful start. It is also useful to have access to a good dictionary (online or a hard copy).

Phonology and morphology, two different systems of language

It might be useful at this point to compare morphology with phonology, a system of language which is more familiar to many. Currently, phonology is much better understood than morphology by educational practitioners. Phonology underpins the teaching of phonics. In response to research, it is embedded in English curriculums in the UK, US, New Zealand and Australia, where it is a foundational methodology for teaching early reading.

While morphology is the system of language by which words are created from units of meaning, phonology is the system of language by which words are broken up into units of sound. According to morphology, words are constructed from units of meaning called morphemes, while phonology separates words into units of sound called phonemes.

Why is morphology important?

Both systems of language are involved in mastering the written English word, but morphology helps us to make sense of language in ways that phonology cannot. Sometimes phonic rules just do not apply. If they did, and words were always spelled as they sound, ***people*** would be spelled ***peeple*** or ***peaple***, ***onion*** would be ***unyun*** or ***unyoon***, ***Christmas*** would be ***crismous***, ***heard*** would be ***herd***, and ***two*** would be ***too***. Yet these words are not spelled as they sound and do not therefore follow phonic rules; they are therefore classed as "exception words". But are they really exceptions? Not if the rules are based on morphology.

Often, morphological principles can be applied to make sense of these "exceptions". Let's look at the word ***onion*** to illustrate this. Morphological rules explain its spelling. They tell us that the root of the word ***onion*** is ***one***, because an onion has one stem, and the suffix ***-ion*** means it is a noun. What we see here is that the word's spelling has evolved from its morphology, not its phonology, and its spelling is therefore not an exception. It makes sense – just with different rules. The trouble with school curriculums is that many words are classed as exceptions. In the British spelling curriculum they are known as Common Exception Words. These exception words can be the hardest words to learn. What if we chose not to call them exceptions, but applied morphological rules instead?

For example, ***people*** is a "Common Exception Word" in the spelling strand of the UK National Curriculum, and this word is a common stumbling block for children in primary school to whom spelling does not come easily. Morphology can help. It tells us that ***people*** derives from the Latin ***populous,*** and relates to ***population,*** which explains the non-phonetic exception **o.** The simple act of linking the exception word ***people*** with its morphological relative ***population*** can remind the learner to insert the **o** when spelling this word. It is no longer an exception.

Here are some more examples. The exception word **Christmas** is easier to learn if linked with the word ***Christ***. ***Heard*** is easier if linked by meaning to ***hear***. The rogue **w** in the word ***two*** is better understood when linked to ***twins*** and ***twice;*** the list could, and does, go on. Teaching these morphological links can dramatically reduce the number of exception words in our language and hence make learning to spell and understand words much easier.

Figure 1.5 further illustrates the problems that pupils encounter when they automatically apply phonics when tackling the spelling of unknown words. When writing the word ***foxes***, for example, a child might sound it out: ***f – o – x – i – z***. The spelling might then be written ***foxiz.*** A morphological approach would avoid this common error. The spelling of the suffix ***-es,*** which sounds like ***/iz/,*** would be taught, as well as its function, which is to create a syllable to make a plural. For example, we hear the /iz/ sound in the words foxes (fox + ***-es***), hisses (hiss + ***-es***), wishes (wish + ***-es***), boxes (box + ***-es***), misses (miss + ***-es***), and dishes (dish + ***-es***). Figure 1.5 provides this, and other examples of how a morphological approach makes it possible to explain and address some common spelling errors. It is by talking about the meaning and/or function of a morpheme as well as how to spell it that we can help pupils to recognise patterns in and between words. Morph Mastery delivers this approach.

Word	**Phonological structure (sounds)**	**Common phonetic error**	**Morphological structure**
Foxes	f + o + x + i + s	foxiz	fox (= fox), es (= plural pronounced /iz/ after certain consonants)
hunted	h + u + n + t + i + d	huntid	hunt(= hunt), ed (= past tense pronounced /id/ after certain consonants)
formless	f + or + m + l + er + ss	formlerss/ formlous	form (= shape), less (= without)

Figure 1.5

The experience for a learner with reading and spelling difficulties during the early primary school years, where there is such a strong focus on phonics, can be a vicious cycle (Figure 1.6). Difficulties grasping phonology and phonics lead to poor decoding and encoding skills for reading and spelling respectively. This can lead to lack of exposure to print, which in turn reduces opportunities to learn decoding for reading and encoding for spelling.

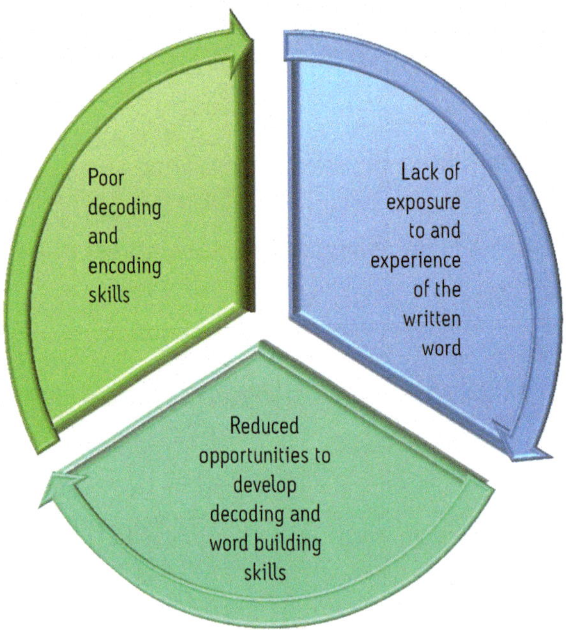

Figure 1.6 The vicious cycle of repeated phonics teaching

This vicious cycle can lead to reduced reading comprehension and vocabulary skills, as illustrated in Figure 1.7 (the legacy of poor reading and spelling). Reduced exposure to print leads to reduced exposure to vocabulary and reduced opportunity to develop higher level reading skills, which are fundamental in reading comprehension. In addition, the repetition of phonics-based intervention throughout Key Stage 2 can further reduce opportunities to link words to meaning.

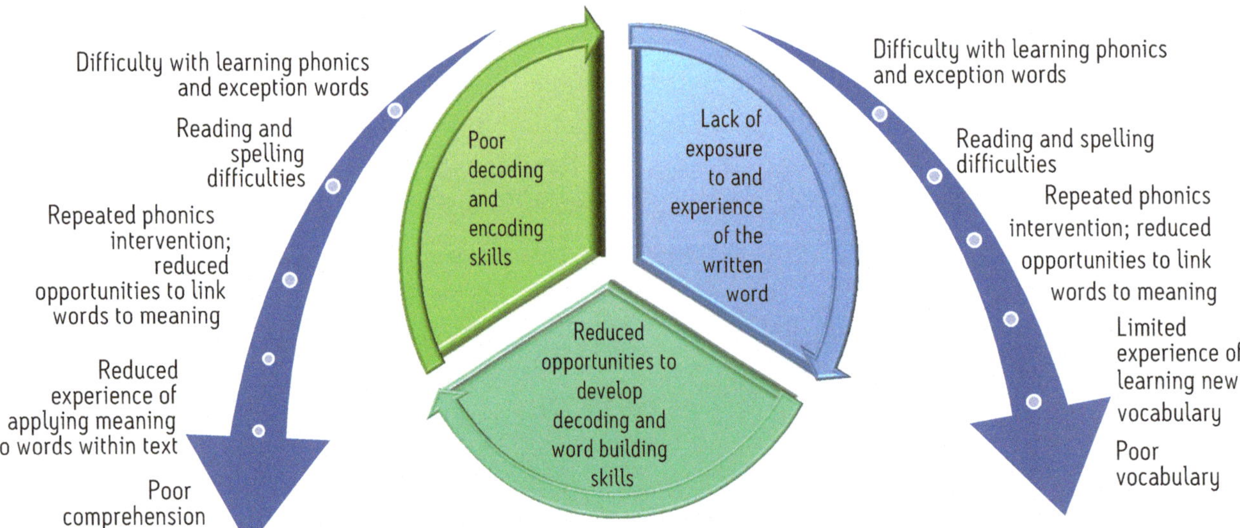

Figure 1.7 The legacy of poor reading and spelling

When learners start to make sense of language in a morphological way, they are relating parts of words to meaning and making sense of words. They develop strategies to analyse, explore and compare words, which help them to understand and tackle new words in reading and spelling in a way that teaching phonics does not. Vocabulary skills and reading comprehension are therefore enhanced. One teacher involved in the Morph Mastery pilot compared the morphological approach to cars. You can have a Vauxhall or a Ford, she said, but ultimately they are the same engine underneath all the bodywork. If we help learners to get underneath the bodywork, which is different in so many cars, we help them see the real structure and make sense of the whole car.

What can we learn from research about the importance of morphology?

We know from a growing and evolving body of research that understanding words morphologically is important in gaining literacy skills. Morph Mastery is founded on this research. There are three main findings which are foundational, as outlined below.

1. **Morphological awareness is highly influential when learning to read and write**
   We know that teaching morphology can support reading comprehension.[1] It supports metalinguistic skills (thinking and talking about words and language) which in turn helps the understanding of texts. We also know that teaching morphology supports vocabulary development.[2] The act of studying words and their different units of meaning through morphology has an obvious and direct link to understanding them. Morphological awareness, research tells us, is also an indicator of a learner's word reading ability[3] and spelling.[4] It is even thought by some researchers that morphological skills have a strong part to play in writing composition.[5]
2. **Morphological awareness can be trained**
   It is well established that poor phonological awareness is often a major stumbling block for many children with reading difficulties, but research also tells us that morphological awareness can help to compensate for this.[6] New research tells us that morphological awareness, like phonological awareness, can be trained through intervention, and that this improves literacy skills.[7]
3. **Pupils with reading difficulties respond particularly well to morphological awareness training**
   It has been recently discovered through research[8] that many poor readers have morphological awareness impairments. The conclusion is that reading difficulties often stem from weakness in some areas of language (and not just decoding and phonics difficulties). The same research found that while the cause of reading difficulties in children does not always stem from language weakness (in some cases early middle ear infections were the cause), a structured approach to morphological training is effective in all cases.

These three findings in research are highly significant in informing educators how to support pupils with weak literacy skills. Morph Mastery works because we know that pupils with reading difficulties respond well to morphological awareness training, and this improves their literacy outcomes.

Introducing The "M" Factor

Morphology can be exciting! In Morph Mastery, we are encouraging learners to become **M**asters of **M**orphology. It is more than a spelling programme; they will do far more than simply attaching prefixes and suffixes to words. A Morph Master develops power over words to transform meaning, comparing them and enjoying the simple complexities of word after word. Words can be analysed, investigated, discussed, and changed in exciting ways. Morph Mastery empowers the learner in the meaningful craft of words. This craft is known in Morph Mastery as The M Factor.

At the end of the Morph Mastery pilot, adults delivering the intervention all commented on this:

> "We've been able to explore words in a way that we wouldn't have been able to explore before."
>
> "We talk about words and meaning and there is so much discussion."
>
> "There is so much more meaning in words when you look at them this way. You aren't just learning spellings by rote but making sense of them."

Introducing the Morph Masters

There are three illustrated Morph Masters, called Prefa, Root and Sufa. They are ninja-like characters who each represent a different type of morpheme. Prefa represents prefixes, Root stands for his namesake, and the character representing suffixes is Sufa. They each carry word sceptres, which they use to craft and transform words and meaning. Their respective colours of green, yellow and blue are used throughout *Morph Mastery*.

Each character has its own symbol which is linked to that part of the word throughout the intervention: the fish, the cross and the star. These symbols have been made into "The Morph", a secret handshake designed for use only by Morph Masters and Morph Masters in training.

The Morph: a secret handshake

Step 1: The Fish (Prefa)

Two hands approach each other like swimming fish.

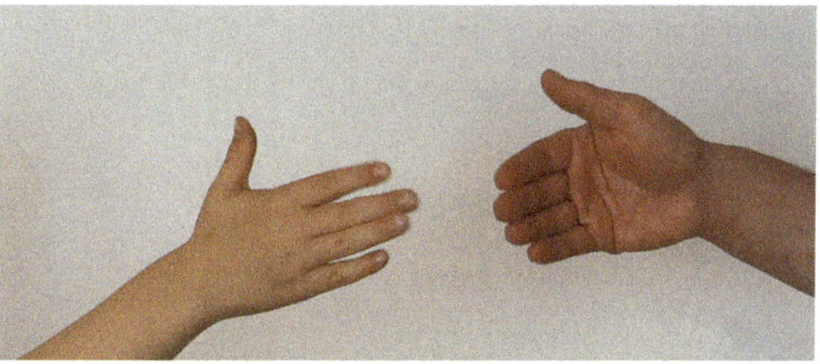

Step 2: The Cross (Root)

Both thumbs interlink to make a cross shape.

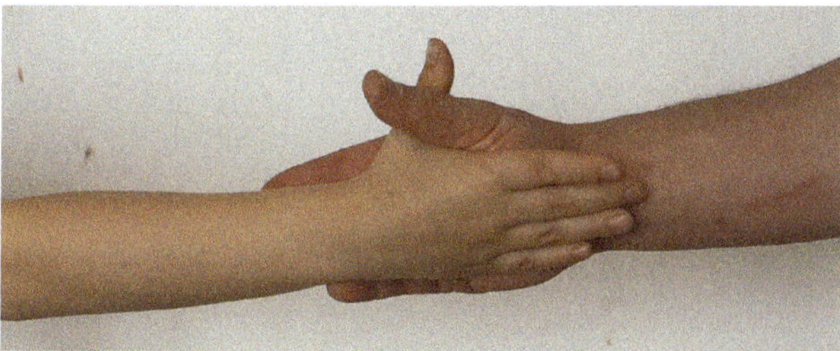

Step 3: The Star (Sufa)

The fingers wiggle and wave like twinkling stars.

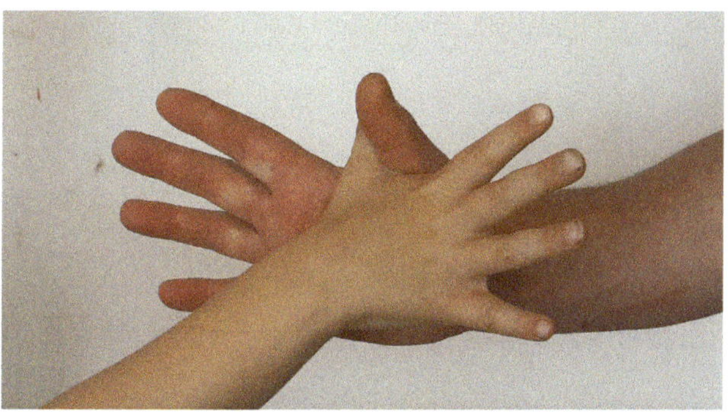

Hopefully this chapter has provided you with an informative introduction to morphology, as well as an understanding of why it is so important. There are so many exciting ways that it can be used in mainstream teaching as well as additional support for pupils with special educational needs. The structure of words can be exciting and empowering. The following chapters will unravel this further, starting in Chapter 2 with a closer look at why spelling is so enormously difficult for so many people.

Endnotes

1 Carroll & Breadmore 2017; Deacon, Kieffer & Laroche 2014; Levesque, Kieffer & Deacon 2017.
2 Nunes & Bryant 2006; Breadmore et al. 2019.
3 Nunes & Bryant 2006; Deacon et al, 2014; Kirby et al. 2012.
4 Nunes & Bryant 2006, Apel et al, 2013.
5 McCutchen et al. 2014.
6 Carroll & Breadmore 2017; Tsesmeli & Seymour 2009.
7 Nunes & Bryant 2006; Bowers, Deacon and Kirby 2010.
8 Carroll & Breadmore 2017.

2. Spelling

Friend or foe?

There are many reasons why spelling is difficult. Imagine you are spelling the word ***helpless***. Here's what might be happening for you if you have spelling difficulties.

Working memory difficulties

Working memory is the ability to store information whilst working on it. Examples of tasks requiring working memory are: remembering a question you have been asked whilst answering it, or remembering sounds whilst writing them down in letter form.

You say the sounds (h – e – l – p – l – e – s – s) but forget them as you attempt to write them. You may either get stuck and simply start again (this might happen more than once, leading to losing the flow of your writing and not writing much in the time allocated), or you write a shorter form of the word, like ***helpl***.

Phonological awareness difficulties

Phonological awareness is the ability to discriminate and manipulate speech sounds. It involves hearing, identifying and playing with them. If you have phonological difficulties, you might struggle to identify or say the sounds in a word that you hear, which means you only manage to write some of them down. Or you might find it hard to know the order of the sounds you hear, or to say them in the right order.

You hear ***helpless***, and maybe can say the two syllables: ***help*** + ***less***. You might then struggle to identify all the sounds in ***help***, so you write only two of them: **he**. You might hear ***less*** but only be able to isolate two sounds, ***ls***. The word you end up writing is ***hels***.

Motor skills and handwriting difficulties

The very act of writing letters and words can help you to remember the spelling. If you have difficulty with the mechanical act of writing, remembering what you have written is much harder. It therefore takes much longer for the correct spelling to be remembered.

You might be able to write ***helpless*** once, when copying, but you forget it easily, or you miss out letters because of the effort needed for concentrating.

Poor visual skills

Some learners' eyes behave differently to others. Some people struggle to hold their vision on single letters or words. Some people say they can see letters from every angle and struggle to remember which way round is the correct one. Some people struggle to see the difference between similar symbols. This makes spelling really difficult.

When spelling ***helpless***, you might reverse letters so the "p" looks like a "d" or "b", and you might write the letters in the wrong order.

Slow processing speed

Processing speed can be visually or verbally slow - or both. This makes spelling laborious and difficult, whether it is because you are slow to recognise and remember the look of the letters and link them together, or because you work slowly when linking the sounds.

You may take longer to spell ***helpless***, and it might take you longer to commit it to your long term memory for instant recall next time.

Phonics dependency

If phonics is your only strategy for spelling, you are likely to spell everything exactly as it sounds. The problem with this is that the English language does not work this way.

You might say each sound in ***helpless*** (h – e – l – p – l – er- s) and write ***helplers***, or ***helpluss***.

Friend or foe?

Spelling can therefore be extremely challenging for some. These challenges lead to reduced fluency, lack of confidence and enjoyment in writing, and the restriction of vocabulary use to the words learners know they can spell. They can lead to learners not achieving their potential and becoming disengaged with the written word. For these learners, spelling becomes the enemy.

However, looking at spelling through a morphological lens can change this. Learners can become friends with words, instead of their enemies, as they analyse them in terms of meaningful chunks. One pupil who had been involved in the pilot commented when she was interviewed at the end that she found spelling much easier now, because she felt she understood the "***real parts of the word***". The focus on meaning instead of sound makes words more real, memorable and easier to process quickly, reducing the effort for those with memory and processing speed difficulties. It also makes them more fun to learn for many learners. Morphology does not rely as much on phonological skills; therefore the phonological load is reduced for those with difficulties in this area.

A morphological approach supports visual skills, because learners are encouraged to look at the morphemes as well as hearing them. For example, if you look at the word ***stealth*** you might see the root ***steal***, enabling you to spell it correctly. Meanwhile, morphology offers an alternative to those who rely too heavily, or unsuccessfully, on phonics and have become disenfranchised with spelling altogether, as described in Chapter 1.

By changing how learners look at words, spelling is no longer an enemy but a friend – it supports understanding and helps with the learning of new words.

3. Key skills in becoming a Morph Master

There are three key skills which you will need to become a Morph Master. These three skills are the main principles and as such they are embedded in Morph Mastery.

1. Word Agility

This is playing games and conducting experiments with word structures and meanings. Word agility involves constructing, deconstructing, comparing and transforming words.

Word agility is about becoming confident with words and morphemes, experimenting with building them, taking them apart, and changing them. For example, experimenting by changing a suffix. What happens if I change the ***-ly*** in ***happily*** to ***-ness***? Does the meaning change? How? Do I still have to apply a spelling rule? Why? Can I change it to ***-ment***? **Word Agility** is developed through games in each lesson; these are presented in detail in Chapter 10. You will find, however, that your learners will begin to exercise their word agility spontaneously in your lessons. In the pilot, for example, one pupil wanted to know if there was such a word as "removement" when she was learning the words related to the root ***move***. Another pupil demonstrated fantastic word agility when he made the following comment: "If you are making a mess you are technically an uncleaner. It should be a word!"

2. Word Mastery

This is the study of words and their parts. It is asking questions about words and the morphemes within them. We discuss what happens to words if we deconstruct them or build them again with different morphemes. We talk about their meaning and how their morphemes contribute to this.

Word mastery concerns actively thinking and talking about the words we use. In Morph Mastery it is developed through a set of questions. For example:

How many morphemes does it have?
Can you add any prefixes?
Can you change the root?
Can you change the prefix or suffix?
What does the suffix mean/do?

The full set of Word Mastery questions can be found on the following page, and in Appendix 12. **Word Mastery** is taught explicitly on **Day 2** each week. A word containing two or more morphemes is chosen in advance and questions are asked and answered. Question cards are provided to support this. More details are in Chapter 9.

In the pilot, pupils began to use their new-found word mastery skills spontaneously. For example, the misleading spelling in the common branding of "**smokey** bacon" crisps was revealed by asking questions about the suffix and spelling rule. The pupil was learning to drop the final "e" when suffixing single syllable words containing a long vowel, so wondered if the correct spelling should be **smoky**? **Smokey** looked right, but the adult and pupil couldn't work out why. Word mastery was then conducted by asking questions: is there a suffix? What is it? Has the root changed when adding a suffix? They discovered together that **smokey** looks right because it is seen so frequently on crisp packets. However, the spelling on crisp packets, they discovered, was incorrect; the correct spelling is in fact **smoky**, which follows the known suffixing drop "e" rule.

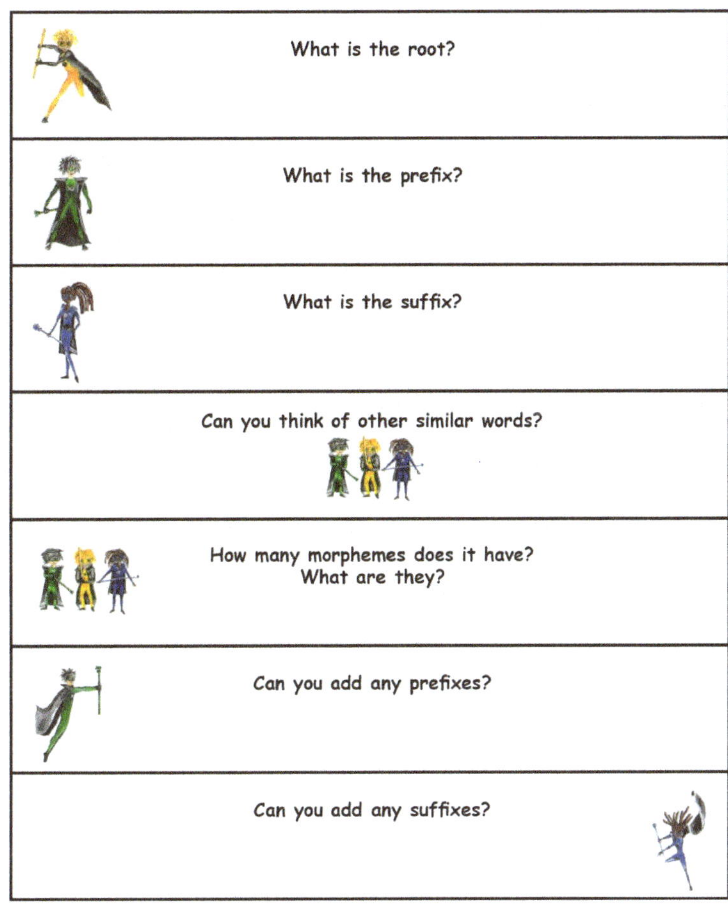

What is the root?

What is the prefix?

What is the suffix?

Can you think of other similar words?

How many morphemes does it have?
What are they?

Can you add any prefixes?

Can you add any suffixes?

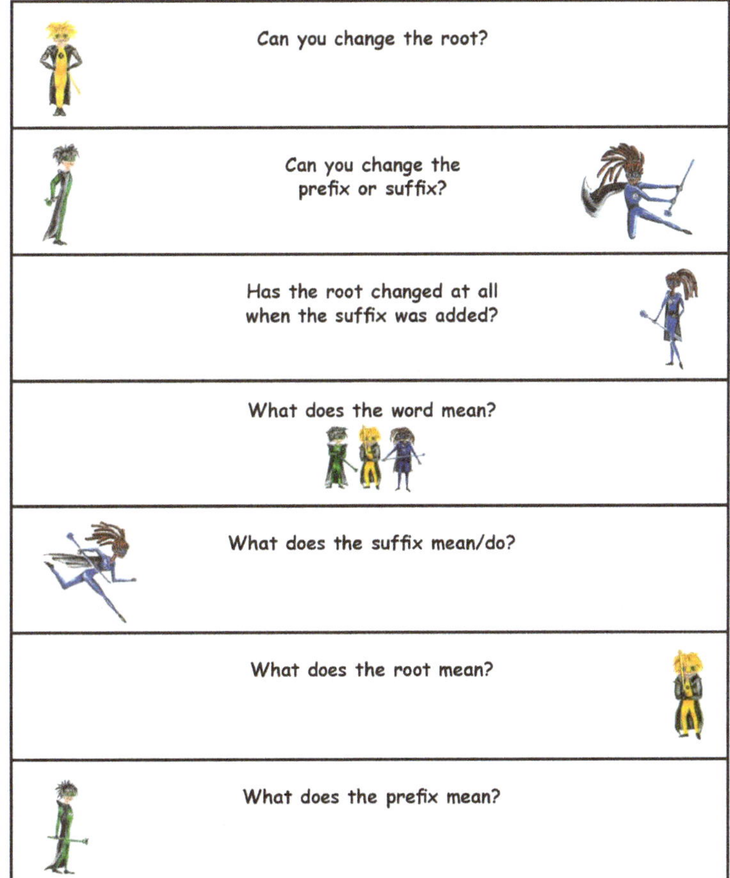

Can you change the root?

Can you change the
prefix or suffix?

Has the root changed at all
when the suffix was added?

What does the word mean?

What does the suffix mean/do?

What does the root mean?

What does the prefix mean?

Word Mastery Questions

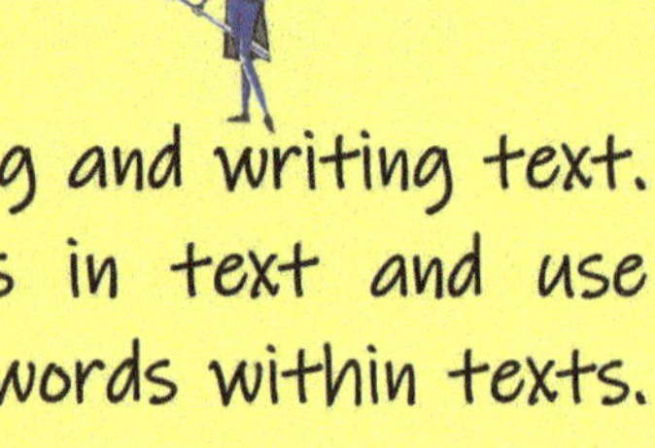

3. Word Espionage

Morph Masters are spies when reading and writing text. We actively look out for morphemes in text and use morphemes to check for meanings of words within texts. We think about what we know about morphemes to help us understand the words we find and to create new words.

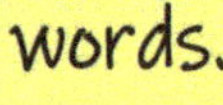

Word espionage entails editing and checking text. Morph Masters are encouraged to examine texts they are reading, or texts they have written, to find morphemes and make observations about what they find. **Word Espionage** is taught on **Day 1** and **Day 3** in Morph Mastery. On **Day 1**, the learner highlights morphemes in a text s/he is reading and comments on them. On **Day 3**, a sample of writing is edited with morphemes in mind. More details can be found in Chapter 9.

These three skills, **Word Agility, Word Mastery** and **Word Espionage**, are all rooted in what we know works; they are each designed to ensure that learning is embedded and consolidated, as follows:

Word Agility adopts the principle that learning needs to be multi-sensory, fun and active. The games use touch, movement, colour, talking and listening. There is an incentive to remember taught words and spellings. They also ensure that what is taught from previous weeks is practised. This is known as overlearning.

Word Mastery adopts the principle of metacognition, in other words thinking and talking about learning, exploring new words and meanings actively.

Word Espionage ensures that learning is meaningful, because it is linked to what the learners are doing in class. It supports making links with classwork and transferring learning in context.

4. Golden rules for becoming a Morph Master teacher

> As soon as I teach something new, they forget the last thing I taught. It feels like running to stand still!

If you have taught any learners who have learning difficulties, you will be very familiar with the feeling of running to stand still. You teach something, for example a spelling rule, and your learners can do it perfectly, so you move on to the next thing. Then, a few weeks later, you notice that, while they have mastered the new learning, the previous spelling rule is completely forgotten! Added to this, no matter how proficient your learners are when in your smaller group or individual lessons, they seem to automatically forget when in class.

This is a very familiar problem for educators. There are three golden rules to help avoid it which, when applied to any intervention, including Morph Mastery, may not completely solve the problem, but will certainly help.

It helps some practitioners to consider that your average learner with specific learning difficulties might take ten times as long as a neurotypical (or, in layperson's terms, normal) learner to commit to long term memory what is learnt. Obviously, this is a vast generalisation; every individual is different and it depends on the nature of what is being taught. Some other aspects of learning might be remembered more quickly by your pupil with specific learning difficulties than your neurotypical learner, for example in music, art or technology. Their brains just learn differently. However, in the realm of spelling, reading and language, you can confidently assume that your learners with specific learning difficulties are going to need Golden Rule 1: **practice, practice and more practice**. And then, after the practice, they will need more practice!

Overlearning is embedded in *Morph Mastery: A Morphological Intervention for Reading, Spelling and Vocabulary*. We use flash cards known as "trigger cards" for revision in each lesson and games which include previously taught words. Dictated sentences are another chance to practise previously taught spellings, whilst looking through texts in the Word Espionage activities encourages the learners to find taught morphemes in contexts that are meaningful to them.

The second Golden Rule to effectively teaching learners with specific learning difficulties, and indeed any kind of learning difficulty, is to provide multi-sensory teaching and learning opportunities to make connections between senses and enhance memory. Say it, make it, hear it, do it, move it, see it.

Multi-sensory learning is embedded in Morph Mastery. Firstly, the three characters that represent the prefix, root and suffix are colour coded. These colours are reinforced throughout the activities using highlighters and coloured pens. Each character also bears a distinctive symbol, which is enacted in The Morph handshake. The colour coding, symbols and handshake can be used throughout the lessons, providing visual and kinaesthetic reinforcement: learners are trained to think of morphemes in colours, symbols and actions as well as language. The games in every lesson are also multi-sensory; they use colour, tactile resources, voice recorders and the opportunity to talk. Remember that asking pupils to say a word as well as read/ write it is an instant way to make the learning experience multi-sensory; speaking while writing ensures that learners are moving and hearing as well as writing and seeing.

Planning precisely is key for learners who already find spelling very difficult. If there is a trap to fall into, they will! Equally, if something is not specifically taught, they are very unlikely to learn it by osmosis! This is where Golden Rule 3, **plan precisely**, comes in. There are two parts to this golden rule.

Firstly, if something is not known, it needs to be explicitly taught. So many interventions are ineffective for learners with significant difficulties because they address needs generally, rather than targeting the specific needs of the pupils. Addressing needs generally is effective for most pupils, but rarely does it work for your pupil with persistent specific learning difficulties. Assessments which inform intervention, followed by the careful setting of targets, are therefore essential, and they must lay the foundations for planning. In Morph Mastery, all lessons are planned according to what your learners need to know, and this is established by assessment.

The second part to golden rule 3 is to stick to what the pupils know, ***except*** the thing you are teaching. In other words, the only challenge for them in that lesson is the targeted piece of learning; nothing else should be new or difficult. In your Morph Mastery lessons, don't expect your learners to write or read words they don't know how to read or spell, ***unless*** they are the words you are teaching. For example, if your prior assessment of the pupils tells you that they cannot spell words containing the "***drop e***" rule (e.g. like – liking) it is essential that you do not include these words in your games, sentences and activities ***unless*** this rule is what you are targeting.

It is very easy to inadvertently slip unknown words into learning activities when they are not the targeted words for that week. It might even be tempting to add other challenges into the lesson in the hope that the pupil might learn other words as well as the targeted spellings. However, this not only confuses both learner and teacher, but it also dilutes the learning potential of the actual targeted word. In addition, and most importantly, this extra challenge is likely to contribute to the pupil's stress and therefore probable failure. Remember that pupils identified for intervention have probably already experienced failure, possibly many times. Your job is to make sure in your planning that the lessons are free of failure! In Morph Mastery, the only tricky aspect of learning should be the spelling that you have identified for explicit teaching.

In Morph Mastery, the golden rule of precision planning is vital in all of the lessons. However, there is one exception to this rule. The morphological awareness games, which are ***not*** reading or spelling games, may include a wider variety of words than those your learner knows how to spell. These activities are much more about words your learners understand than about their ability to spell them; here is your opportunity to expose your learner(s) to richer vocabulary than his or her spelling repertoire would otherwise allow (see Figure 1.7 in Chapter 1, page 6: the legacy of poor reading and spelling). More information about morphological awareness is provided in Chapter 5, and the morphological awareness games are outlined in Chapter 10.

These three golden rules are often the difference between an effective and an ineffective intervention. So don't forget to provide overlearning opportunities, make it multi-sensory and plan precisely.

5. Laying the foundations: what you need to know

There are many books and resources available which can explain all the terminology involved in morphology in far more depth than this manual. Our purpose is the nuts and bolts. What do you ***need*** to know to deliver Morph Mastery effectively?

Need to know 1:

Morpheme, root, prefix, suffix, affix

In Chapter 1 the terms morpheme, root, prefix and suffix were introduced. A morpheme is the smallest possible unit of meaning within a word. It can be a prefix, root or suffix. Here is a visual reminder.

Roots which are words in their own right
run
mount
take

Latin roots

port (carry)

scrib (write)

vac (empty)

Greek roots

biblio (book)

doc (teach)

dyno (power)

An affix is the umbrella term for all prefixes and suffixes, as illustrated below.

Need to know 2:

Transparent and opaque morphemes

Morphemes can be sorted into two types; phonologically transparent and opaque morphemes. This refers to how easily they can be heard within a word. You will need to understand how this works in order to help your learners, but these are not terms you will necessarily need to explain to the learner.

Transparent morphemes

Morphemes are usually smaller units than the whole word (except in words which only contain a root, for example ***run, sing, laugh***). As such, they can usually be detected within a word. For example, if you hear the word ***unhelpful*** you can hear the three morphemes ***un-***, ***help*** and ***-ful***. If you hear the word ***reacting***, you can hear the morphemes ***re-***, ***act*** and ***-ing***. These morphemes are known as phonologically transparent morphemes.

Opaque morphemes

In some cases, the morphemes cannot be heard so easily. These are known as phonologically opaque morphemes. For example, the ***/z/*** sound at the end of ***close*** (as in close the school) changes to a different sound in ***closure.*** The hard **c** in ***politics, magic***, and ***music*** becomes soft in ***politician***, ***magician*** and ***musician.*** They do not sound exactly the same and the morphemes are more difficult to isolate; they are opaque. There are many more examples of phonologically opaque morphemes, where the impact of adding a morpheme ranges from sounding very mildly different (as in ***urgent*** when changed to ***urgency***) to sounding very different, for example when ***heal*** becomes ***healthy*** or ***Christ*** becomes ***Christmas***.

Opaque morphemes are much harder for most pupils because they have been trained to listen to phonemes (sounds) in words in order to read, spell and understand them. This is a major stumbling block and one which needs to be understood, assessed and targeted through teaching in Morph Mastery. Although these morphemes are phonologically opaque, visually they are very easy to see, so a visual approach becomes extremely effective in teaching them. It is worth noting that in Morph Mastery, the terms transparent and opaque refer to the sound only, so these morphemes are ***phonologically*** transparent and opaque. For a full list of examples of phonologically opaque morphemes in Morph Mastery, see Appendix 13, page 239.

Need to know 3:

Morphological awareness

Morphological awareness is the awareness of, and ability to manipulate, the morphemes within words. It concerns understanding the function of each morpheme within a word, and being able to change words by adding or removing morphemes. It is helpful to think of morphological awareness as a continuum whereby children move from implicit to explicit morphological awareness (see below).[1]

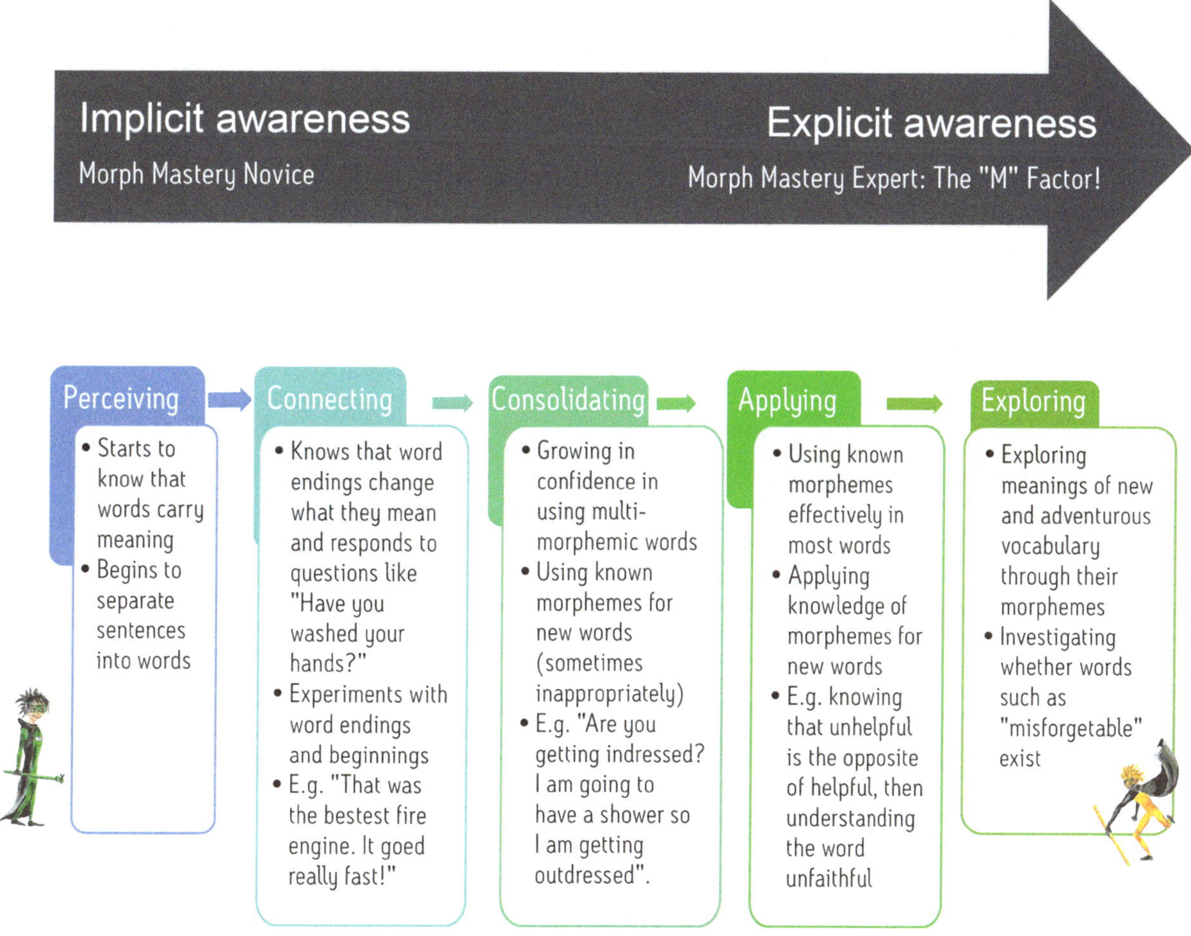

In order become a Morph Mastery expert and gain explicit morphological awareness (or The "M" Factor – see Chapter 1), there is more involved than just knowing how to add prefixes and suffixes and being able to spell them. Explicit morphological awareness is the ability to, for example, make multiple words and analyse them effectively, test out new words and compare and contrast their morphemes. It encompasses metacognition (thinking and talking about words intelligently). It involves word analysis, reflection, enquiry and finding relationships between words.

Notes

1 This continuum is designed to be practical for classroom use – it was influenced by the research of Hannah Leigh Nicholls at the University of Coventry, www.researchgate.net/profile/Hannah_Leigh_Nicholls.

6. Assess – Plan – Do – Review

An Overview of Morph Mastery the Intervention

The Intervention adopts the cycle of ***Assess-Plan-Do-Review*** as identified in the UK Special Educational Needs and Disability (SEND) Code of Practice: 0–25 Years (Government of UK 2015). This is illustrated in Figure 6.1. As you will see, the practitioner is reviewing and assessing throughout the cycle.

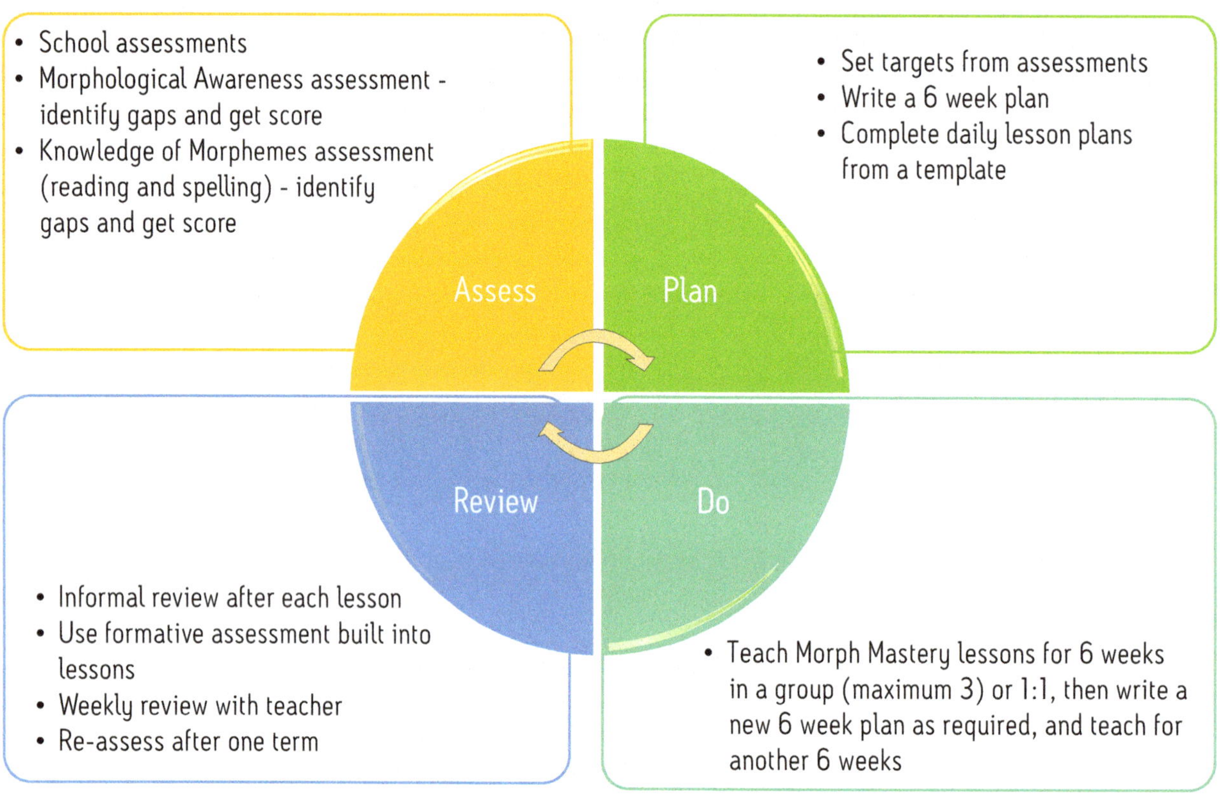

Figure 6.1 Assess - Plan - Do - Review

Assess

In addition to your school assessments, and any assessments administered by your SENCO, you will need to administer the Morph Mastery Assessments. More details can be found in Chapter 7. In brief, there are two main assessments:

1. Morphological Awareness (an oral assessment)
2. Knowledge of Morphemes (reading and spelling)

Plan

Your assessments will identify areas of morphological awareness that need to be taught, and morphemes that need to be taught for reading and spelling. You'll use these to set SMART (Specific, Measurable, Achievable, Realistic and Time Limited) targets, and to write your first six-week plan. It's tempting to plan for 12 weeks, but best practice is to wait until you have completed your first six weeks, as needs can change.

Do

Teach the intervention for six weeks, before writing another six-week plan from the same assessments. **Don't** repeat the assessments until after two sets of six weeks.

Each week you'll teach Lessons 1, 2 and 3. The lessons last 30 minutes and follow the same basic structure; but they are personalised according to your six-week plan. Some activities feature in every lesson, while others are spread out over the week, as illustrated in the overview (Figure 6.2). In brief, lesson 1 introduces a new root, lesson 2 a new affix and lesson 3 consolidates word agility through games and over-learning.

	Day 1	Day 2	Day 3
Morphological Awareness	✓	✓	✓
Test trigger cards	✓	✓	✓
Make a trigger card	✓	✓	
New root	✓		
New affix		✓	
The Morph handshake	✓	✓	✓
Make a portal	✓	✓	
Morph Mastercard	✓	✓	✓
Word Agility game	✓	✓	✓ (extended)
Word Espionage	✓ (reading)		✓ (writing)
Word Mastery		✓	
Writing (sentence dictation)			✓
Review – learner & adult	✓	✓	✓

Figure 6.2

Review

After 12 weeks, repeat the assessments and gather any other progress data. Teachers, the SENCO and the adult delivering the intervention can then evaluate progress and plan whether to continue in the same way, adapt or change the intervention, stop the intervention or seek specialist support. More information about this will be provided in Chapter 12.

7. Measuring, planning and monitoring through assessment

There are two main assessments that you will need to administer for delivering Morph Mastery. These can be found in Appendix 1, 2 and 3 of this book. They are:

- **Morphological Awareness** (Chapter 5 explains what we mean by morphological awareness and why it is important)
- **Knowledge of Morphemes** (reading and spelling)

The other assessment sheet that you will need is the **Assessment Summary Sheet** (Appendix 4). We'll discuss all three of these assessment documents during this chapter. But first, it's important to consider what the assessments are for, and some general guiding principles for administering them.

The assessments are extremely useful before you start teaching because they will show you what your learners know already, and what they still need to learn. They therefore support precision planning because you will know exactly what to teach and what you can assume to be known. You will also be able to set SMART (Specific, Measurable, Achievable, Realistic and Time Limited) targets.

The assessments are also useful during your intervention, to ensure that your learners are making progress, and after teaching to evaluate the programme. It's recommended that you repeat them after each term of teaching, so that you can review your SMART targets and measure progress. The danger with only assessing at the end of a programme is always that you cannot make changes retrospectively; it's far better to find out that the teaching isn't working when you can still make changes or review. Assessing termly means that you can identify if what you have taught has been learnt, and make changes to your teaching if necessary, or simply build in more revision opportunities. This close monitoring will help you to make sure your valuable teaching time has been spent effectively and appropriately, and it will help you to keep a close eye on the impact of your intervention.

General guidelines of assessments

a) Administer the assessments once a term
b) Use them to set your teaching targets – be specific
c) Don't over-assess – once a term is fine and don't ask the pupil to go right to the end of the assessments if there are obvious and considerable difficulties in the early stages of the assessment
d) Have all your resources ready in advance of the assessment
e) Administer the assessment in several sittings if possible, in order to avoid fatigue
f) Write in pencil – you'll find you are always editing!

g) If the answer given is incorrect, don't just write a cross – write down what the learner does for your later analysis
h) Don't be tempted to teach or remind while you are assessing – even if it is something you think the pupil should know!

Now let's look at the two assessments in more detail and how to administer them.

Morphological Awareness Assessment (Appendix 1)

There are nine pages in this assessment. It should take approximately 20 minutes to administer, depending on your learner's speed and ability.

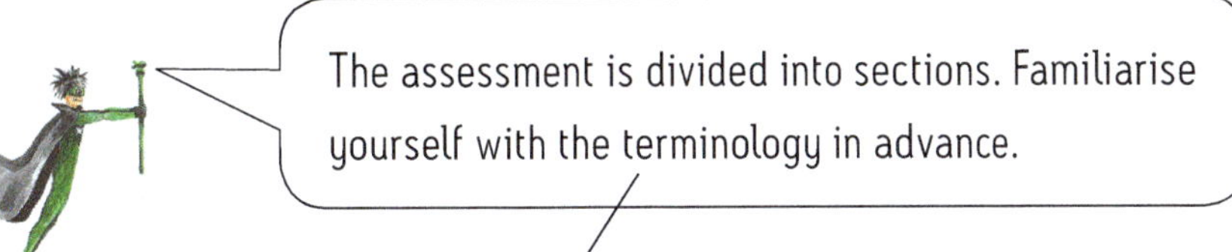

The assessment is divided into sections. Familiarise yourself with the terminology in advance.

Guidelines and terminology for assessment

TRANSPARENT MORPHEMES are morphemes where the root word does not change its sound when affixed, e.g. **like** becomes **dislike**.
OPAQUE (PHONOLOGICALLY COMPLEX) MORPHEMES are morphemes where the root word is not heard or its sound is changed when it is affixed, e.g. **catch** becomes **caught**.
WORD RELATIONSHIPS involve the morphological relationship between words. Specifically, for this assessment, it concerns whether they have the same root.
PSEUDO-WORDS are made up, or nonsense words.

You will need to cut up the picture cards for transparent morpheme sentence tasks in advance. All your instructions and words you will say are written into the assessment – your words are in green.

Some tasks are "**WORD**" tasks. Others are "**SENTENCE**" tasks. Sentence tasks may place additional load on working memory. In order to alleviate this, pictures are provided at the end of the assessment.
All instructions are given with each task. The answers are in orange. The words the adult says are in green.
What you need: Blank copy of the assessment, a pencil, and the pictures for transparent morpheme sentence tasks cut up.
Discontinue rule: Administer all of the transparent and opaque morphemes sections. Discontinue the word relationships and pseudowords sections if the learner makes 4 consecutive errors.
Scoring: Score 1 point for each correct answer and write it in the boxes at the end of each section. Transfer these scores to the scoring box on above and calculate a total score out of 50.

Each section is colour coded and this is shown by the border: green for transparent morphemes, pink for opaque morphemes, lilac for word relationships, turquoise for pesudowords

The answers are in orange.

Write the score and any comments in the box after the assessment has finished.

TRANSPARENT MORPHEMES
(where the root word does not change its sound when affixed)

1. Words: Production

The pupil listens to two words. The second word is the first word with an added affix. The pupil is then given a different word and asked to say an affixed version of it.

Say: *I am going to say two words. Listen to how the first word is changed to make the second word. Ready?* ***High: highest***. *What words did I say?* (if the child doesn't know, repeat them). *Did you hear how the first word changed?* If the child doesn't know: *I added* ***-est***. *Now you try. I will say the first two again to remind you what to do.* ***High, highest, kind...*** *What comes next?* (If the child doesn't know, say ***High, highest, kind, kindest***. *I added* ***-est*** *to* ***kind.***) *So you had these words:* ***High, highest, kind, kindest.*** *Now try these.*

For each question there is an example pair of words and a test word. The adult says the example pair, pauses then says the test word. The pupil must say the missing word (answer in orange)

a) **long: longer**
   short: ___________ (shorter)
b) **happy: happiness**
   kind: _________ (kindness)
c) **appear: disappear**
   trust: ___________ (distrust)
d) **fit: unfit**
e) **friendliness: _______ (unfriendliness)**

Transparent morphemes production score (words) /4
Comments

In the transparent and opaque morphemes sections, there is no need to explain what you mean by transparent and opaque. This terminology is not required for the task and is not taught in the intervention.

OPAQUE (PHONOLOGICALLY COMPLEX) MORPHEMES
(where the root word is not heard or its sound is changed when it is affixed):

1. Words: Production

The pupil is asked to listen to two words. The second word is the first word in a different form. The pupil is then given a different word and asked to generate the same form of that word.

Say: *I am going to say two words. Listen to how the first word is changed to make the second word.* ***Drink: drank****. What words did I say? Did you hear how the first word changed? Now you try. I will say the first two again to remind you what to do.* ***Drink, drank, hide...*** *What comes next? (*If the child doesn't know, say ***Drink, drank, hide, hid.)*** *So you had these words:* ***Drink, drank, hide, hid.*** *Now try these.*

For each question there is an example pair of words and a test word. Adult says the example pair, pauses then says the test word. Pupil must say the missing word (in orange)

a. **Eat: ate. Come: __________ (came)**
b. **Circle: circular, rectangle: ______________ (rectangular)**
c. **King: kingdom, wise: _____________ (wisdom)**

Opaque morphemes production score (words)	/3
Comments	

However, your learners will need to know the meaning of **root, morpheme, prefix, suffix, and affix**. You can explain these terms during the assessment if you need to. In the word relationships assessment, for example, it is fine to explain what you mean by root if it is not already known.

WORD RELATIONSHIPS

In this task the pupil is asked to say if two words have the same root.

> Say: *In this one, I am going to say two words. I will ask you if they come from the same root. The root is the bit of the word where its meaning comes from. Here is an example.* ***Sing*** *and* ***singing*** *come from the same root,* ***sing****. Now try these.* ***Heal*** *and* ***healthy****. Do they words come from the same root? Yes, because* ***heal*** *is about having good health, or being* ***healthy****.*

The adult says the two words then asks if they come from the same root. Answers in orange. Pupil's answer is written in the box.

1. Wish & wishfulness? (yes) ☐
2. Pillow & pill? (no) ☐
3. Pay & repay? (yes) ☐
4. Touch & touchy? (yes) ☐
5. Match & mat? (no) ☐
6. Moth & mother? (no) ☐
7. Cook & cookery? (yes) ☐
8. Mailbag & female? (no) ☐
9. International & nation? (yes) ☐
10. Export & supportive? (yes) ☐
11. Detention & Punishment? (no) ☐

Word relationships score (sentences)	/11
Comments	

After you have administered the **Morphological Awareness Assessment**, transfer your results, with any comments on to the cover page (Figure 7.1).

Morphological Awareness Assessment

Pupil's name:						DOB:		
Completed by:						Date:		
TRANSPARENT MORPHEMES score: /16			OPAQUE MORPHEMES score /12			WORD RELATIONSHIPS score /11	PSEUDOWORDS score /11	TOTAL Score /50
Words	P /4	D /4	Words	P /3	D /3			
Sentences	P /4	D /4	Sentences	P /3	D /3			
Comment			Comment			Comment	Comment	General comments
Strengths						Weaknesses		

Figure 7.1

It's really useful at this point to make any notes on strengths and weaknesses as this will help you to target your teaching. Figures 7.2 and 7.3 show some completed examples:

TRANSPARENT MORPHEMES score: 4 /16			OPAQUE MORPHEMES score 0 /12			WORD RELATIONSHIPS score 10 /11	PSEUDOWORDS score 0 /11	TOTAL Score /50 14
Words	P0/4	D2/4	Words	P0/3	D0/3			
Sentences	P1/4	D1/4	Sentences	P0/3	D0/3			
Comment lacking confidence, not naturally making links			Comment Discontinued – found very hard, not able to make links			Comment Appeared to guess some	Comment Did not administer	General comments Hard work – nothing automatic or fluent
Strengths Word relationships – listens for meaning of words Decomposition better than production						Weaknesses •Making links between morphemes (as opposed to words) •Opaque morphemes •Words and sentences both weak		

Figure 7.2

TRANSPARENT MORPHEMES score: 11 /16			OPAQUE MORPHEMES score 5 /12			WORD RELATIONSHIPS score 7/11	PSEUDOWORDS score 5/11	TOTAL Score /50 28
Words	P3/4	D2/4	Words	P1/3	D0/3			
Sentences	P3/4	D3/4	Sentences	P2/3	D2/3			
Comment Longer word was harder - maybe working memory?			Comment Guessed a lot for meaning.			Comment Hesitant - lots of guesswork.	Comment Really good attempt at making meanings - often close.	General comments Check working memory. Needs confidence.

Strengths	Weaknesses
Transparent morphemes - production. Opaque morphemes - sentences.	Decomposition - transparent & opaque. Opaque morphemes in words pseudowords.

Figure 7.3

Knowledge of Morphemes Assessment (Appendix 2 and 3)

This is a reading and spelling assessment. The morphemes are taken from the English Curriculum (2014) and organised into year groups. There are two sections to this assessment:

1. **The Adult Record Sheet** (Appendix 2)

   The Adult Record Sheet (Figure 7.4, 7.5, 7.6, 7.7, 7.8, 7.9) is used by the adult to make notes. There are three pages of assessment and a cover page which provides a summary. The assessment is not read by the pupil. You will need one copy of this for each pupil you assess.

Morph mastery

Knowledge of Morphemes Reading and Spelling Assessment (Adult Record Sheet)

This is an assessment of spelling and reading of suffixes and prefixes from the National Curriculum (2014) from Year 1 to 4. There are separate pupil sheets for the pupil to read from. To score, award one mark per item, and allow a mark if the suffix/prefix and rule (if relevant) are correctly read or spelled, even if the whole word is not correct. If more than ten spelling errors are made in one set of words, complete the set and score it, but do not continue to the next sets and score 0 for any sets that are not administered.

Summary	Pupil's Name:			Date:	
	Year 1	Year 2	Year 3 & 4	Year 5 & 6	Total Score
Score: Read	/10	/24	/23	/18	/75
Score: Spell	/10	/24	/23	/18	/75

Morphemes to target through teaching: (Highlight/circle if unknown)	
Year 1	**-s** (plural), **-s** (3rd person), **-es**, **-ing**, **-ed** (past tense), **-ed** (added syllable), **-er**, **-est**, **-y**, **un-**
Year 2	**Rule 1) No change to root: -ment, -ness, -ful, -less, -ly** **Rule 2) y →i: -es, -ed, -er, -est, -ness, -ful, -less, -ly** **Rule 3) drop e: –ing, -es, -ed, -er, -est, -y** **Rule 4) double final consonant: –ing, -ed, -er, -est, -y**
Year 3 & 4	**dis-**, **mis-**, **re-**, **in-**, **il-**, **im-**, **ir-**, **sub-**, **super-**, **inter-**, **anti-**, **auto-**, **-ation**, **-ation** (drop e), **-ly** (le → ly), **-ly** (ic →ically), **-ous**, **-ous** (drop e), **-ous** (our → or) **-tion** (t + **-ion**), **-sion** (s + **-ion**), ssion (ss + **-ion**), **-cian** (c + ian)
Year 5 & 6	**-cious**, **-tious**, **-tial**, **-cial**, **-ant**, **-ance**, **-ent**, **-ence**, **-ancy**, **-ency**, **-able**, **-ible**, **-able** (drop e), **-ible** (drop e), **-ability**, **-ibility**, **-ably**, **-ibly**

Figure 7.4 Adult Record Sheet cover page

Year 1

Affix	Meaning/function/rule	Test word	Pupil response: read	Pupil response: spell
-s	Noun plural	cats		
-s	3rd person singular	sits		
-es	Adds a syllable /iz/ when noun plural or verb 3rd person	fixes		
-ing	Verb present continuous tense	jumping		
-ed	Verb past tense	helped		
-ed	Verb past tense when adds extra syllable /id/	hunted		
-er	Makes root word into comparative	burner		
-est	Superlative	quickest		
-y	Makes root into adjective	crispy		
un-	Opposite (not)	unzip		

Summary: highlight if unknown	
Read:	Spell:
-s (plural)	-s (plural)
-s (3rd person)	-s (3rd person)
-es	-es
-ing	-ing
-ed	-ed
-ed (added syllable)	-ed (added syllable)
-er	-er
-est	-est
-y	-y
un-	un-
Total /10	Total /10

Figure 7.5 Adult Record Sheet Year 1

Year 2

Affix	Meaning/function/rule	Test word	Pupil response: read	Pupil response: spell
-ment	Makes root word into a noun	shipment		
-ness	Makes root word into a noun	fitness		
-ful	Makes root word into adjective	wishful		
-less	Makes root word into an adjective	restless		
-ly	Makes root word into adverb	sadly		
-es	If root ends in **y** change to **i**	cries		
-ed	If root ends in **y** change to **i**	dried		
-er	If root ends in **y** change to **i**	luckier		
-est	If root ends in **y** (ee sound) change to i	runniest		
-ness		bendiness		
-ful	If root ends in **y** change to i	plentiful		
-less		penniless		
-ly		angrily		

Summary: highlight if unknown	
Read:	Spell:
-ment	-ment
-ness	-ness
-ful	-ful
-less	-less
-ly	-ly
-es (y → i)	-es (y → i)
-ed (y → i)	-ed (y → i)
-er (y → i)	-er (y → i)
-est (y → i)	-est (y → i)
-ness (y → i)	-ness (y → i)
-ful (y → i)	-ful (y → i)
-less (y → i)	-less (y → i)
-ly (y → i)	-ly (y → i)

Affix	Meaning/function/rule	Test word	Pupil response: read	Pupil response: spell
-ing	If the root has a consonant before the final **e**, drop it if the suffix begins with a vowel or **-y**	liking		
-es		roses		
-ed		saved		
-er		nicer		
-est		latest		
-y		shiny		
-ing	Double the final consonant in one syllable root words ending in a single consonant to keep the vowel short	letting		
-ed		popped		
-er		runner		
-est		saddest		
-y		nutty		

Summary: highlight if unknown	
Read:	Spell:
-ing (drop e)	-ing (drop e)
-es (drop e)	-es (drop e)
-ed (drop e)	-ed (drop e)
-er (drop e)	-er (drop e)
-est (drop e)	-est (drop e)
-y (drop e)	-y (drop e)
-ing (double consonant)	-ing (double consonant)
-ed (double consonant)	-ed (double consonant)
-er (double consonant)	-er (double consonant)
-est (double consonant)	-est (double consonant)
-y (double consonant)	-y (double consonant)
Total /24	Total /24

Figure 7.6 Adult Record Sheet Year 2

Year 3 & 4 (Page 1 of 2)

Affix	Meaning/function/rule	Test word	Pupil response: read	Pupil response: spell
dis-	Opposite/not	dislike		
mis-	Opposite/not	misprint		
re-	Again/back	react		
in-	Not	insane		
il-	Not (when root starts with l)	illegal		
im-	Not (when root starts with m or p)	improper		
ir-	Not (when root starts with r)	irregular		
sub-	Under	submarine		
super-	above	superman		
inter-	Between, among	interact		
anti-	against	antifreeze		
auto-	Self, own	autograph		
-ation	Noun maker	formation		
-ation	Verb maker: If the root has a consonant before the final e drop the e	sensation		
-ly	Adverb maker (if the root ends in -le drop the e)	gently		
-ly	Adverb maker (if the root ends in -ic add al before the -ly)	frantically		

Summary: highlight if unknown	
Read:	Spell:
dis-	dis-
mis-	mis-
re-	re-
in-	in-
il-	il-
im-	im-
ir-	ir-
sub-	sub-
super-	super-
inter-	inter-
anti-	anti-
auto-	auto-
-ation	-ation
-ation (drop e)	-ation (drop e)
-ly (le → ly)	-ly (le → ly)
-ly (-ic → ically)	-ly (-ic → ically)

Figure 7.7 Adult Record Sheet Year 3 & 4

Year 3 & 4 (page 2 of 2)

Affix	Meaning/function/rule	Test word	Pupil response: read	Pupil response: spell
-ous	Adjective maker	poisonous		
-ous	Adjective maker: If the root has a consonant before the final e drop the e	famous		
-ous	Noun maker (if the root ends in -our, drop the u)	humorous		
-tion	Noun maker (use if the root ends in t or te)	action		
-sion	Noun maker (use if the root ends in d, de or se)	erosion		
-ssion	Noun maker (use if the root ends in ss or mit)	procession		
-cian	Noun maker (use if the root ends in c or s)	musician		

Summary: highlight if unknown	
Read:	Spell:
-ous	-ous
-ous (drop e)	-ous (drop e)
-ous (our → or)	-ous (our → or)
-tion	-tion
-sion	-sion
-ssion	-ssion
-cian	-cian
Total /23	Total /23

Figure 7.7 Adult Record Sheet Year 3 & 4 (continued)

Year 5 & 6 (Page 1 of 2)

Affix	Meaning/function/rule	Test word	Pupil response: read	Pupil response: spell
-cious	Adjective maker (when the root ends in **ce** – drop **e**)	spacious		
-tious	Adjective maker (when the root ends in **n** – drop **n**)	infectious		
-tial	Adjective maker (when the root ends in **nce** or **t**)	partial		
-cial	Adjective maker (when the root ends in **ace** or a short vowel + **ce** – drop the **e**)	facial		
-ant	Adjective maker (when the root ends in **t** or **ate**, drop **ate**)	observant		
-ance	Noun maker	brilliance		
-ent	Adjective maker	urgent		
-ence	Noun maker	silence		
-ancy	Noun maker	pregnancy		
-ency	Noun maker	emergency		

Summary: highlight if unknown	
Read:	Spell:
-cious	-cious
-tious	-tious
-tial	-tial
-cial	-cial
-ant	-ant
-ance	-ance
-ent	-ent
-ence	-ence
-ancy	-ancy
-ency	-ency

Affix	Meaning/function/rule	Test word	Pupil response: read	Pupil response: spell
-able	Adjective maker (primarily used with Anglo Saxon roots)	readable		
-ible	Adjective maker (primarily used with Latin roots)	flexible		
-able	Adjective maker (drop the final e)	likable		
-ible	Adjective maker (drop the final e)	sensible		
-ability	Noun maker	notability		
-ibility	Noun maker	reversibility		
-ably	Adverb maker	reasonably		
-ibly	Adverb maker	incredibly		

Summary: highlight if unknown	
Read:	Spell:
-able	-able
-ible	-ible
-able	-able
-ible	-ible
-ability	-ability
-ibility	-ibility
-ably	-ably
-ibly	-ibly
Total /18	Total /18

Figure 7.8 Adult Record Sheet Year 5 & 6

2. **The Pupil Word Lists** (Figure 7.5 and Appendix 3)

These are the lists that the pupil reads for the reading element of the assessment. You only need to print these off once as they can be re-used. It's recommended that you laminate them.

Year 1 Pupil Word List

cats
quickest
sits
crispy
fixes
unzip
jumping
helped
hunted
burner

Year 2 Pupil Word List

shipment	angrily
fitness	liking
wishful	roses
restless	saved
sadly	nicer
cries	latest
dried	shiny
luckier	letting
runniest	popped
bendiness	runner
plentiful	saddest
penniless	nutty

Figure 7.9 Pupil Word Lists Year 1 and 2

Year 3 & 4 Pupil Word List

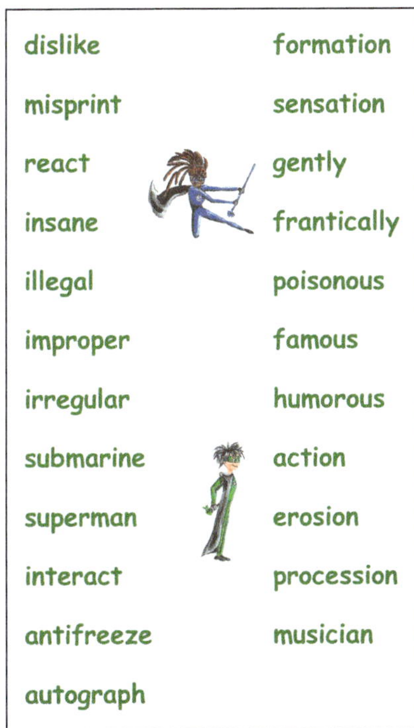

dislike
formation
misprint
sensation
react
gently
insane
frantically
illegal
poisonous
improper
famous
irregular
humorous
submarine
action
superman
erosion
interact
procession
antifreeze
musician
autograph

Year 5 & 6 Pupil Word List

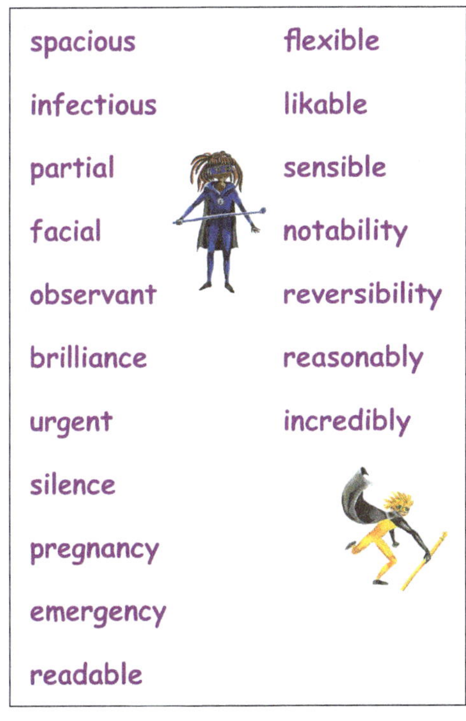

spacious
flexible
infectious
likable
partial
sensible
facial
notability
observant
reversibility
brilliance
reasonably
urgent
incredibly
silence
pregnancy
emergency
readable

Figure 7.10 Pupil Word Lists Year 3 & 4 and 5 & 6

Administering the Knowledge of Morphemes Assessment

If possible, administer the reading and spelling assessments in two separate sittings. If there are ten or more errors in one year group section for ***spelling only***, do not administer the next year group section. Always complete any section that you start so that you can obtain a score. Don't show the pupil the **Adult Record Sheet**. Use the **Pupil Word Lists** for the reading assessment. Provide a separate piece of paper for the pupil to write on for the spelling assessment.

Recording and scoring

If the answer is correct, just ✓. However, for any incorrect answer, don't just ✗. Write down what the pupil says (in the reading tasks) and writes (in the spelling tasks). This makes it easier for you to both to score the assessment and to analyse errors. Not all incorrectly spelled words will count as wrong in this assessment; it depends on whether the targeted morpheme was incorrect. You'll need to check which part of the word was wrong. This is illustrated in Figure 7.11.

In this example, ***burner*** was read as ***brunner.*** In spite of the error in the first part of the word, the pupil has successfully read the targeted ***-er*** so this counts as correct. However, the spelling ***brunah*** for the same word is incorrect as the targeted ***-er*** is not spelled correctly. It may still be useful for the assessor to note that the phonic sound ***ur*** is not secure. As Morph Mastery is not a phonics intervention, this will need to be taught elsewhere. In Morph Mastery, it might be necessary to avoid using words containing the ***ur*** sound until the learner is secure in spelling them.

Year 1

Affix	Meaning/function/rule	Test word	Pupil response: read	Pupil response: spell
-s	Noun plural	cats	✓	✓
-s	3rd person singular	sits	✓	sitz
-es	Adds a syllable /iz/ when noun plural or verb 3rd person	fixes	fixess	fixiz
-ing	Verb present continuous tense	jumping	✓	✓
-ed	Verb past tense	helped	✓	helpt
-ed	Verb past tense when adds extra syllable /id/	hunted	said hunt -ed then ✓	huntid
-er	Makes root word into comparative	burner	brunner	brunah
-est	Superlative	quickest	✓	quickest
-y	Makes root into adjective	crispy	✓	crispiy
un-	Opposite (not)	unzip	✓	✓

Summary: highlight if unknown	
Read:	Spell:
-s (plural)	-s (plural)
-s (3rd person)	-s (3rd person)
-es	-es
-ing	-ing
-ed	-ed
-ed (added syllable)	-ed (added syllable)
-er	-er
-est	-est
-y	-y
un-	un-
Total 9 /10	Total 3/10

If your learner was not right the first time, it's useful to record this. This means the learner is not secure to the point of being fluent and automatic. In this example, the initial attempt to read ***hunted*** was incorrect, but the pupil self-corrected. This counts as correct but this might be a morpheme you would want to include in your games and activities to develop automaticity.

Figure 7.11

You will find that the **Year 2 Knowledge of Morphemes Assessment** of spelling focuses on both the ability to spell the targeted morpheme, and also on the ability to apply spelling rules. Many (but not all) of the suffixes targeted here have already been assessed in the **Year 1 Pupil Word List**, but there no spelling rule was applied. The four spelling rules that are targeted in the Year 2 set of words, are:

I. The root does not change when a suffix is added
II. ***y* → *i***: Where the root word ends in ***y***, it sometimes changes to an ***i*** when suffixed. For example, ***angry*** becomes ***angrily*** (the ***y*** has changed into an ***i***)
III. ***Drop e:*** If the root ends in a consonant + ***e***, the ***e*** is sometimes dropped when suffixed. For example, ***like*** becomes ***liking*** (the final ***e*** in ***like*** is dropped)
IV. ***Double final consonant***: If the root ends in a short vowel + consonant, this consonant is doubled in order to keep the vowel short. For example, ***pop*** becomes ***popped*** (the final ***p*** is doubled to keep the ***o*** vowel sound short)

These are all clearly marked in the assessment. For example, in Figure 7.12 the pupil is tested on the spelling of the morphemes **-es, -ed, -er, -est, -ness, -ful, -less** and **-ly** when applying the **y → i** rule**.** Here, the pupil was successful in spelling each morpheme, except **-ly**. However, the rule was not applied successfully even when the suffix was correct. Therefore none of these spellings can be marked as correct.

-es	If root ends in **y** change to **i**	cries	crease	cryes
-ed	If root ends in **y** change to **i**	dried	dreed	dryed
-er	If root ends in **y** change to **i**	luckier	lucker	luckyer
-est	If root ends in **y** (ee sound) change to i	runniest	runnest	runyest
-ness		bendiness	✓	bendyness
-ful	If root ends in **y** change to i	plentiful	✓	plentyful
-less		penniless	✓	pennyless
-ly		angrily	✓	angryliy

-es (y → i)	-es (y → i)
-ed (y → i)	-ed (y → i)
-er (y → i)	-er (y → i)
-est (y → i)	-est (y → i)
-ness (y → i)	-ness (y → i)
-ful (y → i)	-ful (y → i)
-less (y → i)	-less (y → i)
-ly (y → i)	-ly (y → i)

Figure 7.12

The suffix **-ly** is not tested in the Year 1 assessment, so in the **Year 2 Pupil Word List** it is tested both with and without the application of a spelling rule.

Figure 7.13 shows how to score the **Year 2 Pupil Word List**.

Where a suffix + rule is being assessed, the answer is only counted correct if the suffix is spelled correctly ***and*** rule is applied successfully. So ***bendyness*** in the example below is not correct, even though the suffix is spelled correctly. It's the same for ***pennyless, luckyer, likeing,*** and ***poped.***

Year 2 (Page 1 of 2) Morpha Masters

Affix	Meaning/function/rule	Test word	Pupil response: read	Pupil response: spell
-ment	Makes root word into a noun	shipment	✓	✓
-ness	Makes root word into a noun	fitness	✓	fitrous
-ful	Makes root word into adjective	wishful	✓	wishfull
-less	Makes root word into an adjective	restless	✓	✓
-ly	Makes root word into adverb	sadly	✓	✓
-es	If root ends in y change to i	cries	✓	crize
-ed	If root ends in y change to i	dried	✓	driede
-er	If root ends in y change to i	luckier	✓	luckyer
-est	If root ends in y (ee sound) change to i	runniest	runnesty	runnist
-ness		bendiness	✓	bendyness
-ful	If root ends in y change to i	plentiful	✓	pletifl
-less		penniless	penless	pennyless
-ly		angrily	angry	angroly

Summary: highlight if unknown	
Read:	Spell:
-ment	-ment
-ness	-ness
-ful	-ful
-less	-less
-ly	-ly
-es (y → i)	-es (y → i)
-ed (y → i)	-ed (y → i)
-er (y → i)	-er (y → i)
-est (y → i)	-est (y → i)
-ness (y → i)	-ness (y → i)
-ful (y → i)	-ful (y → i)
-less (y → i)	-less (y → i)
-ly (y → i)	-ly (y → i)

Year 2 (page 2 of 2)

Affix	Meaning/function/rule	Test word	Pupil response: read	Pupil response: spell
-ing	If the root has a consonant before the final **e**, drop it if the suffix begins with a vowel or **-y**	liking	✓	likeing
-es		roses	✓	✓
-ed		saved	✓	savd
-er		nicer	✓	✓
-est		latest	letters	latist
-y		shiny	✓	✓
-ing	Double the final consonant in one syllable root words ending in a single consonant to keep the vowel short	letting	✓	✓
-ed		popped	✓	poped
-er		runner	✓	runah
-est		saddest	✓	sadist
-y		nutty	✓	(nuty, then SC self-corrected) ✓

Summary: highlight if unknown	
Read:	Spell:
-ing (drop e)	-ing (drop e)
-es (drop e)	-es (drop e)
-ed (drop e)	-ed (drop e)
-er (drop e)	-er (drop e)
-est (drop e)	-est (drop e)
-y (drop e)	-y (drop e)
-ing (double consonant)	-ing (double consonant)
-ed (double consonant)	-ed (double consonant)
-er (double consonant)	-er (double consonant)
-est (double consonant)	-est (double consonant)
-y (double consonant)	-y (double consonant)
Total 20 /24	Total 8 /24

Likewise, if the rule is applied successfully but the suffix incorrectly spelled it cannot be marked as correct. In this example, the learner remembered to drop the ***e*** at the end of ***late***, but incorrectly spelled the suffix by writing ***latist.*** It cannot be marked as correct.

Figure 7.13

The **Year 3 & 4 Pupil Word Lists** include some Latin suffixes (Figure 7.14) – for example ***sub-, super-, auto, -anti***. More information about Latin and Greek roots and suffixes can be found in Appendix 15. There will inevitably be a need to teach the meaning of these as well as the spelling. However, the assessment is purely spelling and reading based as this is often where learners stumble the most and require explicit teaching. The vocabulary will still be taught as you progress through your teaching.

Again, if the target morpheme is correctly spelled, the pupil response can be marked as correct, even if the rest of the word is not correct.

Here, ***in-*** is spelled correctly in ***insain*** even though the whole word is not correct. Therefore it can be marked as correct. It's the same for ***submareen*** and ***antifreaze.***

Year 3 & 4 (Page 1 of 2)

Affix	Meaning/function/rule	Test word	Pupil response: read	Pupil response: spell
dis-	Opposite/not	**dislike**	✓	disslike
mis-	Opposite/not	**misprint**	✓	missprint
re-	Again/back	**react**	reeked	reacked
in-	Not	**insane**	✓	insain
il-	Not (when root starts with l)	**illegal**	✓	ilegal
im-	Not (when root starts with m or p)	**improper**	✓	improperr
ir-	Not (when root starts with r)	**irregular**	✓	iregular
sub-	Under	**submarine**	submarny	submareen
super-	above	**superman**	✓	✓
inter-	Between, among	**interact**	intract	interacked
anti-	against	**antifreeze**	✓	antifreaze
auto-	Self, own	**autograph**	photograph	dk
-ation	Noun maker	**formation**	✓	formayshun
-ation	Verb maker: If the root has a consonant before the final e drop the e	**sensation**	✓	sensayshun
-ly	Adverb maker (if the root ends in -le drop the e)	**gently**	✓	✓
-ly	Adverb maker (if the root ends in -ic add al before the -ly)	**frantically**	✓	frantickly

Summary: highlight if unknown	
Read:	Spell:
dis-	dis-
mis-	mis-
re-	re-
in-	in-
il-	il-
im-	im-
ir-	ir-
sub-	sub-
super-	super-
inter-	inter-
anti-	anti-
auto-	auto-
-ation	-ation
-ation (drop e)	-ation (drop e)
-ly (le → ly)	-ly (le → ly)
-ly (-ic → ically)	-ly (-ic → ically)

If the learner doesn't make a response or says "I don't know", record this with a – or ***dk.*** Do this for all the assessments.

Year 3 & 4 (page 2 of 2)

Affix	Meaning/function/rule	Test word	Pupil response: read	Pupil response: spell
-ous	Adjective maker	**poisonous**	✓	poysnus
-ous	Adjective maker: If the root has a consonant before the final e drop the e	**famous**	✓	fameuss
-ous	Noun maker (if the root ends in -our, drop the u)	**humorous**	✓	dk
-tion	Noun maker (use if the root ends in t or te)	**action**	✓	✓
-sion	Noun maker (use if the root ends in d, de or se)	**erosion**	erôssion	irosean
-ssion	Noun maker (use if the root ends in ss or mit)	**procession**	✓	prosesion
-cian	Noun maker (use if the root ends in c or s)	**musician**	✓	musicion

Summary: highlight if unknown	
Read:	Spell:
-ous	-ous
-ous (drop e)	-ous (drop e)
-ous (our → or)	-ous (our → or)
-tion	-tion
-sion	-sion
-ssion	-ssion
-cian	-cian
Total 19 /23	Total 8 /23

Figure 7.14

If your pupil makes more than ten errors in the spelling section of any set of words, finish the set and score it but do not administer the next set. Score 0 for any sets of words that have not been administered. If you do get as far as the Year 5 & 6 assessment, the same principles apply in assessing and scoring.

Knowledge of Morphemes: transferring the scores to the cover sheet

The first page of the **Adult Record Sheet** (Figure 7.15) serves as a summary sheet for the **Knowledge of Morphemes Assessment** (not to be confused with the separate **Assessment Summary Sheet** which is a summary of all the assessments). It offers a total score out of 75, and itemises which morphemes need to be taught.

Morph mastery
Knowledge of Morphemes Reading and Spelling Assessment (Adult Record Sheet)

This is an assessment of spelling and reading of suffixes and prefixes from the National Curriculum (2014) from Year 1 to 4. There are separate pupil sheets for the pupil to read from. To score, award one mark per item, and allow a mark if the suffix/prefix and rule (if relevant) are correctly read or spelled, even if the whole word is not correct. If more than ten spelling errors are made in one set of words, complete the set and score it, but do not continue to the next sets and score 0 for any sets that are not administered.

Summary	Pupil's Name:			Date:	
	Year 1	Year 2	Year 3 & 4	Year 5 & 6	Total Score
Score: Read	/10	/24	/23	/18	/75
Score: Spell	/10	/24	/23	/18	/75

Morphemes to target through teaching: (Highlight/circle if unknown)	
Year 1	**-s** (plural), **-s** (3rd person), **-es**, **-ing**, **-ed** (past tense), **-ed** (added syllable), **-er**, **-est**, **-y**, **un-**
Year 2	**Rule 1) No change to root: -ment, -ness, -ful, -less, -ly** **Rule 2) y →i: -es, -ed, -er, -est, -ness, -ful, -less, -ly** **Rule 3) drop e: –ing, -es, -ed, -er, -est, -y** **Rule 4) double final consonant: –ing, -ed, -er, -est, -y**
Year 3 & 4	**dis-**, **mis-**, **re-**, **in-**, **il-**, **im-**, **ir-**, **sub-**, **super-**, **inter-**, **anti-**, **auto-**, **-ation**, **-ation** (drop e), **-ly** (le → ly), **-ly** (ic →ically), **-ous**, **-ous** (drop e), **-ous** (our → or) **-tion** (t + **-ion**), **-sion** (s + **-ion**), ssion (ss + **-ion**), **-cian** (c + ian)
Year 5 & 6	**-cious**, **-tious**, **-tial**, **-cial**, **-ant**, **-ance**, **-ent**, **-ence**, **-ancy**, **-ency**, **-able**, **-ible**, **-able** (drop e), **-ible** (drop e), **-ability**, **-ibility**, **-ably**, **-ibly**

Figure 7.15

We'll now look at an imaginary learner's **Knowledge of Morphemes Assessment** to show how to complete this page. In Morpha Masters' assessment, illustrated in Figures 7.16, 7,17, and 7.18, you will note that the assessment was discontinued at the end of the **Year 2 Pupil Word List** because she had made more than 10 spelling errors in this set (Figure 7.18).

It is assumed that any morpheme that is not secure in ***either*** reading ***or*** spelling, or both, will need teaching. The cover page is intended to be a summary of these**,** so that you can see at a glance what you need to teach**.** You therefore don't need to indicate on this page whether it was reading or spelling that was insecure, just to highlight the morphemes which were not secure in either (or both). This is illustrated in Figure 7.17.

Year 1 *Morpha Masters*

Affix	Meaning/function/rule	Test word	Pupil response: read	Pupil response: spell
-s	Noun plural	cats	✓	✓
-s	3rd person singular	sits	✓	✓
-es	Adds a syllable /iz/ when noun plural or verb 3rd person	fixes	✓	fixis
-ing	Verb present continuous tense	jumping	✓	✓
-ed	Verb past tense	helped	✓	✓
-ed	Verb past tense when adds extra syllable /id/	hunted	✓	huntid
-er	Makes root word into comparative	burner	✓	✓
-est	Superlative	quickest	✓	quickist
-y	Makes root into adjective	crispy	✓	✓
un-	Opposite (not)	unzip	✓	✓

Summary: highlight if unknown	
Read:	Spell:
-s (plural)	-s (plural)
-s (3rd person)	-s (3rd person)
-es	-es
-ing	-ing
-ed	-ed
-ed (added syllable)	-ed (added syllable)
-er	-er
-est	-est
-y	-y
un-	un-
Total 10 /10	Total 7 /10

Figure 7.16

Morpha read all the Year 1 words correctly and scored 10/10. She incorrectly spelled 3 words and scored 7/10 for this (above). The morphemes she cannot spell have been highlighted on the cover sheet (below). These are the morphemes that need teaching. Although she can read them, they still need teaching.

This is an assessment of spelling and reading of suffixes and prefixes from the National Curriculum (2014) from Year 1 to 4. There are separate pupil sheets for the pupil to read from. To score, award one mark per item, and allow a mark if the suffix/prefix and rule (if relevant) are correctly read or spelled, even if the whole word is not correct. If more than ten spelling errors are made in one set of words, complete the set and score it, but do not continue to the next sets and score 0 for any sets that are not administered.

Summary	Pupil's Name:	Morpha Masters		Date:	
	Year 1	Year 2	Year 3 & 4 not tested	Year 5 & 6 not tested	Total Score
Score: Read	/10 10	/24 20	/23 0	/18 0	/175 30
Score: Spell	/10 7	/24 8	/23 0	/18 0	/175 15
Morphemes to target through teaching: (Highlight/circle if unknown)					
Year 1	-s (plural), -s (3rd person), -es, -ing, -ed (past tense), -ed (added syllable), -er, -est, -y, un-				
Year 2	Rule 1) No change to root: -ment, -ness, -ful, -less, -ly Rule 2) y → i: -es, -ed, -er, -est, -ness, -ful, -less, -ly Rule 3) drop e: –ing, -es, -ed, -er, -est, -y Rule 4) double final consonant: –ing, -ed, -er, -est, -y				
Year 3 & 4 (not tested)	dis-, mis-, re-, in-, il-, im-, ir-, sub-, super-, inter-, anti-, auto-, -ation, -ation (drop e), -ly (le → ly), -ly (ic → ically), -ous, -ous (drop e), -ous (our → or) -tion (t + -ion), -sion (s + -ion), ssion (ss + -ion), -cian (c + ian)				
Year 5 & 6 (not tested)	-cious, -tious, -tial, -cial, -ant, -ance, -ent, -ence, -ancy, -ency, -able, -ible, -able (drop e), -ible (drop e), -ability, -ibility, -ably, -ibly				

Figure 7.17

Year 2 (Page 1 of 2) *Morpha Masters*

Affix	Meaning/function/rule	Test word	Pupil response: read	Pupil response: spell
-ment	Makes root word into a noun	shipment	✓	✓
-ness	Makes root word into a noun	fitness	✓	fitnous
-ful	Makes root word into adjective	wishful	✓	wishfull
-less	Makes root word into an adjective	restless	✓	✓
-ly	Makes root word into adverb	sadly	✓	✓
-es	If root ends in y change to i	cries	✓	crise
-ed	If root ends in y change to i	dried	✓	driede
-er	If root ends in y change to i	luckier	✓	luckyer
-est	If root ends in y (ee sound) change to i	runniest	runnest	runnist
-ness		bendiness	✓	bendynous
-ful	If root ends in y change to i	plentiful	✓	pletifl
-less		penniless	penless	pennyls
-ly		angrily	angry	angrly

Summary: highlight if unknown	
Read:	Spell:
-ment	-ment
-ness	-ness
-ful	-ful
-less	-less
-ly	-ly
-es (y → i)	-es (y → i)
-ed (y → i)	-ed (y → i)
-er (y → i)	-er (y → i)
-est (y → i)	-est (y → i)
-ness (y → i)	-ness (y → i)
-ful (y → i)	-ful (y → i)
-less (y → i)	-less (y → i)
-ly (y → i)	-ly (y → i)

Year 2 (page 2 of 2) *Morpha Masters*

Affix	Meaning/function/rule	Test word	Pupil response: read	Pupil response: spell
-ing	If the root has a consonant before the final **e**, drop it if the suffix begins with a vowel or -y	liking	✓	liking
-es		roses	✓	✓
-ed		saved	✓	savd
-er		nicer	✓	✓
-est		latest	letters	laitist
-y		shiny	✓	✓
-ing	Double the final consonant in one syllable root words ending in a single consonant to keep the vowel short	letting	✓	✓
-ed		popped	✓	popt
-er		runner	✓	runah
-est		saddest	✓	sadist
-y		nutty	✓	✓

Summary: highlight if unknown	
Read:	Spell:
-ing (drop e)	-ing (drop e)
-es (drop e)	-es (drop e)
-ed (drop e)	-ed (drop e)
-er (drop e)	-er (drop e)
-est (drop e)	-est (drop e)
-y (drop e)	-y (drop e)
-ing (double consonant)	-ing (double consonant)
-ed (double consonant)	-ed (double consonant)
-er (double consonant)	-er (double consonant)
-est (double consonant)	-est (double consonant)
-y (double consonant)	-y (double consonant)
Total 20/24	Total 8 /24

Figure 7.18

Morpha correctly read some Year 2 words that she couldn't spell (for example fitness, bendiness). On the cover sheet (Figure 7.17) these are all highlighted. Although she can read them, she cannot spell them, so they need teaching. The highlighted morphemes will need to be taught. Conversely, if Morpha had been able to spell a morpheme but not read it, this would also be highlighted.

Once this cover page is complete, it will be easy to set targets for teaching. The scores can be compared each term to evaluate progress. However, a more comprehensive summary of the whole assessment can be found in the **Assessment Summary Sheet**, which we will discuss now.

Assessment Summary Sheet

Pupil's name:	Year group:	Date:	Weeks of intervention:	Working within phonics phase:
Morphological awareness Total Score /50	Transparent morphemes Areas of difficulty: Score /16	Opaque morphemes Areas of difficulty: Score /12	Word relationships Comments: Score /11	Pseudowords Comments: Score /11
Morphemic knowledge total score:			Reading /75	Spelling /75

Year 1 scores: Reading /10 Spelling /10	Difficulty with (highlight if the pupil has a difficulty in either spelling, reading or both): **-s, (plural) -s (3rd person), -es, -ing, -ed (past tense),** **-ed (added syllable) -er, -est, -y, -un**
Year 2 scores: Reading /24 Spelling /24	Difficulty with (highlight if the pupil has a difficulty in either spelling, reading or both): **Rule 1) No change to root: -ment, -ness, -ful, -less, -ly** **Rule 2) y →i: -es, -ed, -er, -est, -ness, -ful, -less, -ly** **Rule 3) drop e: –ing, es, -ed, -er, -est, -y** **Rule 4) double final consonant: –ing, -ed, -er, -est, -y**
Year 3 & 4 scores: Reading /23 Spelling /23	Difficulty with (highlight if the pupil has a difficulty in either spelling, reading or both): **dis-, mis-, re-, in-, il-, im-, ir-,** **sub-, super-, inter-, anti-, auto-** **-ation, -ation (drop e), -ly (le → ly), -ly (ic →ically),** **-ous, -ous (drop e), -ous (our → or)** **-tion (t + -ion), -sion (s + -ion), ssion (ss + -ion), -cian (c + ian)**
Year 5 & 6 scores: Reading /18 Spelling /18	Difficulty with (highlight if the pupil has a difficulty in either spelling, reading or both): **-cious, -tious, -tial, -cial,** **-ant, -ent, -ance, -ence, -ancy, -ency** **-able, -ible, -able (drop e), -ible (drop e)** **-abiliy, -ibility, -ably, -ibly**

The **Assessment Summary Sheet** (Appendix 4) is a useful overview of both assessments; the **Morphological Awareness Assessment** and the **Knowledge of Morphemes**. It can be used to set targets and plan teaching. It's also useful to know at a glance what your pupil can already do. This will help you to plan games and dictated sentences; but we will cover this in Chapter 8. Figure 7.19 is an example of Morpha's completed **Assessment Summary Sheet**.

4. Assessment Summary Sheet

Pupil's name: Morpha Masters	Year group:	Date:	Weeks of intervention: 0	Working within phonics phase:
Morphological awareness Lacks fluency & automaticity but seeks word meanings Total Score 28 /50	Transparent morphemes Areas of difficulty: • Decomposition • Longer words Score 11 /16	Opaque morphemes Areas of difficulty: • Decomposition • Sentences Score 5 /12	Word relationships Comments: Words that sound the same are problematic Score 7 /11	Pseudowords Comments: Most of these problematic Score 5 /11
Morphemic knowledge total score:			Reading /75	Spelling /75
Year 1 scores: Reading 10 /10 Spelling 7 /10	Difficulty with (highlight if the pupil has a difficulty in either spelling, reading or both): -s, (plural) -s (3rd person), -es, -ing, -ed (past tense), -ed (added syllable) -er, -est, -y, -un			
Year 2 scores: Reading 20 /24 Spelling 8 /24	Difficulty with (highlight if the pupil has a difficulty in either spelling, reading or both): Rule 1) No change to root: -ment, -ness, -ful, -less, -ly Rule 2) y → i: -es, -ed, -er, -est, -ness, -ful, -less, -ly Rule 3) drop e: -ing, es, -ed, -er, -est, -y Rule 4) double final consonant: –ing, -ed, -er, -est, -y			
Year 3 & 4 scores: Reading /23 Spelling /23 not tested	Difficulty with (highlight if the pupil has a difficulty in either spelling, reading or both): dis-, mis-, re-, in-, il-, im-, ir-, sub-, super-, inter-, anti-, auto- -ation, -ation (drop e), -ly (le → ly), -ly (ic → ically), -ous, -ous (drop e), -ous (our → or) -tion (t + -ion), -sion (s + -ion), ssion (ss + -ion), -cian (c + ian)			
Year 5 & 6 scores: Reading /18 Spelling /18 not tested	Difficulty with (highlight if the pupil has a difficulty in either spelling, reading or both): -cious, -tious, -tial, -cial, -ant, -ent, -ance, -ence, -ancy, -ency -able, -ible, -able (drop e), -ible (drop e) -abiliy, -ibility, -ably, -ibly			

Figure 7.19

Once you have completed the summary sheet you are ready to set SMART (Specific, Measurable, Achievable, Realistic and Time Limited) targets and objectives for teaching. Some examples of targets for Morpha, taken from this assessment, may be as follows:

Decompose words containing transparent morphemes (morphological awareness)
Read and spell words containing the following morphemes: **-es, -ed** (added syllable), **-est**, **-ness**, **-ful**, **-less**, **-ly**
Apply the y → I rule when suffixing with **-ful**, **-less**, **-ly**, **-es**, **-ed**, **-er**, **-est**

Now you have completed your assessments, you are ready to start planning.

8. Using the assessments to plan

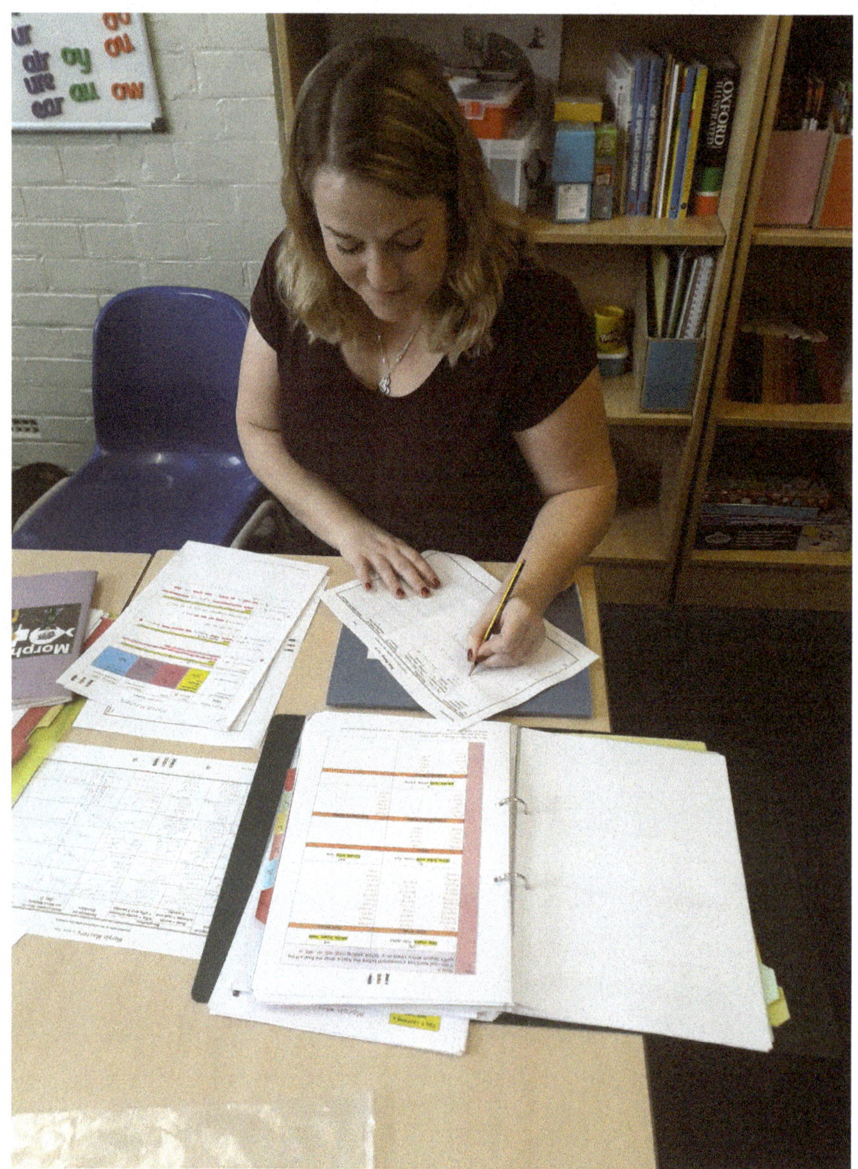

Once you have used your assessments to identify what needs to be taught, you are ready to complete the **Six-week Plan** for Morph Mastery (Figure 8.1). A photocopiable master copy of this can be found in Appendix 5.

Pupil name(s): Morph Mastery: 6week plan Date:

Shaded cells to be completed after the lessons

Week no.	Morphological Awareness Focus & games:	Morphemes		Sentence for dictation	Word chosen for Word Mastery (Day 2)	Notes (after the lessons)
		Day 1: root + words (choose 1 root and 2–12 words)	Day 2: affix + words (choose 1 affix and 3–12 words)			

Figure 8.1

Figure 8.2 shows a completed **Six-week Plan** for our imaginary pupil, Morpha Masters. A larger version of Morpha's **Six-week Plan** can be found on page 52 (Figure 8.5)

Pupil name(s): Morpha Masters Date:

Shaded cells to be completed after the lessons

Week no.	Morphological Awareness Focus & games:	Morphemes		Sentence for dictation	Word chosen for Word Mastery (Day 2)	Notes (after the lessons)
		Day 1: root + words (choose 1 root and 2–12 words)	Day 2: affix + words (choose 1 affix and 3–12 words)			
1	Transparent Morphemes.	wish wish, wishes wishing, wished	-es wishes, boxes, fixes, mixes, foxes, rushes, hisses, brushes, watches	He wishes for boxes and brushes.		
2	Production & decomposition • Morph Match	wait waits, waiting, waited, wait	-ed (added syllable) waited, rested, treated, wanted, sorted, hunted, tested, floated	I waited for boxes and wanted watches.		
3	Game 2 & 3 • Spinner Game 1–6	clean cleans, clean, cleaning, cleaned	-est richest, coldest, cleanest, tallest, lightest, strongest, longest, quickest	I hunted for the quickest, strongest foxes.		
4	• Happy Families	fit fit, fits, unfit	-ness fitness, madness, rudeness, kindness, darkness, fairness hardness	Fitness is madness for the weakest.		
5	• Pairs Down Game 1, 2, 4	pain pain, pains, pained, painful, painfulness	-ful painful, wishful, fitful harmful, careful, helpful, forgetful, hopeful	I wanted kindness from the harmful, painful foxes.		
6	↓	happy, beauty happy, beauty, unhappy, beautiful happiness unhappiness	-ness (y-i), -ful (y-i) happiness, emptiness, silliness, tidiness, laziness, plentiful, beautiful, pitiful	Happiness is beautiful and plentiful for the richest.		

Figure 8.2

This chapter will take you through how to complete the **Six-week Plan**, step by step. You will need your pupil's completed **Assessment Summary Sheet** (Figure 8.3, see Chapter 7 for details) along with SMART targets, if you have set them. The final two columns on the **Six-week Plan** are completed retrospectively each week; they are shaded to indicate this.

4. Assessment Summary Sheet

Pupil's name: Morpha Masters	Year group:	Date:	Weeks of intervention: 0	Working within phonics phase:
Morphological awareness Lacks fluency & automaticity but seeks word meanings Total Score 28 /50	**Transparent morphemes** Areas of difficulty: • Decomposition • Longer words Score 11 /16	**Opaque morphemes** Areas of difficulty: • Decomposition • Sentences Score 5 /12	**Word relationships** Comments: • Words that sound the same are problematic Score 7 /11	**Pseudowords** Comments: Most of these problematic Score 5 /11
Morphemic knowledge total score:			**Reading /75**	**Spelling /75**

Year 1 scores: Reading 10/10 Spelling 7 /10	Difficulty with (highlight if the pupil has a difficulty in either spelling, reading or both): **-s, (plural) -s (3rd person), -es, -ing, -ed (past tense),** **-ed (added syllable) -er, -est, -y, -un**
Year 2 scores: Reading 20/24 Spelling 8 /24	Difficulty with (highlight if the pupil has a difficulty in either spelling, reading or both): **Rule 1) No change to root: -ment, -ness, -ful, -less, -ly** **Rule 2) y → i: -es, -ed, -er, -est, -ness, -ful, -less, -ly** **Rule 3) drop e: –ing, es, -ed, -er, -est, -y** **Rule 4) double final consonant: –ing, -ed, -er, -est, -y**
Year 3 & 4 scores: Reading /23 Spelling /23 not tested	Difficulty with (highlight if the pupil has a difficulty in either spelling, reading or both): **dis-, mis-, re-, in-, il-, im-, ir-,** **sub-, super-, inter-, anti-, auto-** **-ation, -ation (drop e), -ly (le → ly), -ly (ic → ically),** **-ous, -ous (drop e), -ous (our → or)** **-tion (t + -ion), -sion (s + -ion), ssion (ss + -ion), -cian (c + ian)**
Year 5 & 6 scores: Reading /18 Spelling /18 not tested	Difficulty with (highlight if the pupil has a difficulty in either spelling, reading or both): **-cious, -tious, -tial, -cial,** **-ant, -ent, -ance, -ence, -ancy, -ency** **-able, -ible, -able (drop e), -ible (drop e)** **-abiliy, -ibility, -ably, -ibly**

Figure 8.3

We will now go through how to complete the plan, column by column.

First Column: Week No

This indicates which week of the intervention you are on. For your first plan this will be 1–6.

Second Column: The Morphological Awareness Focus & Games

Morphological awareness is taught using games. This column will identify your focus for teaching and the games you will use. It will normally be filled out as one block of learning for six weeks, rather than six individual targeted areas for each week, as illustrated in Figure 8.5.

To inform your choice of focus, use your **Assessment Summary Sheet**. Figure 8.4 illustrates how this has been done for Morpha Masters. Morpha's assessments show that she has difficulty with decomposition of transparent morphemes. This has therefore been targeted for the first six weeks of intervention, along with production of morphemes (Figure 8.5). This is because decomposition of morphemes goes hand in hand with production.

Pupil's name: Morpha Masters	**Year group:**	**Date:**	**Weeks of intervention:** 0	**Working within phonics phase:**
Morphological awareness Lacks fluency & automaticity but seeks word meanings **Total Score** 28 **/50**	**Transparent morphemes** **Areas of difficulty:** • Decomposition • Longer words **Score** 11 **/16**	**Opaque morphemes** **Areas of difficulty:** • Decomposition • Sentences **Score** 5 **/12**	**Word relationships** **Comments:** • Words that sound the same are problematic **Score** 7 **/11**	**Pseudowords** **Comments:** Most of these problematic **Score** 5 **/11**

Figure 8.4

Pupil name(s): Morpha Masters

Date:

Shaded cells to be completed after the lessons

Week no.	Morphological Awareness Focus & games:	Morphemes		Sentence for dictation	Word chosen for Word Mastery (Day 2)	Notes (after the lessons)
		Day 1: root + words (choose 1 root and 2–12 words)	Day 2: affix + words (choose 1 affix and 3–12 words)			
1	Transparent Morphemes.	wish wish, wishes, wishing, wished	-es wishes, boxes, fixes, mixes, foxes, rushes, hisses, brushes, watches	He wishes for boxes and brushes.		
2	Production & decomposition • Morph Match	wait waits, waiting, waited, wait	-ed (added syllable) waited, rested, treated, wanted, sorted, hunted, tested, floated	I waited for boxes and wanted watches.		
3	game 2 & 3 • Spinner Game 1–6	clean cleans, clean, cleaning, cleaned	-est richest, coldest, cleanest, tallest, lightest, strongest, longest, quickest	I hunted for the quickest, strongest foxes.		
4	• Happy Families	fit fit, fits, unfit	-ness fitness, madness, rudeness, kindness, darkness, fairness, hardness	Fitness is madness for the weakest.		
5	• Pairs Down Game 1, 2, 4	pain pain, pains, pained, painful, painfulness	-ful painful, wishful, fitful, harmful, careful, helpful, forgetful, hopeful	I wanted kindness from the harmful, painful foxes.		
6	↓	happy, beauty happy, beauty, unhappy, beautiful, happiness, unhappiness	-ness (y-i), -ful (y-i) happiness, emptiness, silliness, tidiness, laziness, plentiful, beautiful, pitiful	Happiness is beautiful and plentiful for the richest.		

Figure 8.5

Once you have written down your target area(s) for the six weeks, you will need to identify which games you will use. Choose a selection of games (for more detail, see Chapter 10) that target your focus area and write them down in this column, as illustrated in Figure 8.5.

Third Column: Morphemes

This column is divided into two (for a completed example, see Figure 8.6). On the left-hand side, the targeted roots for each week are identified for Day 1. One root is taught each week. The second sub-column lists the targeted affix (prefix or suffix) for the week, which is taught on Day 2. Again, identify just one affix for each week. You'll need to complete the right-hand side first, because the targeted affixes on this side dictate which roots you choose for the left hand side. In both sub-columns you will also write a list of words you will teach. This is illustrated in Morpha's **Six-week Plan** (Figure 8.6).

Morphemes	
Day 1: root + words (choose 1 root and 2–12 words)	**Day 2: affix + words (choose 1 affix and 3–12 words)**
wish wish, wishes, wishing, wished	-es wishes, boxes, fixes, mixes, foxes, rushes, hisses, brushes, watches
wait waits, waiting, waited, wait	-ed (added syllable) waited, rested, treated, wanted, sorted, hunted, tested, floated
clean cleans, clean, cleaning, cleaned	-est richest, coldest, cleanest, tallest, lightest, strongest, longest, quickest
fit fit, fits, unfit	-ness fitness, madness, rudeness, kindness, darkness, fairness, hardness
pain pain, pains, pained, painful, painfulness	-ful painful, wishful, fitful, harmful, careful, helpful, forgetful, hopeful
happy, beauty happy, beauty, unhappy, beautiful, happiness, unhappiness	-ness (y-i), -ful (y-i) happiness, emptiness, silliness, tidiness, laziness, plentiful, beautiful, pitiful

Figure 8.6

There are two documents that you will need to look at when you complete the Morphemes columns, in addition to your **Assessment Summary**. These are:

1. **Suggested Teaching Sequence: affixes with roots** (Figure 8.7 and Appendix 6)
2. **Word Lists** for planning (Appendix 7), available either for Year 1 (Figure 8.8), Year 2 (Figure 8.9), Years 3 & 4 (Figure 8.10) and Years 5 & 6 (Figure 8.11). Note that these word lists are extensive so only the first page is shown in these pages but they can all be found in Appendix 7.

Optional: choose as appropriate for the pupil(s). These have been chosen for potential flexibility with word play as the programme continues. Words in red are listed in the National Curriculum as common exception words for that year group (Year 1 & 2) or 100 words that children are expected to spell by the end of that year group (Year 3 & 4, Year 5 & 6).

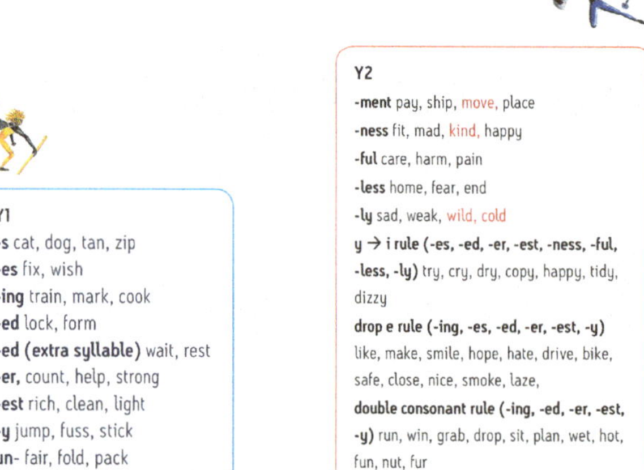

Y3 & 4
dis- connect, continue
mis- spell, calculate
re- visit, appear
in- correct, direct
il- legal
ir- regular, relevant
im – perfect, possible
sub- scribe, merge
super- market, star
inter- act, -rupt
anti- freeze
auto- graph
-ation inform, commend
-ation (drop e) create, educate
-ly (le → ly) idle, simple
-ly (ic → ically) basic
-ous danger, poison
-ous (drop e) fame, adventure
-ous (our → or) humour
-tion elect, act
-sion tense, comprehend, decide
-ssion admit, possess
-cian music, electric
Y5 & 6
-cious grace, space
-tious caution
-cial face, office
-tial part, essence
-ant observe, expect
- ent depend, exist
- ance attend, (re)sist (stand)
-ence indulge, compete
-ancy hesitate, expect
-ency fluent, urgent
-able port (carry), enjoy
-ible struct (build), flex
-able (drop e) love, excite
-ible (drop e) sense, force
-ability read
-ibility cred (believe)
-ably reason, note
-ibly leg (read)

Figure 8.7 Suggested Teaching Sequence

Year 1 & 2

Words in bold have phonics and/or spelling rules that relate to that year group or below. Words in red are common exception words for that year group. *Highlighted words in italics* have more possibilities for word building and are in the suggested teaching sequence for word roots, with further word lists below for playing games and spelling lists.

Year 1	-s ***cat, dog, tan, zip***		_es ***fix, wish,*** **box, mix, rush, hiss**
	Plural maker (noun)		**Plural maker (noun)**
	cats	rats	boxes
	dogs	ribs	ashes
	bags	vets	bushes
	fans	vans	churches
	fins	wigs	foxes
	hats	zips	brushes
	huts	shops	dishes
	jugs	days	kisses
	tans	schools	patches
	logs	friends	lunches
	legs	pens	glasses
	mats	toys	watches
	mugs	games	
	nets	cups	
	pans	ponds	
	pits	books	
	pins	boys	
	rags	desks	
	Verb tense		**Verb tense**
	digs	sits	fizzes
	bats	sobs	wishes
	bets	kicks	mixes
	gets	spins	rushes
	hits	runs	catches
	jogs	cooks	buzzes
	tips	plays	hisses
	licks	jumps	fixes
	mops	drags	touches
	pats	drops	washes
	picks	grabs	
	quits	hugs	
		stops	

Figure 8.8 Word Lists for Planning

Year 2	Rule 1: No change to the root If a suffix starts with a consonant, it is added to the root word without any change in the spelling of the root word.	
	-ment *pay, ship, move, place*	**-ness** *mad, rude, fit, kind, happy,* empty, silly
	Noun maker	**Noun maker**
	movement, replacement, placement, payment, enjoyment, shipment, employment, amazement, management	rudeness, hardness, neatness, fitness, madness, sadness, kindness, softness, strictness, greatness, gladness, shyness, darkness, flatness, loudness, fairness
	-ful *care, harm, pain*	**-less** *home, fear, end*
	Adjective maker – means full of	**Adjective maker – means without**
	careful, wishful, fearful, restful, hopeful, shameful, fitful, hateful, faithful, useful, forgetful, handful, harmful, hurtful, colourful, painful, thankful, mouthful, helpful, playful	homeless, careless, fearless, blameless, endless, formless, restless, hopeless, helpless, painless, speechless, sleepless, homeless, thoughtless
	-ly *sad, weak, wild, cold*	
	Adverb maker	
	Sadly, weekly, Badly, properly, madly, normally, weakly, kindly, wildly, quickly, coldly, thickly, friendly, really	

Figure 8.9 Word Lists for Planning

Morph Mastery

Word Lists for Teaching Prefixes and Suffixes (Year 3 & 4)

Year 3 & 4

Words in bold have phonics and/or spelling rules that relate to that year group or below. Words in red are on the list of 100 words in the National Curriculum that children in England are expected to be able to spell by the end of Year 4. *Highlighted words in italics* have more possibilities for word building and are in the suggested teaching sequence for word roots, with further word lists below for playing games and spelling lists.

Year 3 & 4	dis- *connect*, *continue*, **agree, like, trust**			mis- *spell*, *calculate*, **behave, fire, use**		
	Opposite, not			**Opposite, not**		
	disagree	disown	disapprove	misunderstand	misfire	misguide
	disobey	displease	discomfort	misspell	misfortune	mislead
	discover	disqualify	distrust	misdeed	mishear	misprint
	dislike	disappear	discontinue	misbehave	misinform	mistrust
	dishonest	disconnect		miscalculate	misread	misuse
	dishearten	disinfect		misplace	mistake	
	dislodge	disembark		miscount	misfortune	
	re- *visit*, *appear*, **make, place, act, call, bound**					
	Again			**Back**		
	remake	relive	rebuild	retreat		
	redo	revisit	recycle	recede		
	regrow	rewrite	refill	return		
	replace	refresh	reform	recall		
	reawaken	reappear	replay	reflect		
	react	redecorate		rebound		

Figure 8.10 Word Lists for Planning

Year 5 & 6[1]

Words in bold have phonics and/or spelling rules that relate to that year group or below. Words in red are on the list of 100 words in the National Curriculum that children in England are expected to be able to spell by the end of Year 6. *Highlighted words in italics* have more possibilities for word building and are in the suggested teaching sequence for word roots, with further word lists below for playing games and spelling lists.

Year 5 & 6		
	-cious (c + ious) ***grace, space,* malice**	**-tious (t + ious)** ***caution,* superstition**
	Adjective maker (when the root ends in ce – remove the e)	**Adjective maker (when the root ends in n – remove the n)**
	vicious gracious spacious officious malicious	rebellious repetitious superstitious cautious infectious nutritious
	-cial ***face,* office, prejudice, race**	**-tial** ***part, essence,* existence, evidence**
	Adjective maker (when the root ends in ace or a short vowel sound followed by ce – remove the e)	**Adjective maker (when the root ends in nce or t)**
	facial prejudicial beneficial official artificial racial commercial financial sacrificial	existential partial essential confidential evidential substantial inferential torrential sequential
	Exception: Spatial	
	-ant ***observe, expect,* tolerate, hesitate**	**-ance** ***attend, resist,* defy, guide**
	Adjective maker (when the root ends in t or ate – remove ate. **Often made from roots that can also be used with -ation)**	**Noun maker** **Used when related adjective ends in -ant** **Refers to action, state or quality**
	observant participant hesitant tolerant abundant distant dominant expectant pregnant buoyant	hesitance tolerance resistance brilliance attendance ignorance elegance arrogance alliance defiance distance guidance

Figure 8.11 Word Lists for Planning

There are four steps to completing the Morphemes column. They are:

1. Choose your six targeted affixes for the right-hand column. Select them from your completed **Assessment Summary Sheet**. You will teach one of these each week; list one in each row of this column (demonstrated in Figure 8.12). Don't choose your words yet!

Year 1 scores: Reading 10/10 Spelling 7/10	Difficulty with (highlight if the pupil has a difficulty in either spelling, reading or both): **-s, (plural) -s (3rd person), -es, -ing, -ed (past tense),** **-ed (added syllable) -er, -est, -y, -un**
Year 2 scores: Reading 20/24 Spelling 8/24	Difficulty with (highlight if the pupil has a difficulty in either spelling, reading or both): **Rule 1) No change to root: -ment, -ness, -ful, -less, -ly** **Rule 2) y →i: -es, -ed, -er, -est, -ness, -ful, -less, -ly** **Rule 3) drop e: –ing, es, -ed, -er, -est, -y** **Rule 4) double final consonant: –ing, -ed, -er, -est, -y**

Morphemes	
Day 1: root + words (choose 1 root and 2–12 words)	**Day 2: affix + words (choose 1 affix and 3–12 words)**
	-es
	-ed (added syllable)
	-est
	-ness
	-ful
	-ness (y-i), -ful (y-i)

Figure 8.12

2. Choose your six roots for the left hand column (Day 1). You don't need to look at the **Assessment Summary** for this: you can take these directly from the **Suggested Teaching Sequence**, as illustrated in Figure 8.13.

The **Suggested Teaching Sequence** provides roots to teach alongside your targeted affixes. In Figure 8.13, Morpha's first targeted affix is **-es.** The Suggested Teaching Sequence provides a choice of **fix** or **wish;** here, **wish** has been chosen. In this case, wish was preferred because of the potential words in future weeks (e.g. **wishfulness**) but there are many possible reasons for preferring one of the suggested roots. You might wish to practise a letter sound or formation, or you might wish to use particular vocabulary with your pupil. Use your judgement. The other roots for Weeks 2–6 are chosen in the same way.

Notice that in Morpha's case, two affixes with corresponding roots have been chosen for Week 6. Normally one affix is enough, but in this case Morpha will already have been taught **-ness** and **-ful**; Week 6 tackles them both with the addition of a spelling rule (**y – i**).

Morphemes	
Day 1: root + words (choose 1 root and 2–12 words)	**Day 2: affix + words (choose 1 affix and 3–12 words)**
wish	-es
wait	-ed (added syllable)
clean	-est
fit	-ness
pain	-ful
happy, beauty	-ness (y-i), -ful (y-i)

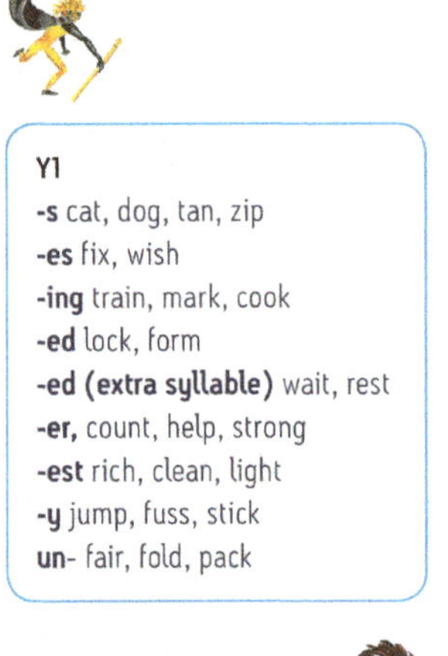

Y1
-s cat, dog, tan, zip
-es fix, wish
-ing train, mark, cook
-ed lock, form
-ed (extra syllable) wait, rest
-er, count, help, strong
-est rich, clean, light
-y jump, fuss, stick
un- fair, fold, pack

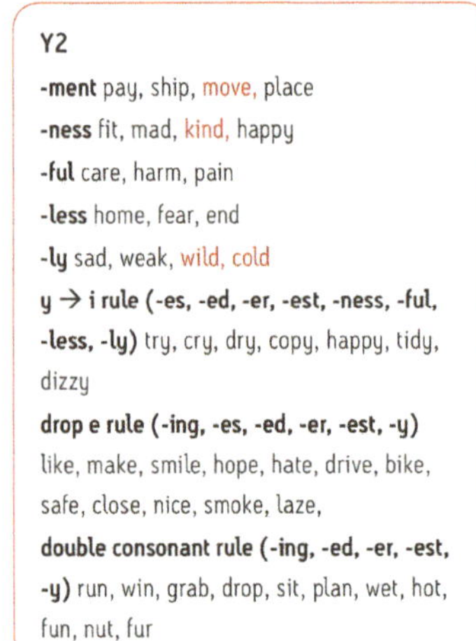

Y2
-ment pay, ship, move, place
-ness fit, mad, kind, happy
-ful care, harm, pain
-less home, fear, end
-ly sad, weak, wild, cold
y → i rule (-es, -ed, -er, -est, -ness, -ful, -less, -ly) try, cry, dry, copy, happy, tidy, dizzy
drop e rule (-ing, -es, -ed, -er, -est, -y) like, make, smile, hope, hate, drive, bike, safe, close, nice, smoke, laze,
double consonant rule (-ing, -ed, -er, -est, -y) run, win, grab, drop, sit, plan, wet, hot, fun, nut, fur

Figure 8.13

3. Choose the words you will teach with your target root (left hand column, Figure 8.14). Choose between

two and 12 words derived from your root. These should not be challenging words, because on Day 1 you are just learning a root and practising word building. Therefore, you should make sure the words you choose are within your learner's grasp. Remember the golden rule of precision planning (Chapter 4)! Don't include words containing affixes that were insecure in assessment, except the affix you are targeting on Day 2. So, Morpha can learn ***painfulness*** in week 5, because she has already learnt ***-ness*** in week 4, and ***-ful*** is targeted on Day 2 of week 5. However, it would be unwise to ask her to learn ***wishfulness*** in week 1; that would be too much of a challenge (Figure 8.14).

Morphemes	
Day 1: root + words (choose 1 root and 2–12 words)	**Day 2: affix + words (choose 1 affix and 3–12 words)**
wish wish, wishes, wishing, wished	-es
wait waits, waiting, waited, wait	-ed (added syllable)
clean cleans, clean, cleaning, cleaned	-est
fit fit, fits, unfit	-ness
pain pain, pains, pained, painful, painfulness	-ful
happy, beauty happy, beauty, unhappy, beautiful, happiness unhappiness	-ness (y-i), -ful (y-i)

Figure 8.14

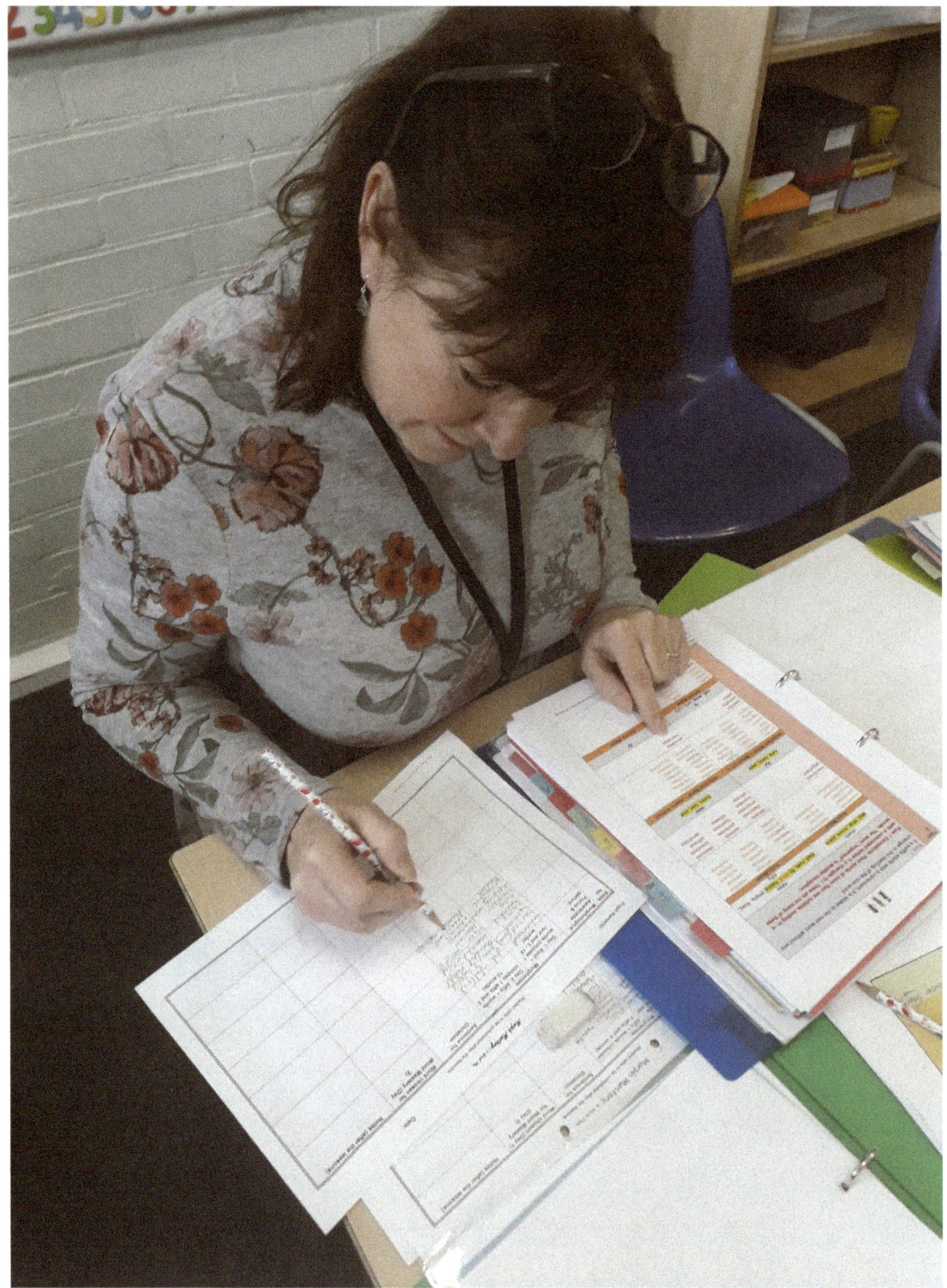

4. List your words derived from your affix for Day 2 (right hand column, see Figure 8.15). To do this, you will need a copy of the **Word Lists** for planning (Figure 8.8, 8.9, 8.10, 8.11). Find the relevant list of words on this document and choose between three and 12 words for your pupil to learn, depending on the availability of words and your learner's ability. Figure 8.15 illustrates how Morpha's words have been chosen for the affixes ***-es*** and ***-ed*** (added syllable) from the relevant pages of the **Year 1 Word Lists**.

Morphemes	
Day 1: root + words (choose 1 root and 2–12 words)	**Day 2: affix + words (choose 1 affix and 3–12 words)**
wish wish, wishes, wishing, wished	-es wishes, boxes, fixes, mixes, foxes, rushes, hisses, brushes, watches
wait waits, waiting, waited, wait	-ed (added syllable) waited, rested, treated, wanted, sorted, hunted, tested, floated
clean cleans, clean, cleaning, cleaned	-est richest, coldest, cleanest, tallest, lightest, strongest, longest, quickest
fit fit, fits, unfit	-ness fitness, madness, rudeness, kindness, darkness, fairness, hardness
pain pain, pains, pained, painful, painfulness	-ful painful, wishful, fitful, harmful, careful, helpful, forgetful, hopeful
happy, beauty happy, beauty, unhappy, beautiful, happiness, unhappiness	-ness (y-i), -ful (y-i) happiness, emptiness, silliness, tidiness, laziness, plentiful, beautiful, pitiful

_es *fix*, *wish*, box, mix, rush, hiss
Plural maker (noun)
boxes ashes bushes churches foxes brushes dishes kisses patches lunches glasses watches

-ed (when an extra syllable is created after t) *wait*, *rest*, treat	
treated	sorted
rested	waited
hunted	floated
wanted	tinted
hinted	tested
rented	

Figure 8.15

Fourth Column: Sentence for Dictation

This is a sentence used on Day 3, which contains the words you have been teaching and the words you are targeting. Aim to include some words from previous weeks; this overlearning will be essential. In keeping with the golden rule of planning precisely (Chapter 4), be careful not to include words that are too challenging for your learner. The only challenging words in these sentences should be the targeted learning and revision of what you have taught. You may need to refer back to your assessments to make sure you are not adding in affixes your learner doesn't yet know. Keep the sentences **short** and **simple**. It doesn't matter if they don't make complete sense. The sillier they are, the more your learner will have the opportunity to laugh! In Figure 8.16, you will see how the sentence chosen for Week 3 includes words from previous weeks.

Now that you have completed your fourth column, you are ready to plan your lessons.

Pupil name(s): Morpha Masters

Date:

Shaded cells to be completed after the lessons

Week no.	Morphological Awareness Focus & games:	Morphemes Day 1: root + words (choose 1 root and 2–12 words)	Morphemes Day 2: affix + words (choose 1 affix and 3–12 words)	Sentence for dictation	Word chosen for Word Mastery (Day 2)	Notes (after the lessons)
1	Transparent Morphemes.	wish wish, wishes, wishing, wished	-es wishes, boxes, fixes, mixes, foxes, rushes, hisses, brishes, watches	He wishes for boxes and brushes.		
2	Production & decomposition • Morph Match	wait waits, waiting, waited, wait	-ed (added syllable) waited, rested, treated, wanted, sorted, hunted, tested, floated	I waited for boxes and wanted watches.		
3	Game 2 & 3 • Spinner Game 1–6	clean cleans, clean, cleaning, cleaned	-est richest, coldest, cleanest, tallest, lightest, strongest, longest, quickest	I hunted for the quickest, strongest foxes.		
4	• Happy Families	fit fit, fits, unfit	-ness fitness, madness, rudeness, kindness, darkness, fairness, hardness	Fitness is madness for the weakest.		
5	• Pairs Down Game 1, 2, 4	pain pain, pains, pained, painful, painfulness	-ful painful, wishful, fitful, harmful, careful, helpful, forgetful, hopeful	I wanted kindness from the harmful, painful foxes.		
6	↓	happy, beauty happy, beauty, unhappy, beautiful, happiness, unhappiness	-ness (y–i), -ful (y–i) happiness, emptiness, silliness, tidiness, laziness, plentiful, beautiful, pitiful	Happiness is beautiful and plentiful for the richest.		

Figure 8.16

Planning for groups

When working with groups on Morph Mastery, the smaller your group is, the more effective your intervention is likely to be. If you are delivering the intervention precisely, make sure your group is not bigger than four. In larger groups it is still possible to play some of the games and teach the words, but you would not be planning precisely for this number of children. Any group method is recommended only for pupils with less severe difficulties with spelling.

When you are working with groups, your planning will need to be more flexible, because none of your **Assessment Summaries** will be the same. Ideally you will have a group of learners at a similar stage. If this is not the case, you should reconsider your group, or your task of finding suitable learning for all of them will be too mammoth for the intervention to be effective.

General guidelines are to go with the majority. In other words, choose areas of teaching that most, or all, of your pupils need to learn. Learners identified for this intervention are going to benefit from any practice and over-learning, so don't worry about focussing on what is already known by one or more members of your group, if it is needed by other members.

When choosing a morphological awareness focus, be aware that any practice in this area will be beneficial, so choose the focus that is most needed. If in doubt, any work on production and decomposition of morphemes will link with the other areas in the assessment anyway, so this might be a good place to start.

When targeting your affixes, again go with the majority. Sometimes learners working on Year 2 spelling of morphemes are not secure in a couple of the morphemes on the Year 1 list. If you find that some of the morphemes in the Year 1 list are not known by just one of your learners, make a judgement whether you need to teach it. It might be that the morpheme is targeted anyway in the Year 2 list, but with a spelling rule, in which case you could teach it alongside the Year 2 spelling rule. If the morphemes ***-ed, -er, -est*** or ***-y*** were unknown by one or more members of your group, it would be advisable to teach these, even if most of your group know them. These can be known for spelling but they hold important grammatical functions, and security in this can be helpful when moving on to the Year 2 morphemes. If your group of learners is particularly weak, you may need to teach every morpheme that was unknown by your group, even if it was just one learner. If this is the case, consider making the group smaller or even teaching them 1:1.

9. The lessons in detail

This chapter looks at the individual lesson plans and how to complete them. A step by step, detailed description on each element of the lessons is provided, as well as example lesson plans.

The lesson plans

You will need to print off the **Lesson Plan Masters** (see Figure 9.1), as well as the **Lesson Plan Masters with guidance** (see Figure 9.2). The guidance sheets can be laminated and kept to hand as a reference, especially when you are starting off. Photocopy masters of all of these can be found in Appendix 8 and 9. You will also need your ***completed*** **Six-week Plan** (Appendix 5).

Much of the lesson plan is already completed for you. You'll just need to write specific details in some of the boxes, for example the words or sentence you have chosen, and indicate your choice of game by highlighting it in the relevant section. There are also some boxes for you to write notes during and/or after the lesson.

Day 1: Learning a new root

Name:	**Year group/class:**	**Week no.:**	**Date:**
New word root:	**Word list:**		
Notes from previous lesson(s):			
Resources: Alphabet arc set out, trigger cards, blank trigger card, Morpheme Cards (chosen in advance), book to write in, pencil/pen, ruler, highlighter pens (green, yellow, blue), **Word Agility** game & resources, text or book for **Word Espionage** (reading), Morph Mastercard			

Morphological awareness (6 mins)	**Targeted area:**	**Activity/game:** e.g.: Morph Match, Spinner Games for Morphological Awareness Development, Happy Families, Pairs Down
Notes:		

Test trigger cards (spell + meaning/function if relevant) (2 mins)
Any problems?

Word root work (11 mins)	Include previously taught affixes/root • Introduce this week's root: Read it (use Morpheme Card or write it on whiteboard for pupil to read). What does it mean? Pupil makes it with tactile letters. • What other words can you make with this root? Pupil uses Morpheme Cards (roots and affixes) to make them and say them each time using The Morph handshake. • Learners make a portal in books for the root (keep Morpheme Cards in view). Include any other words learners can think of. • Dictate the words for pupil to write. Highlight the root. Make a trigger card. • Write the root on the Morph Mastercard (centre).	Word Agility: quick game – reading or spelling. (Highlight one): Morph Guess Morph Match & Spell Spin Words Spin Words Trick Spinner Match/Dice Match Spinner Match Trick Voice Families (voice recorder)
Notes:		

Word espionage (reading text) (10 mins)	Book:	Morphemes found: (If appropriate, adult picks a word for Word Mastery activity in Day 2)
Any identified vocabulary?		Any tricky words identified?

Review with learner (1 min): What word root did you learn today? Which words are derived from this root? Which word did you find tricky to spell/understand? How will you remember it next time?
Adult review

Figure 9.1

Day 1: Learning a new root (page 1 of 2)

Name:	Year group/class:	Week no.:	Date:
New word root: Choose one – use planning	**Word list:** Between 2–12 words containing this week's root depending on learner's speed and size of group. In the first few weeks there may only be 3 possible words		
Notes from previous lesson(s):	Write here anything that came up needing reinforcing or practice, any tricky words or morpheme		
Resources: Alphabet arc set out (set out before lesson using tactile letters), trigger cards, blank trigger card, Morpheme Cards (chosen in advance), book to write in, pencil/pen, ruler, highlighter pens (green, yellow, blue), **Word Agility** game & resources, text or book for **Word Espionage** (reading), Morph Mastercard			

Morphological Awareness (6 mins)	Targeted area:	Activity/game: This can be a few quick questions or a game. EG: Morph Match, Spinner Games for Morphological Awareness Development, Happy Families, Pairs Down Games may need adapting according to time
Notes: Choose a game from the appendix to match your targeted area directly from the assessment. Example: Targeted area: word relationships. Game: voice recorder game 1		

Test trigger cards (spell + meaning/function if relevant) (2 mins)

Any problems? Learners spell the **word** on the front of the trigger card. If forgotten or not correct, turn card over to use trigger on the back and make a note for future teaching.

Day 1: Learning a new root (page 2 of 2)

Word Root Work (11 mins)	Include previously taught affixes/root Use colour coding where possible. Reinforce with The Morph handshake to ensure this activity is kinaesthetic • Introduce this week's root: Read it (use Morpheme Card or write it on whiteboard for pupil to read). What does it mean? Pupil makes it with tactile letters. • What other words can you make with this root? Pupil uses Morpheme Cards (roots and affixes) to make them and say them each time using The Morph handshake. • Learners make a portal in books for the root (keep Morpheme Cards in view). Include any other words learners can think of: limit this to words using today's root as long as they include known morphemes. • Dictate the words for pupil to write. Highlight the root. Make a trigger card. The learners write the morpheme with a word on one side, and decide on a "trigger" to draw/write on the back which will help them remember. • Write the root on the Morph Mastercard (centre). On the centre page of the Mastercard, write it in the appropriate box for the initial letter of the root.	**Word Agility**: quick game – reading or spelling. Highlight one: Morph Guess Morph Match & Spell Spin Words Spin Words Trick Spinner Match/ Dice Match Spinner Match Trick Voice Families (voice recorder)

Word Espionage (reading text) (10 mins)	Learners read their individual reading books OR a text from a lesson - either previous or future lesson. They hunt morphemes and write them down in words on whiteboards, as well as any tricky words.	Morphemes found: (If appropriate, adult picks a word for Word Mastery activity in Day 2.) Choose one linked to current learning if possible. If no word from this text is appropriate, just choose a different word for Day 2.
Any identified vocabulary? Note any interesting words containing taught or discussed morphemes.		Any tricky words identified? Note any words the learners found difficult to read for future teaching.

Review with learner (1 min): What word root did you learn today? Which words are derived from this root? Which word did you find tricky to spell/understand? How will you remember it next time?
Adult Review

Figure 9.2

Preparation before you begin teaching

There are some resources you will need to prepare before you start any teaching. These are:

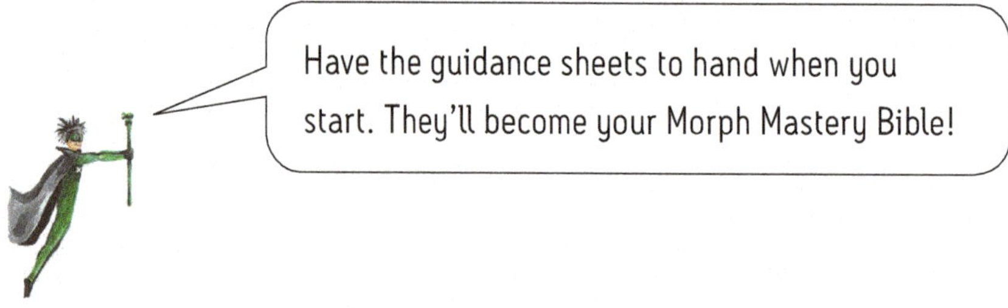

Have the guidance sheets to hand when you start. They'll become your Morph Mastery Bible!

- Blank copies of the **Lesson Plan Masters, Day 1, 2 and 3** (Appendix 9) – enough for each week you are planning to teach
- One copy of the **Lesson Plan Masters with guidance** (Appendix 8) – these are really handy single page crib sheets which detail everything you need and do for each part of each lesson. There is one page for each lesson. It's recommended you laminate them and keep them handy every lesson
- **Morpheme Cards Roots** (Appendix 14) – printed double sided and laminated. Make sure you prepare all the cards for the year group words you are targeting and previous year group(s). These cards are cumulative, so you'll still need to prepare the cards for Years 1 and 2 if you are working on Years 3 and 4 morphemes, as they are used in most of the games, and they are embedded in the lessons
- **Morpheme Cards: Prefix and Suffix** (Appendix 14)
- **Word Mastery Question Cards** (Appendix 12) – laminated or printed on strong card
- **Morph Race Track** and **Stealth** Stronghold Grids please make Stronghold Grids in bold, printed and laminated (Chapter 10)
- **Spinner Base Masters** for Spinner Games, printed and laminated (Chapter 10)
- **Blank Spinner Base Masters,** printed on to paper (Chapter 10)
- **The Morph Mastercard** (Appendix 11) – 1 per learner, printed double sided onto pastel or cream card
- Print off the **Meet the Masters** file, one for each learner (Appendix 10)
- Dice and counters for games
- Voice recorders – you are likely to need voice recorders with the potential to record 12 or more sound bites. These can be bought as two recorders with six sound bite options (e.g. a dice) or 12 individual voice recorders. Choose recorders that are easy to use – you'll want to be able to just press a button and hear the recording

It's always good practice to use pastel or cream paper – this reduces the visual glare and can make a huge difference to some learners.

- Sets of tactile letters – at least two sets of the alphabet will be useful
- Green, yellow and blue highlighters
- Mini whiteboards and pens, or paper and pencils
- Lined exercise book for each learner
- Sets of blank trigger cards – to make these, you'll need pastel green, yellow and blue card cut up into small cards approximately 8cm x 5cm, hole punched at the narrow end, and some treasury tags
- Lots of blank cards/ paper for games

A list of where some of these items can be purchased in available in Appendix 18.

Morph Mastercard – before your first lesson

Before your first lesson, you'll need to meet with your learner(s) to make the Morph Mastercard together. In advance, print the **Morph Mastercard** (Appendix 11) on cream or pastel coloured card or paper, double sided at the short edge.

Fold the card so that the title box with name and class is the front page (Figure 9.3). The centre spread will be the blank **Roots and Derivatives** chart (Figure 9.4). The back page should be the **Affixes I Know with Roots** table (Figure 9.5).

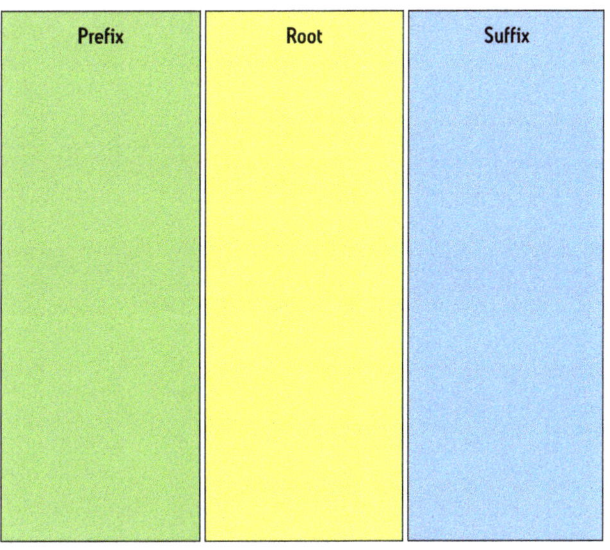

Figure 9.3

Roots and derivatives

These are the roots I already know and interesting derivatives

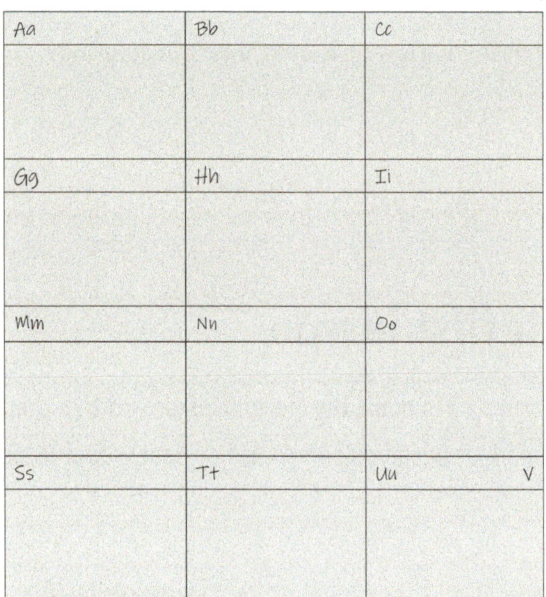

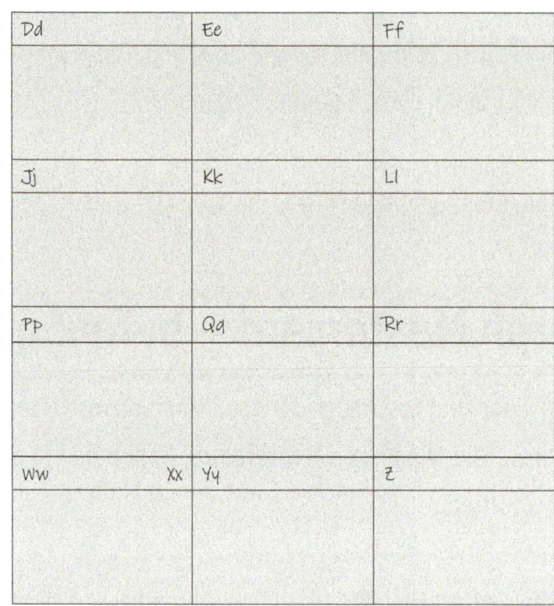

Figure 9.4

Figure 9.5

Using the **Meet the Masters** page (Figure 9.6, Appendix 10), introduce your learners to Prefa, Root and Sufa. The pupil can choose a favourite pose for each character, which is then cut out and stuck into the table on the front page of the booklet (Figure 9.7).

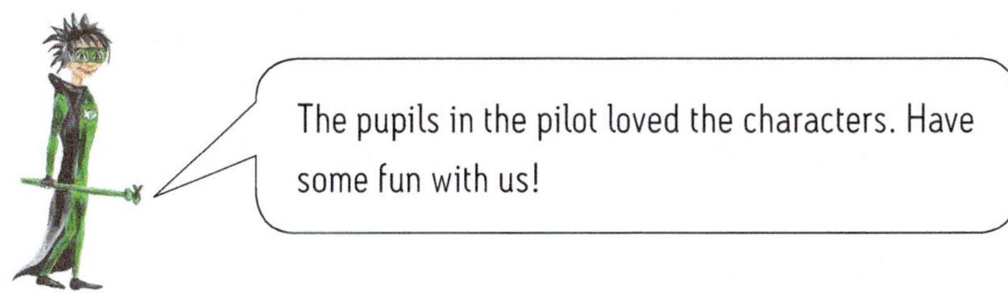

The pupils in the pilot loved the characters. Have some fun with us!

Figure 9.6

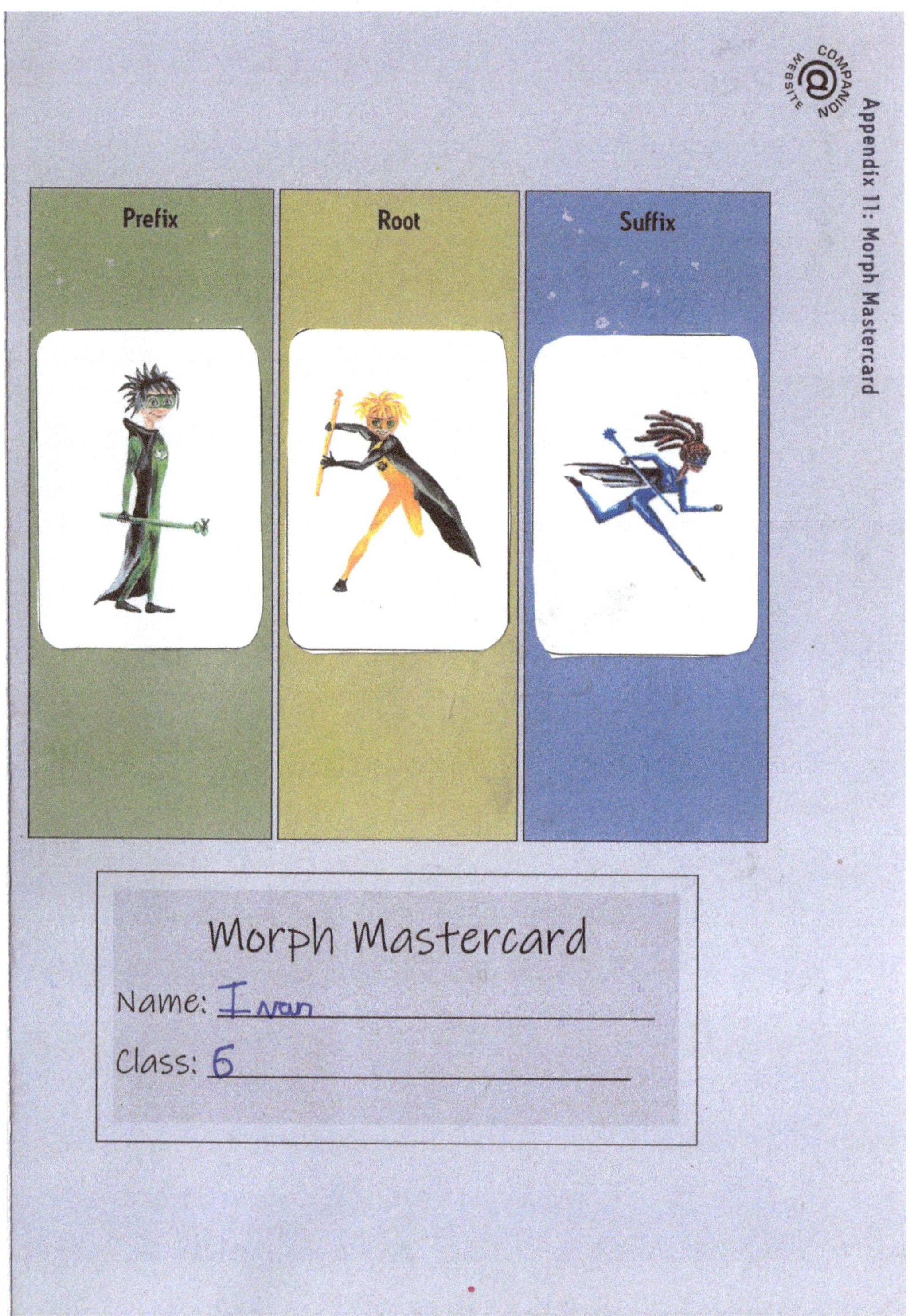

Figure 9.7

The front page can now serve as a visual aid for the three characters, their colours and position in a word. The centre page serves as both spelling and vocabulary aid – a reminder of interesting words as well as spellings. The back page serves as a record of what has been taught for the class teacher.

Preparation before each lesson

On the lesson plan, write the child's name, class, the week number and date. From your completed six-week plan, write in the targeted root and/or affix for the week you are on and your word list. It is also extremely useful to write in any notes from the previous lesson that will be helpful to you. This could be anything: a tricky spelling, something you want to practise, or a word that was discussed and requires follow up. The resources you need are then listed for you on the plan. Before you start teaching, make sure you have all the resources you need for the games you will play, and check the Resources section of the lesson plan to see if you have missed anything else.

Figure 9.8 and Figure 9.9 show examples of how this section might look for **Day 1** and **Day 2**.

Day 1: Learning a new root

Name: S	**Year group/class:** 5	**Week no.:** 5	**Date:** 26 · 2 · 21
New word root: stick	**Word list:** stick, sticks, sticking, unstick, sticky		
Notes from previous lesson(s):	Need to practise qu + x		
Resources: Alphabet arc set out, trigger cards, blank trigger card, Morpheme Cards (chosen in advance), book to write in, pencil/pen, ruler, highlighter pens (green, yellow, blue), **Word Agility** game & resources, text or book for **Word Espionage** (reading), Morph Mastercard			

Figure 9.8

Day 2: Learning a new suffix/prefix

Name: S	**Year group/ class:** 5	**Week no.:** 5	**Date:** 27 · 2 · 21
Targeted root (from day 1): stick **New affix:** -y	**Word list:** sticky, bendy, bossy, smelly, jumpy		
Notes from previous lesson(s):	practise qu, x, box, fix, light, -es		
Resources: Alphabet arc set out, trigger cards, Morpheme Cards (root and affix, chosen in advance), book to write in, pencil/pen, ruler, highlighter pens (green, yellow, blue), **Word Agility** game and resources, chosen word for **Word Mastery** (may have been chosen in **Word Espionage** section of lesson 1), **Word Mastery** cards, Morph Mastercard			

Figure 9.9

Figure 9.10 is an example of a prepared table before a **Day 1** (one learner). The adult sits at right angles to the learner. This learner is right-handed. A left-handed learner would sit on the other side, so that the adult can see what s/he is writing.

Figure 9.10

We'll now go through each section of the lesson plans. For each section we'll ask the following three questions:

What is it? How do I teach it? How do I plan it?

Sections 1 and 2 (Morphological Awareness and Test Trigger Cards) of each lesson are the same in Day 1, 2 and 3 lessons.

Section 1 (Day 1, 2 & 3): Morphological Awareness (5–8 minutes)

Morphological Awareness: What is it?

For more about what morphological awareness is and why we teach it, see Chapter 5. In brief, morphological awareness is not reading or spelling. Instead, you are explicitly teaching a sense of words, their meanings, how they are constructed and how they are related.

Morphological Awareness: How do I teach it?

In Morph Mastery, morphological awareness is always taught through games. There are lots of games to choose from, listed in Chapter 10. Although morphological awareness is not a reading exercise, some of the games do involve reading. If your learner is a weak reader, it's fine to read the

Sections 1 and 2 of each lesson are the same in Day 1, 2 and 3 lessons.

words to your learner during the game, or choose games with limited reading requirements, like the games using voice recorders. All the games are structured but generic. In other words, the structure of the game is always the same, but you will personalise it by adding different words that are appropriate to your learners. It's fine to use the same game again and again; just change the words that you choose.

The key thing to remember about morphological awareness is that it's oral and you can use any words – not just words you have been teaching. They're great games for vocabulary development.

Morphological Awareness: How do I plan it?

The practitioners on the pilot commented that highlighting the lesson plans is fast and easy – a bonus!

On the lesson plan, write down the targeted area from your six-week plan, then choose a game and highlight accordingly (demonstrated in Figure 9.11), writing any additional notes if necessary. You will need to choose the words you wish to use for the game in advance. Remember, this is not a spelling activity, so choose words which will stretch your learner's oral vocabulary, even if they are words your learners won't manage to spell. Most games have suggested words, or you can go to your **Word Lists for planning (Appendix 7)** if you are stuck.

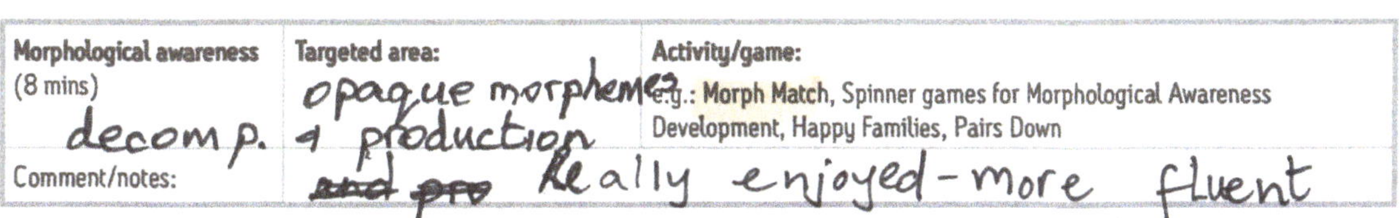

Morphological awareness (8 mins) decomp.	Targeted area: opaque morphemes + production	Activity/game: e.g.: Morph Match, Spinner games for Morphological Awareness Development, Happy Families, Pairs Down
Comment/notes:	~~and pro~~ Really enjoyed – more fluent	

Figure 9.11

There are two traps you could fall into in planning this section of the lesson:

1. Trying to teach spelling of morphemes or spelling rules. Don't! This will detract from the exploration of words and meaning
2. Restricting the activity to words you have targeted for spelling. Don't! You can use longer and more exciting words here – you are stretching vocabulary and word sense, not teaching spelling

Section 2 (Day 1, 2 & 3): Test Trigger Cards (2 minutes)

Test Trigger Cards: What is it?

Each week, on **Day 1** and **2**, learners create two new trigger cards, a yellow card for the targeted root, and a green card for a prefix or blue card for a suffix. The trigger cards are made from blank pastel coloured card (green, blue or yellow), which is cut up into approximately 8cm x 5cm. Targeted morphemes are written on the front, with a word containing that morpheme and a "trigger" to aid memory on the other side. Examples of triggers can be found later in this chapter, in Figures 9.22, 9.28, 9.29 and 9.30. They are kept altogether in a cumulative pack, on a treasury tag or key ring (Figure 9.12).

Colour coding your trigger cards to match the colours with Prefa, Root and Sufa will help your learners to remember.

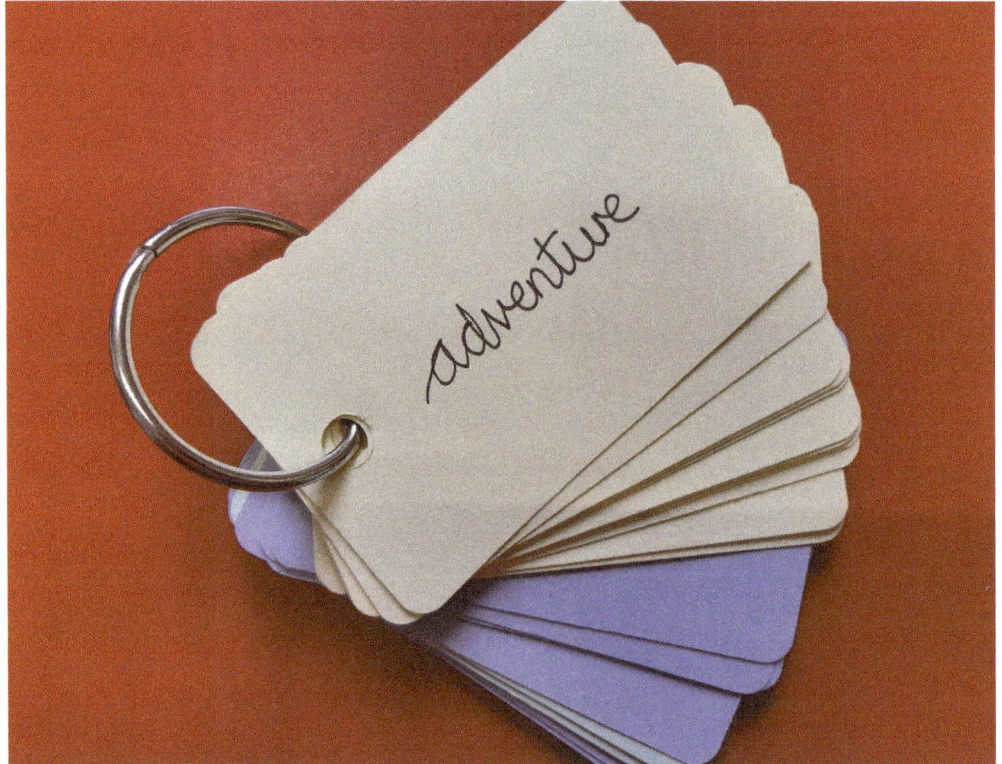

Figure 9.12

Sections 1 and 2 of each lesson are the same in Day 1, 2 and 3 lessons.

Revision using trigger cards is built into every lesson to ensure that you apply Golden Rule 1 in Chapter 4: **Provide Overlearning Opportunities**. The cards keep a record of, and provide a revision prompt for, all the taught morphemes in previous weeks. As you progress through the intervention, your learner's pack of trigger cards will grow.

On **Day 1** and **Day 2** trigger cards come up twice, firstly for testing and secondly to make new ones. This first part of the lesson is for revision, and it involves the learner's whole pack of trigger cards. The task is to spell them on **Day 1** and **3**, and to read them on **Day 2** (but feel free to be flexible with when you ask them to read and spell).

Test Trigger Cards: How do I teach it?

Go through the following procedure for each trigger card in the pack.

1. Ask the learners to read or spell the morpheme on the front of the trigger card
2. Ask them to read or spell the word written on the back
3. Check that the learners know what the morpheme means, or in the case of some suffixes, what it does (for example, **-ness** is a noun maker; it turns an adjective into a noun)
4. If the trigger card represents one of the spelling rules, make sure the learner(s) can apply the rule – the spelling of the word on the back should cover this

If the learners are unsuccessful in any point of this procedure, use the memory aid (trigger) they have written on the back to help them, and make a note for re-teaching at a later stage (Figure 9.13).

For example, let's say the trigger card is for the suffix **-est** with the spelling rule y - i. Here's the procedure.

1. Ask the learners to read or spell **-est** on the front
2. Ask them to read or spell the word on the back, which might be **happiest**
3. Ask them to tell you what **-est** means (they will hopefully say **the most**)
4. Ask them what spelling rule they applied when they wrote the word **happiest**

Again, if your learner is unsuccessful at any stage from 1 - 4, use the trigger they have written or drawn on the back as a prompt.

Don't forget to test spelling of trigger cards! For most learners, spelling is much harder than reading.

Sections 1 and 2 of each lesson are the same in Day 1, 2 and 3 lessons.

Test trigger cards (spell + meaning/function if relevant) (2 mins)
Any problems? placement – placment

Figure 9.13

Test Trigger Cards: How do I plan it?

No advance planning is required for testing trigger cards, but you will need to have the learners' cards ready.

Depending on whether you are teaching **Day 1**, **Day 2** or **Day 3**, each section of the lessons from this point onwards is different. Let's look at each day separately.

Depending on whether you are teaching Day 1, Day 2 or Day 3, each section of the lessons from this point onwards is different. Let's look at each day separately.

Day 1 Lesson

Section 3 (Day 1): Word Root Work (11 minutes)

Word Root Work (Day 1): What is it?

This is when you teach your targeted root. You'll teach the root using Morpheme cards, tactile letters and the Morph handshake. The learners will make a portal, write the words, make a trigger card, write the root into their Morph Mastercard, and play a Word Agility game.

Word Root Work (Day 1): How do I teach it?

The procedure for teaching a new root is detailed in the Lesson Plan Masters with Guidance, as shown in Figure 9.14.

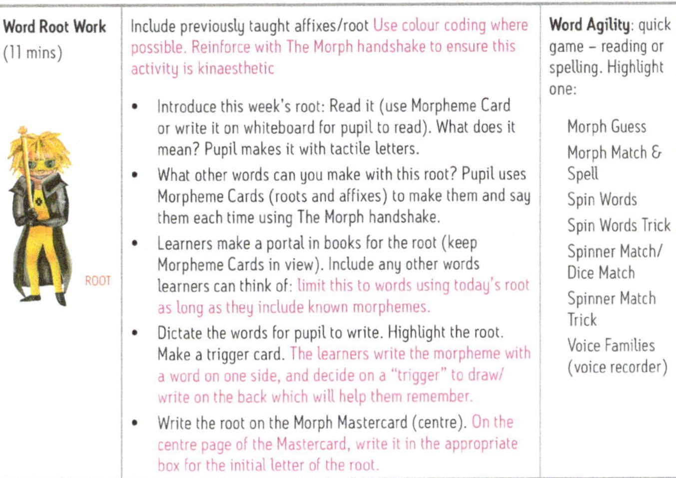

Word Root Work (11 mins) ROOT	Include previously taught affixes/root Use colour coding where possible. Reinforce with The Morph handshake to ensure this activity is kinaesthetic • Introduce this week's root: Read it (use Morpheme Card or write it on whiteboard for pupil to read). What does it mean? Pupil makes it with tactile letters. • What other words can you make with this root? Pupil uses Morpheme Cards (roots and affixes) to make them and say them each time using The Morph handshake. • Learners make a portal in books for the root (keep Morpheme Cards in view). Include any other words learners can think of: limit this to words using today's root as long as they include known morphemes. • Dictate the words for pupil to write. Highlight the root. Make a trigger card. The learners write the morpheme with a word on one side, and decide on a "trigger" to draw/write on the back which will help them remember. • Write the root on the Morph Mastercard (centre). On the centre page of the Mastercard, write it in the appropriate box for the initial letter of the root.	**Word Agility**: quick game – reading or spelling. Highlight one: Morph Guess Morph Match & Spell Spin Words Spin Words Trick Spinner Match/ Dice Match Spinner Match Trick Voice Families (voice recorder)

Figure 9.14

As illustrated in Figure 9.15, you will need to have your alphabet laid out in sequence (preferably in an arc shape). Use the Morpheme card to show the learner the root, then go through the procedure listed in Figure 9.14.

When you ask what other words can be made with your root, have some relevant Morpheme cards ready, in view, on the table. Figure 9.15 shows an example of some Morpheme cards ready for teaching the root **run.** Don't ask your learners to come up with words without providing these cards as a prompt. They may well come up with their own as well, which is great. However, this can be very difficult for learners with word-finding difficulties, so avoid asking them to do this. If there are any tricky words, morphemes or rules, ask the learner to make the word with tactile letters, which will aid learning (Figure 9.16).

Don't be tempted to skip using the tactile letters. They enhance the multi-sensory learning experience and the learners enjoy the sense of word play that they provide.

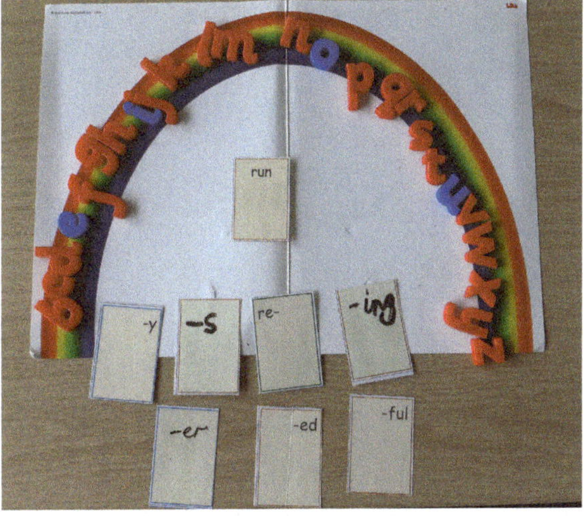

Figure 9.15

Figure 9.16

Word Root Work: the Morph handshake

The Morph handshake is a really important part of the lessons, partly because the pupils enjoy it so much, but also because it provides a kinaesthetic way to remember words and their component morphemes. You'll find that the children are much better at remembering the Morph than the adults! It corresponds with the emblems for each of the characters Prefa, Root and Sufa, who represent prefixes, roots and suffixes. These emblems are the fish, the cross and the star respectively (Figure 9.17). In the handshake, make the shape of the fish, the cross and the star in sequence as you say each part of the word slowly. If the word does not contain a prefix or suffix, simply omit that part of the handshake. Figure 9.17 gives illustrations of this.

All the pupils on the pilot loved the handshake. They learnt it much more quickly than the adults so it was something in which they could be the experts!

Word	prefix	root	suffix
	Hands move forward in zigzags as if swimming like a fish	Thumbs lock and point upwards to make a cross	With thumbs still locked, fingers wave like twinkling stars
unhelpful	un-	help	-ful
reactive	re-	act	-ive
unzips	un-	zip	-s
reform	re-	form	*no action*
teacher	*no action*	teach	-er

Figure 9.17

Word Root Work: making a portal (Day 1)

This is a three (or more as pupils advance in their learning) columned table representing the morphemes in the word. The learner draws the table – but the adult may need to draw it at first until the learner feels ready. The concept is that morphemes can be "inputted" with multiple possibilities of their "output"; a simple root can be transformed into many words with the addition of prefixes, suffixes, or both. At the end of this chapter you'll find the photocopiable guidance sheet: **Steps to Making a Portal,** and some examples are in Figures 9.19–9.22.

On **Day 1**, first input (write) the targeted root in the centre column, then input any relevant prefixes in the left column and suffixes in the right column. Make sure you hyphenate suffixes and prefixes as in Figures 9.19–9.22. This helps the learner to see that prefixes and suffixes are not whole words, as well as to have a visual reminder of their placement in words. Ask the pupil to say the whole word each time they input a morpheme. Once your morphemes are in the portal, use highlighters according to the Morph Mastery colour coding: green for prefixes, yellow for roots and blue for suffixes. In Figure 9.18, the targeted root was **help,** and in Figure 9.19 it was **stick**. Once the portal is made, dictate the words for the pupil to write and highlight.

Figure 9.18

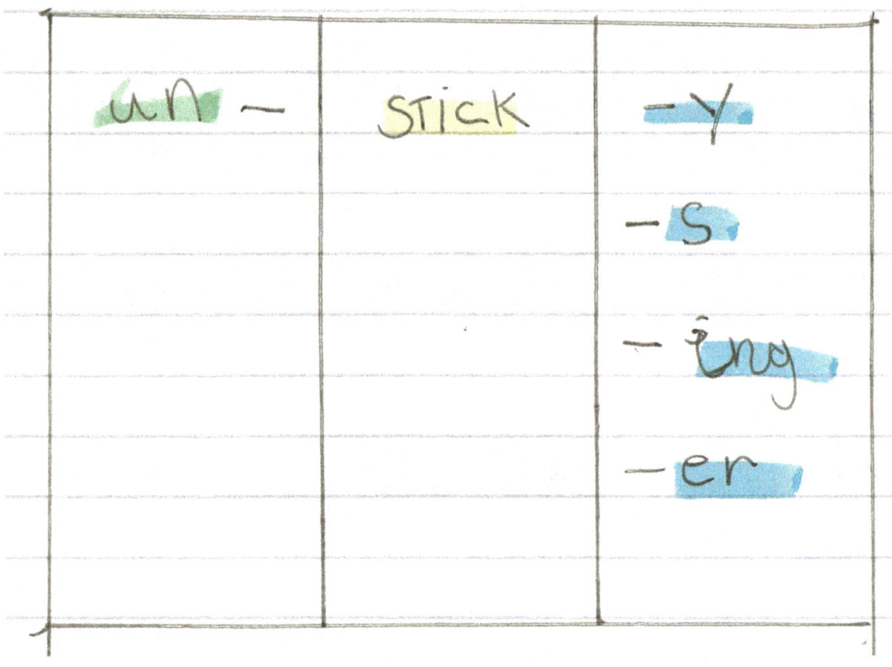

Figure 9.19

How to represent the spelling rules in a portal

Morph Mastery focusses heavily on spelling rules. It's important to represent them in an accurate and helpful way on the portal. Figure 9.20 shows an example of a portal using the double consonant rule with the root **wet,** and Figure 9.21 shows an example of a portal using the drop e rule.

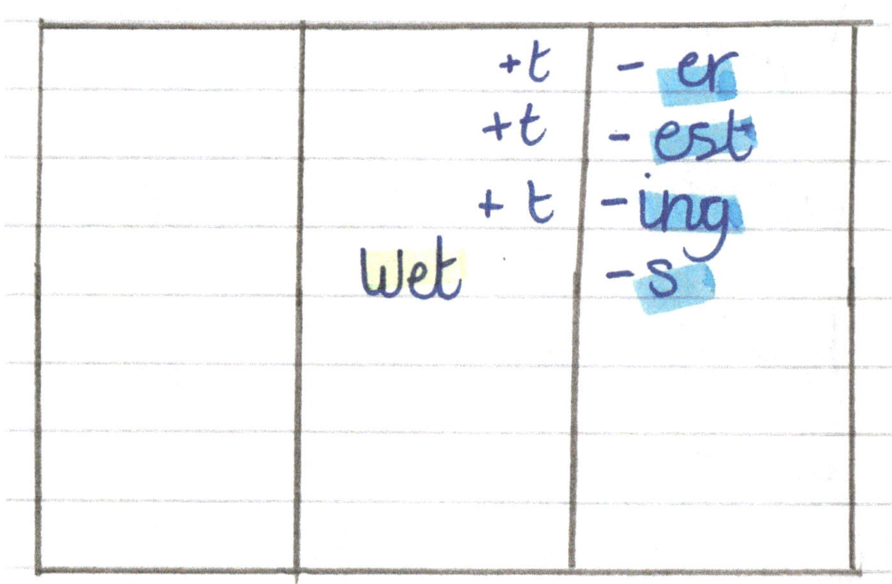

Figure 9.20

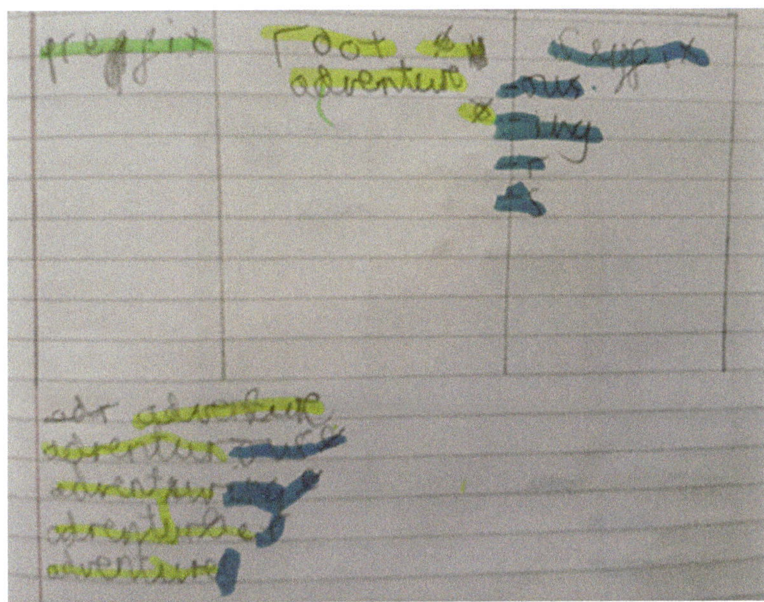

Figure 9.21

Key things to remember when making a portal

1. Keep it simple
2. Don't forget the hyphen
3. Show the spelling rule clearly (if there is one)
4. Allow the pupil to think of his/her own words (but limit tricky spellings)
5. On the first few weeks you may not have many words – this is fine
6. Remember the colour coding
7. Ask the pupil to say the word each time

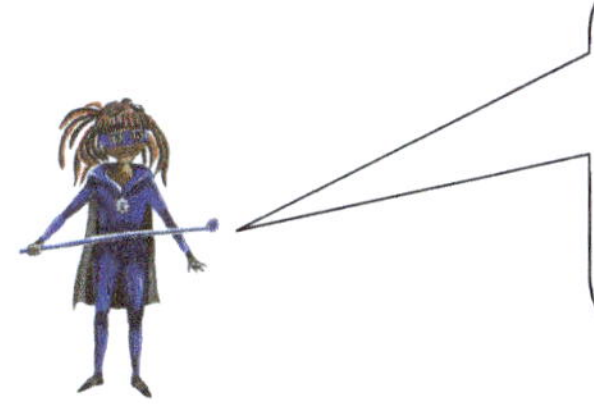

The hyphen before a prefix and after a suffix serve as a visual reminder to the learner that they are only parts of words, and where they are placed in words.

Word Root Work: making a Trigger Card (Day 1: root)

If possible, use a yellow card for the root, (green for a prefix and blue for a suffix). On one side of the trigger card, write the targeted root. On the back, ask the learners to choose a word from the portal and write it on the back of the trigger card. Decide together what the tricky bit of the root is. This could be the meaning or the spelling. Then, ask the learners to write or draw a "trigger" to help them remember the tricky bit. If there is no tricky bit at all (which often happens on **Day 1**), there is no need to draw or write anything on the back. Figure 9.22 shows an example of the back of a trigger card for the root **lock**.

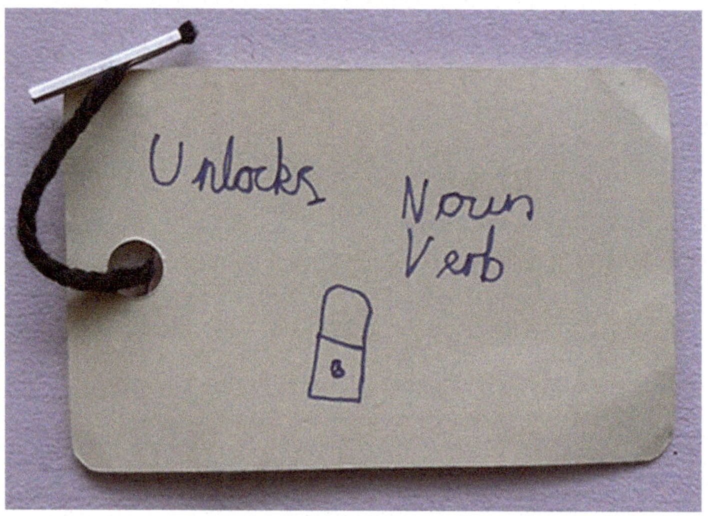

Figure 9.22

Word Root Work (Day 1): Write the root on the Morph Mastercard

Roots are written in the box corresponding to the word's first letter on the alphabetical table (centre pages). This should now be a useful prompt for supporting spelling in class and in the intervention (Figure 9.23).

> Class teachers on the pilot commented that the Mastercard was useful back in class and was used by the pupils independently.

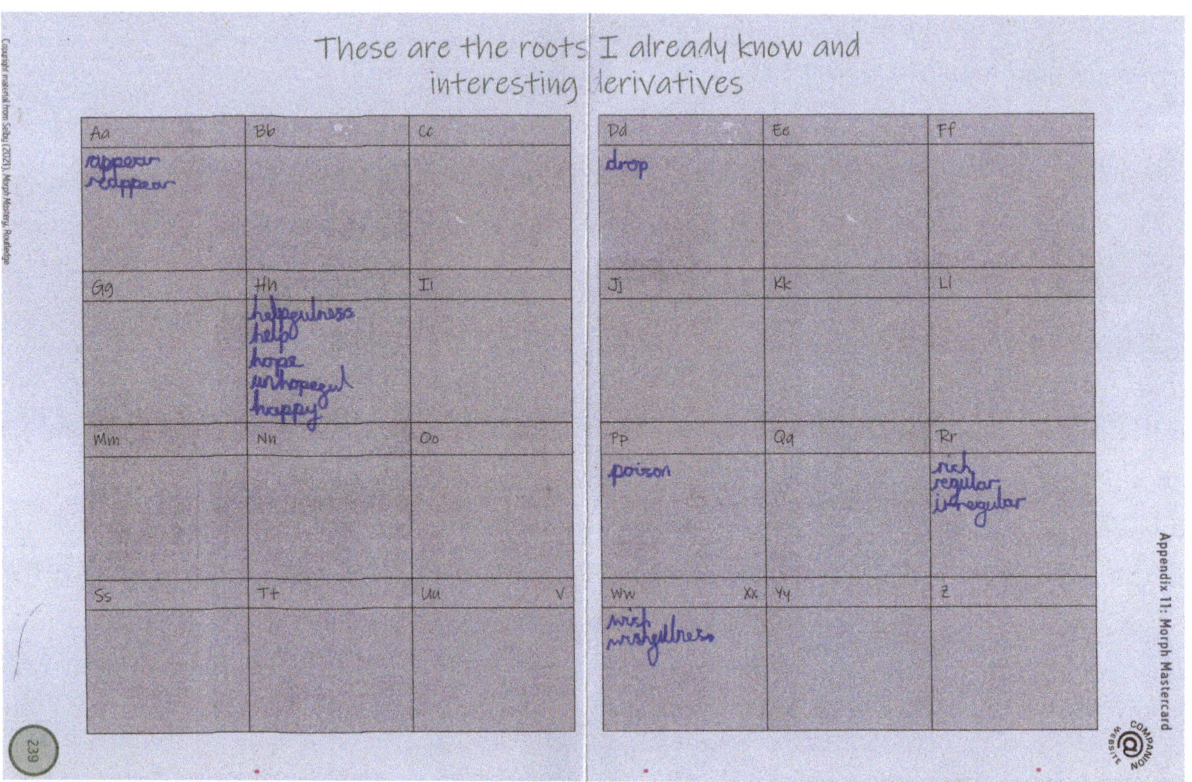

Figure 9.23

Word Root Work (Day 1): the Word Agility game

As illustrated in Figure 9.14, you have a choice of games to play after teaching your new root.

Word Root Work (Day 1): How do I plan it?

In advance, you'll need to select up to 12 Morpheme Cards (but probably fewer depending on your word list and the speed of your learner). On **Day 1**, choose the card for your targeted root and some affix cards. Base the affixes you choose on your word list. Choose a few "red herrings" as well. In Figure 9.24, for example, Sarah was learning the root **light**. Her word list was **light**, **lights**, **lighter** and **lightest**. The Morpheme Cards with suffixes **-s**, **-er** and **-est** were used, because they featured in her word list. In addition, a red herring was thrown in: **-es**. Sarah had already been taught this suffix and knew that it is only used when it adds a syllable to the word (as in **foxes**). She would therefore be capable of trying it together with **light** and saying it does not make a real word.

Name: S	Year group/class: 5	Week no.: 4	Date: 10·2·21
New word root: light	Word list: light, lights, lighter, lightest		

Figure 9.24

You'll also need to plan your game in advance. The games are all detailed in Chapter 10. Choose one of the games listed on the plan (Figure 9.14) and highlight it. You might choose a game which practises applying spelling rules, a game which practises your word list for today or simply a favourite game. It's fine to play the same game for a few weeks if the learners enjoy it; you'll just need to change the words you use. Like the Morphological Awareness games, these games are structured but generic to allow you to personalise them. Remember Golden Rule 1 (provide overlearning opportunities) by making sure you include some words containing previously taught morphemes in all the Word Agility games. Keep the game brief but fun.

The games take a bit of planning when you start but they are essential. All the learners on the pilot commented on how much they loved them. They are not just fun but they make the learning multi-sensory and provide over-learning opportunities.

Section 4 (Day 1): Word Espionage (Reading – 10 minutes)

Word Espionage (reading text) (10 mins)	Learners read their individual reading books OR a text from a lesson - either previous or future lesson. They hunt morphemes and write them down in words on whiteboards, as well as any tricky words.	Morphemes found: (If appropriate, adult picks a word for Word Mastery activity in Day 2.) Choose one linked to current learning if possible. If no word from this text is appropriate, just choose a different word for Day 2.
Any identified vocabulary? Note any interesting words containing taught or discussed morphemes.		Any tricky words identified? Note any words the learners found difficult to read for future teaching.

Word Espionage (Day 1, Reading): What is it?

In the Word Espionage section of **Day 1**, the learners read a text to look for morphemes and talk about what they have found. You can choose a current book they are reading or a text from a lesson. It can be a text they have already read or a text they are going to read. This is a really worthwhile exercise as it helps them to transfer their learning to class work. If working with a group, the learners can all read the same text, or different ones. If working with just one text, and you have time, photocopy the page so that the learners can highlight what they find.

Word Espionage (Day 1, Reading): How do I teach it?

The learners read as much as time allows, even if just a few sentences. They independently highlight or make a note of morphemes that they find, according to the Morph Mastery colour code, and if working in a group, write any interesting words or morphemes on their whiteboard. Discuss these at the end of the read. The adult may wish to draw attention to morphemes in the text, especially if the targeted morphemes and/or spelling rules have been used. If appropriate, you could choose a word from the text for the Word Mastery section of your **Day 2** lesson, when the learners will study a multi-morphemic word (containing at least two morphemes).

For example, Jane had been learning the suffixes **-ed** (including when it adds a syllable, as in wanted), **-s**, **-ing** and **-est**. In a text she saw a number of these and highlighted them. The adult noticed that she had highlighted the **-ed** in word **scared**, and chose to discuss this word as it uses the drop e rule, which was due to be taught the following week. The word chosen for Word Mastery the following day was **unscary**.

Word Espionage (Day 1, Reading) How do I plan it?

If possible, photocopy the text(s) in advance.

Section 5 (Day 1): Review (1 minute)

Review with learner (1 min): What word root did you learn today? Which words are derived from this root? Which word did you find tricky to spell/understand? How will you remember it next time?
Adult Review

The Review is an essential part of any lesson because your learners are always likely to remember the last thing you discussed. This is your chance to remind them of the targeted root and see which words they can remember. It's an oral activity. It's always worthwhile asking if there was anything tricky in the lesson, and how the learners will remember it next time.

We'll now look at the Day 2 lesson. Don't forget that Section 1 and 2 are the same in each lesson, so turn back to page 76 to see the guidance for those sections in your Day 2 lesson.

Day 2 Lesson

Section 3 (Day 2): Word Affix Work (14 minutes)

Word Affix Work (Day 2): What is it?

This is when you teach your affix. You will follow a very similar procedure to Day 1, as you will see in Figure 9.25. You'll use morpheme cards, tactile letters and The Morph handshake. Your learners will make a portal and write down the words. They'll make a trigger card and play a word agility game.

Word Affix Work (Day 2): How do I teach it?

Word Affix Work (14 mins) Targeted affix:   	Use colour coding where possible. Reinforce with The Morph handshake to ensure this activity is kinaesthetic. • Introduce this week's affix. Read it (use Morpheme Cards or write it on the whiteboard for the pupil to read). What does it mean? Pupil makes it with tactile letters. • What other words can you make with this affix? Aim to include this week's targeted root. • Pupil uses Morpheme Cards (root and affix) to make them and say them each time using The Morph handshake. • Pupils make a portal for the affix. Include any other words learner can think of. • Dictate the words for pupil to write. Highlight the affix. Make a trigger card. The learners write the morpheme with a word on one side, and decide on a "trigger" to draw/write on the back which will help them remember. • Write the affix on the Morph Mastercard (back page). Write the suffix or prefix in the relevant column along with the targeted root (Day 1).	**Word Agility**: spelling game Highlight one: Spinner Match Spinner Match Trick Spin Words Spin Words Trick Morph Guess Morph Connect Morph Match & Spell Stealth Voice Families

Figure 9.25

In the same way, use the tactile letters and Morpheme Cards. The Morph handshake from **Day 1** also features in **Day 2**, along with colour coding, saying the words and writing them. The portal is very similar with some slight differences, as outlined in the photocopiable guidance sheet **Steps to Making a Portal** at the end of this chapter. Figure 9.26 is an example of a portal which was made on **Day 2**, when the suffix **-ment** was being taught. Figure 9.27 shows a **Day 2** portal where a spelling rule was applied.

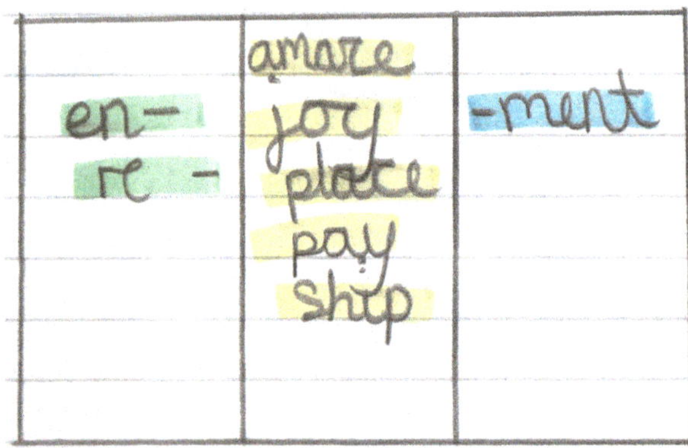

Figure 9.26

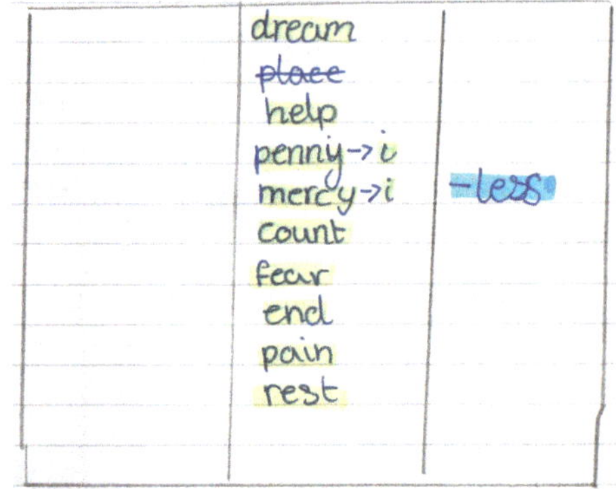

Figure 9.27

The trigger card that you make on **Day 2** follows the same principles as **Day 1**. If possible, use a green card for a prefix, or a blue card for a suffix. On **Day 2**, the learners write the affix on the front of the card, remembering the hyphen to indicate its placement in a word. Next, they write a word containing the affix on the back (they each choose one from their portal). Choose the tricky bit together, then, on the back, write or draw a trigger to help them remember this. Add the card to the pack.

The more your learners are involved in making the trigger card, the more they'll remember them. They love to see the pack build up each week.

If you are teaching a suffix with a spelling rule, the learners write the rule with the suffix on the front of the card. For example, on the front they might write **-er** (**drop e**). On the back it might be **baker**. The trigger might be a picture of a baker dropping a letter e. Figure 9.28 illustrates this.

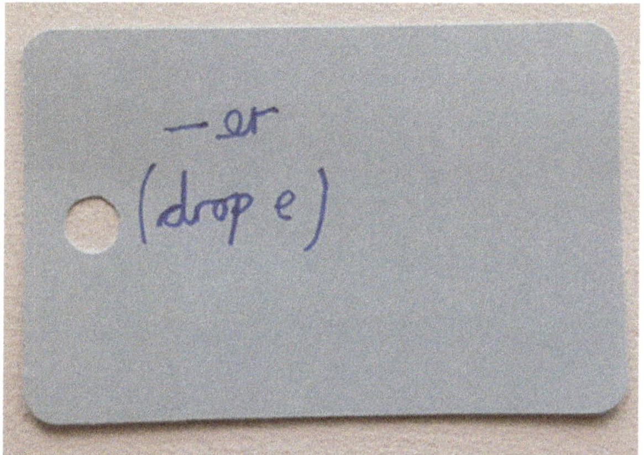

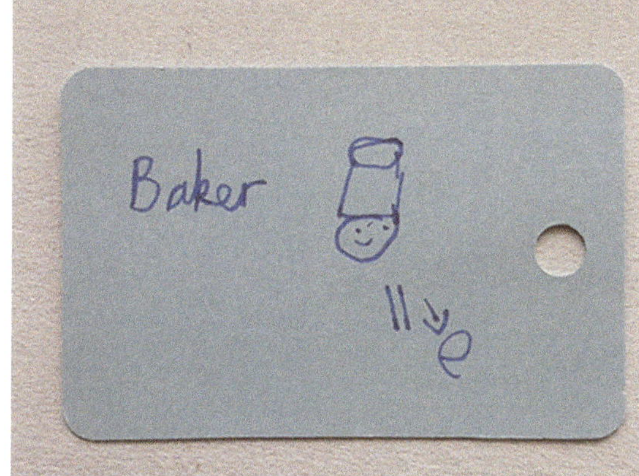

Figure 9.28

Figures 9.29 and 9.30 shows more examples of triggers created by children on **Day 2**.

Figure 9.29

Figure 9.30

On **Day 2**, write the affix that you have taught on the back of the Morph Mastercard, in the relevant column (Figure 9.31). Write the corresponding root that was taught alongside this affix next to it. The list will increase as the weeks go on.

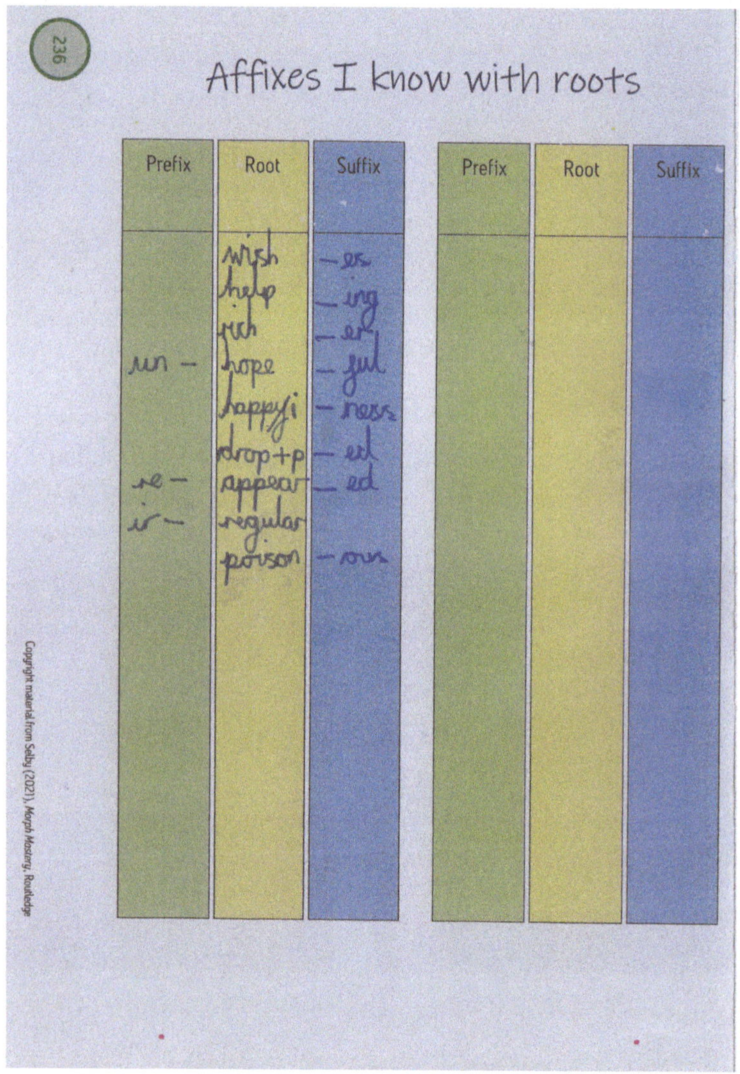

236

Affixes I know with roots

Prefix	Root	Suffix	Prefix	Root	Suffix
	wish	-es			
	help	-ing			
	rich	-er			
un-	hope	-ful			
	happy/i	-ness			
	drop+p	-ed			
re-	appear	-ed			
ir-	regular				
	poison	-ous			

Copyright material from Selby (2021), Morph Mastery, Routledge

Figure 9.31

The Word Agility games listed on **Day 2** are slightly different, but the same principles as **Day 1** apply.

Word Affix Work (Day 2): How do I plan it?

In advance, as for **Day 1**, you will select up to 12 Morpheme Cards (but probably fewer depending on your learner and your word list). On **Day 2**, one of these cards will be your targeted affix; the others will be roots, taken from your word list. As for **Day 1**, choose a few red herrings. In Figure 9.32, for example, Sarah had learnt the root **light** on **Day 1. On Day 2,** she was learning the suffix **-est**. Her word list for **Day 2** was **lightest**, **coldest**, **tallest**, **longest**, **quickest**, **hardest**, **kindest**. The Morpheme Card with the suffix **-est** was used, as well as the Morpheme cards with the roots **light**, **cold**, **tall**, **long**, **quick**, **hard** and **kind**, because they featured in her word list. In addition, a red herring was thrown in: **farm**. Sarah's vocabulary is strong enough for her to know that **farmest** is not a word. Figure 9.32 (previously named 9.36 but corrected) should go beneath this paragraph before Section 4 (Day 2).

Name: S	**Year group/ class:** 5	**Week no.:** 4	**Date:** 10·2·21
Targeted root (from day 1): light **New affix:** -est	**Word list:** lightest, coldest, tallest, longest quickest, hardest, kindest		
Notes from previous lesson(s):	practise -y (spell)		
Resources: Alphabet arc set out, trigger cards, Morpheme Cards (root and affix, chosen in advance), book to write in, pencil/pen, ruler, highlighter pens (green, yellow, blue), **Word Agility** game and resources, chosen word for **Word Mastery** (may have been chosen in **Word Espionage** section of lesson 1), **Word Mastery** cards, Morph Mastercard			

Figure 9.32

Section 4 (Day 2): Word Mastery (5 minutes)

Word Mastery (5 mins)
Study a multi-morphemic word (at least 2 morphemes) linked to this week's root or affix, splitting it into its morphemes, considering its meaning and the meaning of its morphemes (if appropriate). The word may have been chosen in Lesson 1 from **Word Espionage** text. Use **Word Mastery** cards – choose 3 or more cards. Use word chosen from Lesson 1 **Word Espionage** activity (reading). Use word mastery cards – choose two or more depending on learners' ability. Learners ask the questions – prompt where necessary. Pupils may think of their own questions in addition.

Word Mastery (Day 2): What is it?

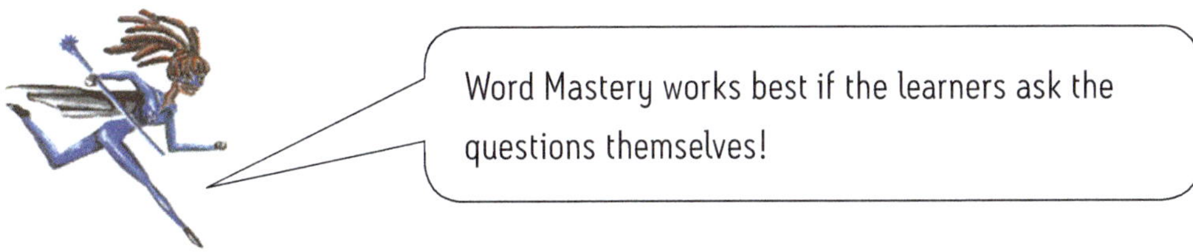

Word Mastery works best if the learners ask the questions themselves!

The adult and learners discuss and analyse a multi-morphemic word (in other words, a word with more than one morpheme, for example **unkindest**, **remaking**), chosen by the adult in advance, using structured question cards (Appendix 12), which are brightly coloured and appealing to the learners. The aim of this activity is to encourage your learners to identify the morphemes within words, make links between words from their morphemes and explore meanings. By discussing words and their components you are not only reinforcing spelling and reading, but you will develop vocabulary as well as explicit morphological awareness (Chapter 5).

Word Mastery (Day 2): How do I teach it?

Write the word on a whiteboard and choose three or more questions. Place them under the word, one at a time (Figure 9.33). Either the adult or the learner(s) ask the question and it is answered.

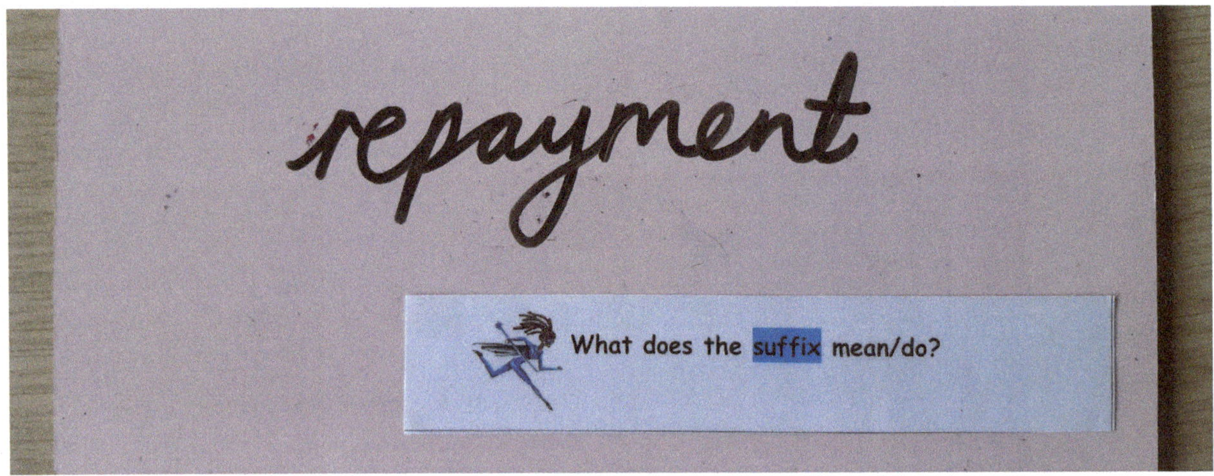

Figure 9.33

Word Mastery (Day 2): How do I plan it?

For this part of the lesson you will need the Word Mastery questions (Figure 9.34). Before you start first lesson, print, laminate and cut them up.

Choose a word linked with your targeted root and affix, but it can be a more tricky or complex word. For example, if you have been teaching the root **form** and the suffix **-er**, you might choose **reformer** or **transformer**. If you have been teaching the suffix **-ness** and the root **help**, you might choose **unhelpfulness** or **helplessness**. Alternatively, you can choose a word containing just the targeted root or affix, or even just the spelling rule. For example, if teaching **form** with **-er**, you might choose the word **reformation** or **remaker**, if teaching **help** and **-ness**, you might choose **unhelpable** or **selfishness**. Choose a word which will be partly familiar, but which has something new to your learner.

What is the root?
What is the prefix?
What is the suffix?
Can you think of other similar words?
How many morphemes does it have? What are they?
Can you add any prefixes?
Can you add any suffixes?

Can you change the root?
Can you change the prefix or suffix?
Has the root changed at all when the suffix was added?
What does the word mean?
What does the suffix mean/do?
What does the root mean?
What does the prefix mean?

Figure 9.34

Section 5 (Day 2): Review (1 minute)

As in **Day 1**, end the lesson with a Review.

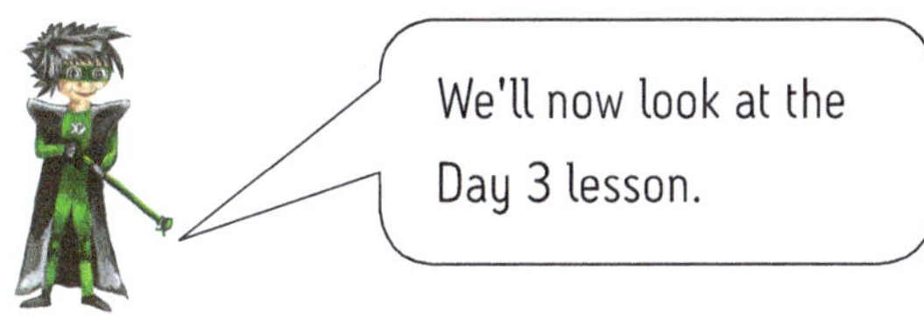
We'll now look at the Day 3 lesson.

On Day 3, there's no new learning. It's a chance to play with words and extend vocabulary.

Lesson 3 Section 3

On **Day 3**, you are not teaching anything new, but extending opportunities for word building and consolidation. **Day 3** also features the **Word Espionage** for writing, where the learners look for morphemes in their own writing. The Morphological Awareness section of the lesson is ***the same as in Day 1 and 2***. The trigger cards section is also the same, except that on Day 3 you may choose to add new words to the Morph Mastercard. These should be any interesting vocabulary or words you have enjoyed investigating, and they should be added to the centre pages of the Mastercard. The plan might look something like this:

Test trigger cards (read or spell + meaning/function if relevant) (2 mins)
Any problems? Forgot y → i in happiness. Revise.
Morph mastercard: Any new words to add? – reformer, transformer.

Day 2 Lesson, Section 5 (Review)

Section 3 (Day 3): Word Agility: Extended Word Building Game (8 minutes)

This is where you can really have some fun!

Word Agility Extended word building game (Day 3): What is it?

Here you will play a longer game than there is opportunity for in **Day 1** and **2**. All the games that you can play on **Day 3** are longer games with a heavier focus on word building than spelling, though spelling is involved. This part of the lesson is about playing with words, exploring them, changing them and transforming them.

Word Agility Extended word building game (Day 3): How do I teach it?

This is taught exclusively by playing a game. Enjoy!

Word Agility Extended word building game (Day 3): How do I plan it?

There is a list of options for games on the lesson plan. As for **Day 1** and **2**, these games are all detailed in Chapter 10. Choose the game you would like to play and highlight it. Personalise the game for your learners by choosing morphemes and words you have taught. Make sure you remember Golden Rule 1 (providing opportunities for overlearning) by including learning from previous weeks as well. Ensure you have all the appropriate materials for your chosen game before the lesson.

Section 4 (Day 3): Writing Sentence Dictation (5 minutes)

Writing Sentence Dictation (Day 3): What is it?

This is a sentence which the adult has prepared in advance. The learners are led through the process of remembering the sentence before writing it independently. They then edit and highlight morphemes. Figure 9.35 is an example of a completed sentence dictation.

Figure 9.35

Writing Sentence Dictation (Day 3): How do I teach it?

1. Read the sentence to the learners
2. Ask the learners to say the sentence. Repeat if necessary
3. Ask the learners to say the sentence back in different voices (e.g. high voice, silly voice, deep voice) and/or while doing different actions (e.g. patting head and/or rubbing tummy, jumping, wrist circles)
4. Ask the learners to write the sentence. Remind them about punctuation
5. Ask learners to check their sentence and edit – this can include spellings and punctuation
6. Ask the learners to highlight morphemes they have been taught according to the Morph colour code

Writing Sentence Dictation (Day 3): How do I plan it?

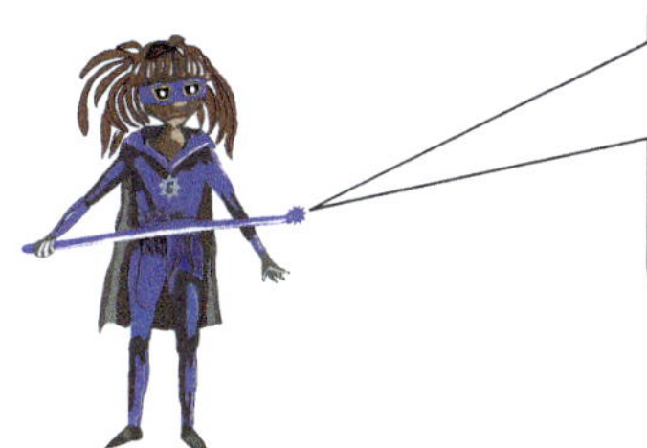

Be careful not to trip your learners up with the dictated sentence! Choose words they know or are learning.

The sentence for dictation is planned when you complete your six-week plan (Chapter 8). You can change it if necessary, to include words that have proven tricky or need over-learning.

Section 4 (Day 3): Word Espionage Writing Check (6 minutes)

Word Espionage (Day 3, Writing): What is it?

The learners look at a piece of writing from class work (preferably photocopied) and hunt for morphemes. Prefixes, roots and suffixes are highlighted. One or two words of interest are identified and discussed.

Word Espionage (Day 3, Writing): How do I teach it?

1. Ask the learners to read the writing quietly to themselves and highlight prefixes, roots and suffixes. If time is limited, this can be just a couple of sentences
2. Ask them if they have found any morphemes that you have taught
3. Ask them if they have found any interesting morphemes/words
4. The adult chooses one word from the text to discuss in terms of its morphemes

For example, in Figure 9.36 the learner highlighted the roots and suffixes in **eaten** (spelled eatan), **bellowed**, **nubbly**, **shouted** and **breeches**. The learner commented that he had learned the suffixes **-ed** and **-ly**. Together they then discussed the word **nubbly.** The adult pointed out that this word, meaning lumpy, comes from the noun **nubble**. They then discussed the drop e rule (which had been taught in a previous lesson) and the learner was praised for applying this rule.

"The whale spoke "I'm hungry!" The small stute fish spoke in a small stute fish voice "Have you ever eatan man?"
"No," bellowed the whale "What is it like?"
"Nice," "Nice but nubbly"
"Then fetch me some!" spoke the whale. He made the waves froth up with his tale.
"One at a time!" shouted the stute fish. "If you go 50 longitude 50 north latitude 40 west and in the middle of the sea with nothing to wear but a pair of suspenders a jack knife and blue canvas breeches on a

Figure 9.36

In Figure 9.37, the adult assessed that the learner had applied the drop e rule in the word **having (**which had been taught previously). She then drew attention to the mis- spelled word **cheesey**, explaining that the drop e rule was also required in this word. A new teaching point was made from the mis-spelled word **realy** by pointing out that the root is **real** and the suffix is **-ly**. This helped the learner to understand the spelling of **really.**

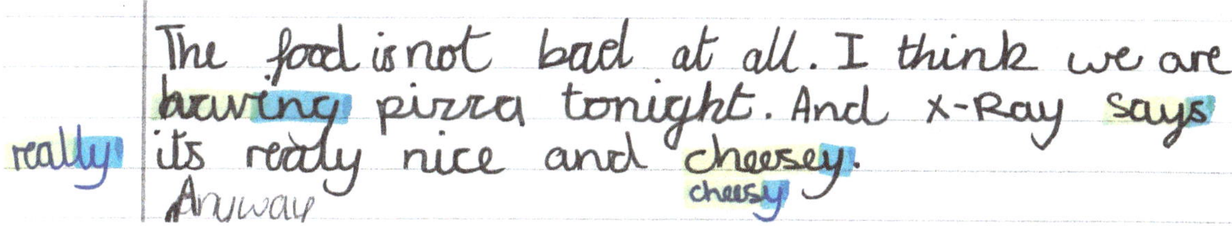

Figure 9.37

Word Espionage (Day 3, Writing): How do I plan it?

If possible, choose the piece of writing in advance. It should be a recent piece of work done in class, so ideally, you'll need to liaise with the learners' teachers. If you have a choice, look for morphemes or spelling rules you have been teaching, but this is not essential. If you are teaching a group, it's most practical to use one piece of writing for all the learners to analyse, and photocopy it. However, if time is limited, just ask them to bring their books and choose the writing at the time of the task.

Section 5 (Day 3): Review (4 minutes)

Review with learner (4 min): What word root did you learn this week? What affix did you learn? Which words are derived from this root or affix? Which other morphemes have you learnt this week? What did you find tricky to spell and how will you remember it? Discuss the root and affix that you have learned this week. Write any related words of interest or tricky words in the appropriate box in the centre of the Morph Mastercard.
Adult Review

As in **Day 1** and **2**, end the lesson with a review. On **Day 3**, you will ask your learners to write any additional words of interest that are related to the taught morphemes onto the centre page of the Morph Mastercard. For example, the might write **friendless** if they have been learning the suffix **-less**, or **villainous** if they have learned **-ous**. In Figure 9.23 (page 86), the learner wrote **tidiness** and **tidied** in the **t** section, to remind himself of these spellings. During the review on **Day 3**, you can also encourage your learner to look for morphemes in their reading and writing over the coming days.

Steps to Making a Portal: Day 1 (Root)

1. The pupil draws three columns with a ruler.

2. The pupil writes the root in the centre column and highlights it in yellow.

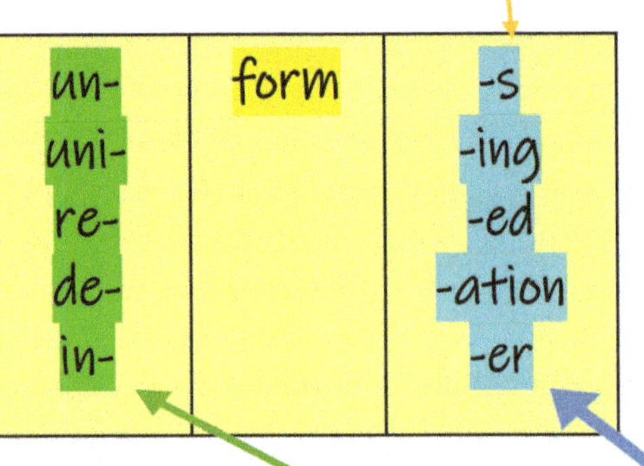

3. The pupil orally recalls words containing this root (use Morpheme Root cards if needed)

4. Pupil writes the relevant affixes with a hyphen in the appropriate column and highlights them according to Morph colour code.

5. Adult dictates words for pupil to write. Pupil highlights the root in yellow, suffixes in blue and prefixes in green.

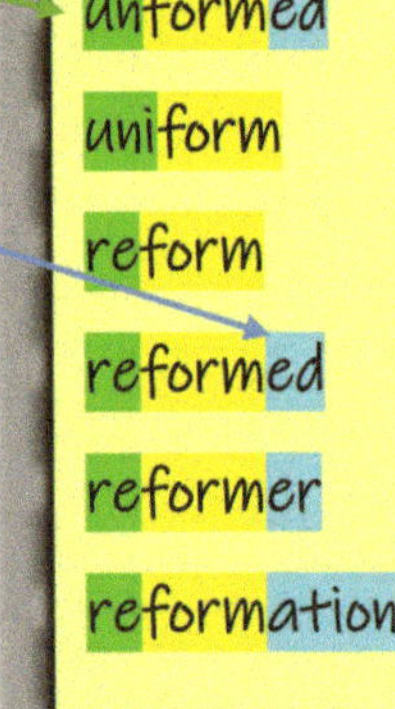

forms
forming
formed
formation
unformed
uniform
reform
reformed
reformer
reformation

Steps to Making a Portal: Day 2 (Affix)

1. The pupil draws three columns with a ruler.

2. The pupil writes the targeted affix with a hyphen in the relevant column and highlights it.

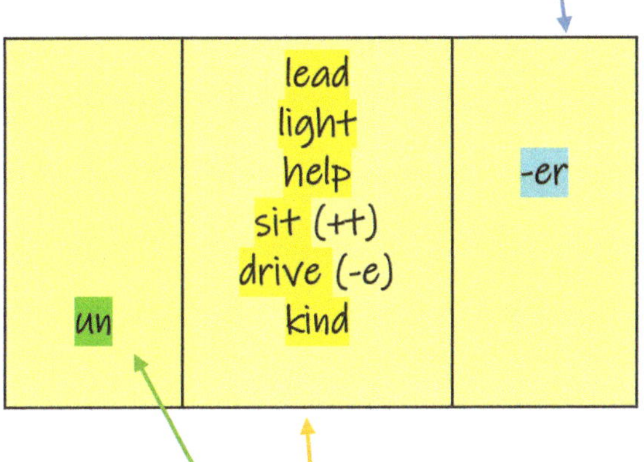

3. The pupil orally recalls words containing this affix (use Morpheme Prefix and Suffix cards if needed).

4. Pupil writes the relevant roots and affixes, if relevant, in the appropriate column and highlights them according to Morph colour code.

5. Adult dictates words for pupil to write. Pupil highlights the targeted affix, roots and any extra affixes according to the Morph colour code.

10. Games and resources

All the games used in Morph Mastery are extremely adaptable. They have been created in a way that allows you to personalise them for your learners, by using morphemes and words they are working on. Most of them are also extremely adaptable for groups and classes.

This chapter begins with the **Index of Games**. Use the Index to select your games. The following factors should influence which games you select:

- Which section of the lesson is it for: **Morphological Awareness** or **Word Agility**?
- Lesson 1, 2 or 3? (there is a suggested choice of games on each lesson plan)
- Whole class or intervention – or both?
- What is the targeted area for your pupil? (Use your **Six-week Plan**)

After the **Index of Games,** you'll find photocopiable instructions for each game. At the end of the chapter you'll find some the photocopiable resources for the games. There are many more of these available on the companion website. Some of the games also have been filmed and these, along with all the photocopiable resources, are available to watch on www.routledge.com/cw/speechmark. These games are marked with the symbol .

Index of Games

Name of game	Page No.	Targeted area	More specifically...	Played in lesson...	Adaptable for whole class?	Film available?
Morph Match Game 1		Morphological Awareness	Word relationships	1, 2, 3	Yes	
Morph Match Game 2 & 3		Morphological Awareness	Decomposition & production (transparent morphemes)	1, 2, 3	Yes	(Game 2)
Morph Match Game 4		Morphological Awareness	Decomposition & production (opaque morphemes)	1, 2, 3	Yes	

Name of game	Page No.	Targeted area	More specifically...	Played in lesson...	Adaptable for whole class?	Film available?
Spinner Game 1 & 2		Morphological Awareness	Decomposition & production	1, 2, 3	Yes	
Spinner Game 3, 4, 5 & 6		Morphological Awareness	Decomposition & production (nonsense words)	1, 2, 3	Yes	 (Game 6)
Voice Families		Morphological Awareness	Word relationships, decomposition & production of words	1, 2, 3	Yes	
Voice Families with spelling		Word Agility	Spelling practice – roots with affixes, can be used to practise spelling rules	1, 2	Yes	
Happy Families		Morphological Awareness	Word relationships, decomposition & production of words	1, 2, 3	Yes (in groups)	
Happy Families with spelling		Word Agility	Spelling practice – roots with affixes, can be used to practise spelling rules	3	Yes (in groups)	
Pairs Down Game 1		Morphological Awareness	Recognise words containing the same root (word relationships, decomposition of morphemes)	1, 2, 3	No	
Pairs Down Game 2		Morphological Awareness	Recognise words containing the same affix (word relationships, decomposition of morphemes)	1, 2, 3	No	
Pairs Down Game 3		Morphological Awareness	Word relationships, decomposition & production (opaque morphemes)	1, 2, 3	No	
Pairs Down Game 4		Morphological Awareness	Build words by adding an affix (production of morphemes)	1, 2, 3	No	

Name of game	Page No.	Targeted area	More specifically...	Played in lesson...	Adaptable for whole class?	Film available?
Pairs Down Game 5		Word Agility	Applying spelling rules by adding an affix to a root	3	Yes	
Pairs		Word Agility	Reading and spelling – using suffix -s or -es	3	No	
Morph Connect		Word Agility	Practise reading and spelling by combining morphemes to build words	2	Yes	
Morph Guess Game 1 & 2		Word Agility	Practise spelling words containing one affix	2	Yes	
Morph Guess Game 3		Word Agility	Practise spelling words containing more than one affix	2	Yes	
Morph Guess Game 4		Word Agility	Practise spelling words containing one root	1	Yes	
Morph Guess Game 5		Word Agility	Practise spelling words containing one root and/or one affix	1, 2	Yes	
Morph Match and Spell		Morphological Awareness and Word Agility	Production of and spelling words containing targeted morphemes	2	Yes	
Spin Words		Word Agility	Word building and spelling	1, 2	Yes	
Spin Words Trick		Word Agility	Word building and applying rules in spelling	1, 2	Yes	
Spinner Match		Word Agility	Word building and spelling	1, 2	Yes	
Spinner Match Trick		Word Agility	Word building and applying rules in spelling	1, 2	Yes	

Name of game	Page No.	Targeted area	More specifically...	Played in lesson...	Adaptable for whole class?	Film available?
Stealth Games 1		Word Agility	Building and spelling words containing taught morphemes (can be used to teach spelling rules also)	2	Yes (in groups)	
Stealth Game 2		Word Agility	Spelling practice of words containing taught morphemes	2	Yes (in groups)	
Stealth Game 3		Word Agility	Building and spelling words containing taught morphemes where rules are applied	2	Yes (in groups)	
Word Morph		Word Agility	Extended word building and spelling	3	Yes	
Wordcraft		Word Agility	Extended word building and spelling	3	Yes	

Morph Match

(games to support morphological awareness development)
In this game players match two spoken morphemes to make, or to link words. There are several variations of the game. The game is all oral – there's no writing involved.

- **You will need:** a set of voice recorders with options for a minimum of 12 recordings (see Appendix 18 for a list of where to source these). You can either use two voice recorders with a capacity of six recordings each, or two recorders (e.g. microphone, dice) with a minimum of 6 separate buttons each, or use 12 individual sound buttons. Whichever option you choose, make sure you have ***two sets*** of six recordings. In advance, choose which game you are playing, then decide on your pairs of words (or morphemes), depending on what you are targeting (examples are provided for each game). Arrange the voice recorders into two sets (unless you already have two recorders with six sound bites). Record spoken versions of each word (or morpheme) on your voice recorders, making sure that one recording from each pair is in each set.
- **How to play:** players take turns to press two buttons, one from each set. If the words/morphemes that they hear match, the player gets a point. Continue until one player gets an agreed total number of points, e.g. 3 or 5. Alternatively, use the Morph Race Track Game Board (page X) instead of giving points if time allows.

Morph Match Game 1: to develop awareness of word relationships

Pre-record pairs of words that are related because they have a morpheme in common. They could have the same root ***or*** affix. Players take turns to press two buttons. If the two words are related, players get a point.

Here are some example word pairs:

For ***transparent morphemes***:

- (roots only) run –running, learn – learnt, help – helper, fit – unfit, long – longest, fox – foxes
- (suffixes only) helping – seeing, farmer – teacher, hopped – cooked, shiny – sleepy, shortest – hardest, works – drives
- (prefixes only) unfit – unkind, misbehave – misprint, react – rewrite, disappear – disown, superstar – superhero, submarine – subway
- (mixed) rotted – wanted, unhelpful – unkind, shiny – shining, runner, rerun, misbehaving, miscounted, rebuilding, returned

For ***opaque morphemes***, choose any pairs of words from the **Examples of phonologically opaque morphemes** list (Appendix 13).

Morph Match Game 2: to develop production and decomposition of transparent morphemes

Each pair that you pre-record on your voice recorders should consist of one root and one affix. For example, one pair could be **form** and **re-**. Record all the roots on one set of recorders, and all the affixes in the other set. Players take turns to press two buttons, one from each set. If they can make a word with their two voice recordings, they get a point.

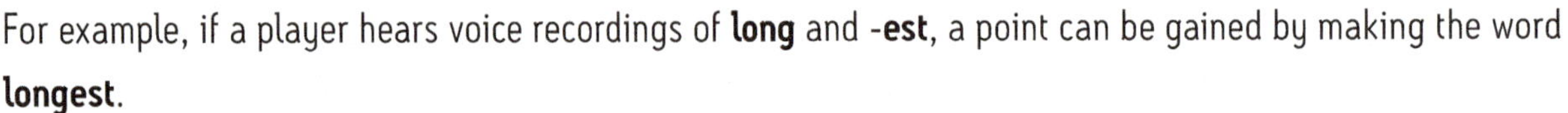

For example, if a player hears voice recordings of **long** and **-est**, a point can be gained by making the word **longest**.

Morph Match Game 3: to develop production and decomposition of transparent morphemes

For each pre-recorded pair, choose one root and one word which is that root with an affix added. For example, you might choose **play** and **played**. Players take turn to press two buttons. If one word can be changed to make the other word, they get a point.

(Optional for added difficulty) If the player can say how the first word is changed to make the second, get two points. For example, if the words are **run** – **running**, the player says "add **–ing** to **run** to make **running**".

Examples of word pairs:

run – running, act – react, sing – singer, unkind – kind, hat – hats, wish – wishes

Morph Match Game 4 (more advanced): to develop production and decomposition of opaque morphemes

This game is very similar to game 3, but it focuses on opaque morphemes. For each pre-recorded pair of words, choose one root and one word which is the root with an affix added. Record the roots all in one set of recorders, and the roots with affixes all in another set. Players take turns to press two buttons. If one word can be changed to make the other word, they get a point.

(Optional for added challenge) If the player can say how the sound has changed, award two points. For example, if the words are **child** – **children**, the player says "the long **i** sound in **child** changes to a short sound **i**".

Use **Examples of phonologically opaque morphemes, Appendix 13** to choose words.

How to adapt Morph Match for the whole class

Option 1: play the game as a whole class with two sets of voice recorders – in teams, pupils take turns to choose two recordings and try to match them.

Option 2: play the game in teams with human voice recorders! Split the class into 12 teams. Play Morph Match as above, but instead of recording your words or morphemes on voice recorders, each team has a morpheme to say. Choose one team who must pick two other teams to say their morphemes. The picking team gets a point if they have a pair.

Spinner Games

(games to support morphological awareness development)

Games to support decomposition, production and manipulation of morphemes

All these games require a spinner (see Appendix 18 for where to source these and the photocopiable spinner bases at the end of this chapter). All of them are purely oral – no writing is involved.

Spinner Game 1 (decomposition and production of real words)

- **You will need:** Real Words Cards (cut up) and Spinner Base 4.

Real Words

disliked	unties
unhappiness	reacted
unzips	untying
distrusted	mishits
remaking	refills
replaying	reliving

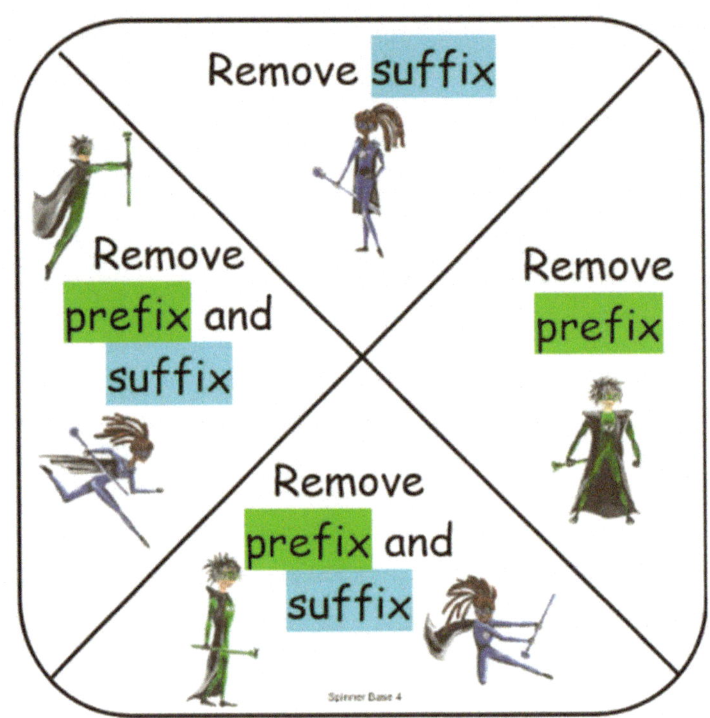

- **How to play:** take turns to pick up a word card and read it to the player on your left (adult may help reading). That player spins the spinner and changes the word s/he has heard from the word card by doing what the spinner says, then saying the new word (no writing required).

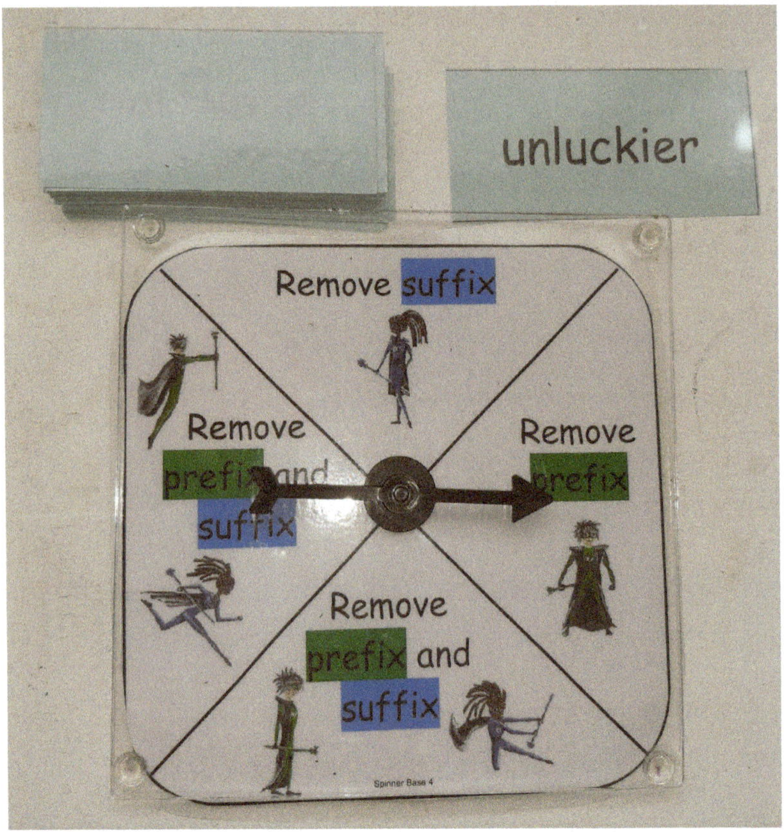

For example, If the word that is read from the card is **disliked**, and the spinner instruction is **remove suffix**, the answer will be **dislike**. If the spinner instruction is **remove suffix and prefix**, the answer is **like**. When they are correct, each player either gets a point or gets to move along a general game board, for example the **Morph Race Track Game** or **Craft**.

Spinner Game 2 (decomposition and production of real words)

- **You will need:** a selection of Morpheme Cards (roots) and Spinner Base 5 (this may need to be amended according to the pupils, for example fewer options – or use a **Blank Spinner Base** to adapt).

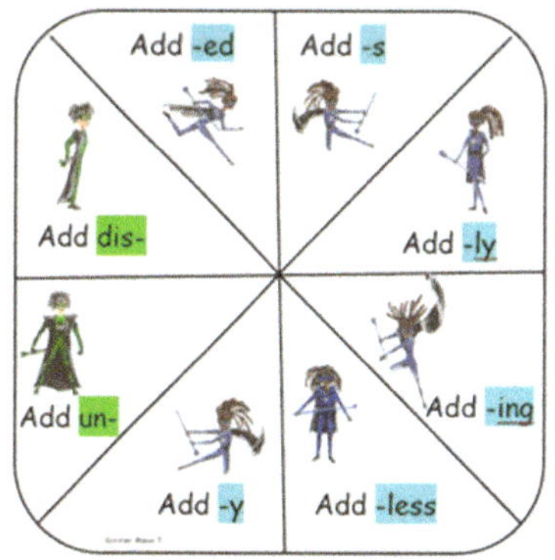

- **How to play:** take turns to pick up a root word card and read it to the player on your left (adult may help with reading). That player spins the spinner and changes the root s/he has heard according to what the spinner says, then says the new word (no writing required). If the word you have made is a real word, you get a point.

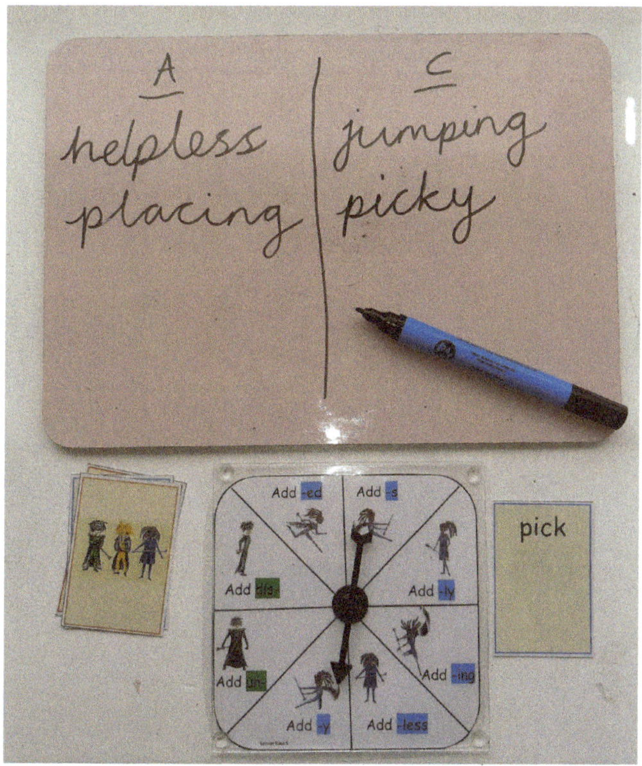

For example, if the root on the Mastery card is **fit**, and the spinner says **add -s**, the player says **fits**. A point is awarded. If the spinner says **add -y**, the player says **fitty**. No point is awarded.

Spinner Game 3 (decomposition and production of nonsense words)

- **You will need:** Spinner Base 1 and Nonsense Word Cards Set 1 (cut up). Depending on your learners' ability, you may choose to use a blank spinner base to vary the suffixes.

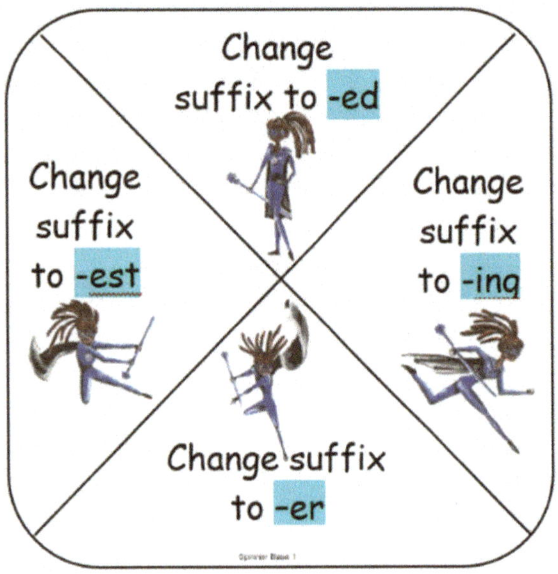

pons	gegs
fuds	beffs
teshes	puxes
wosses	nisses
lenging	roating
hicking	saiting

- **How to play:** shuffle the word cards and place them in a pile face down on the table. Player 1 picks up a card and spins the spinner. Follow the instructions on the spinner base and say the answer (no writing). Example: The word card is **pons**. The spinner's instruction is change suffix to **-ing**. The answer is **ponning**.
- **Easier version for weaker readers:** adult reads the card every time.

Spinner Game 4 (decomposition and production of nonsense words)

- **You will need:** Spinner Base 2 and shuffled Nonsense Word Cards set 2. If preferred, use a Blank Spinner Base to vary the prefixes on the spinner according to what you have been teaching. Choose to use 2, 3 or 4 prefixes depending on the child's ability.

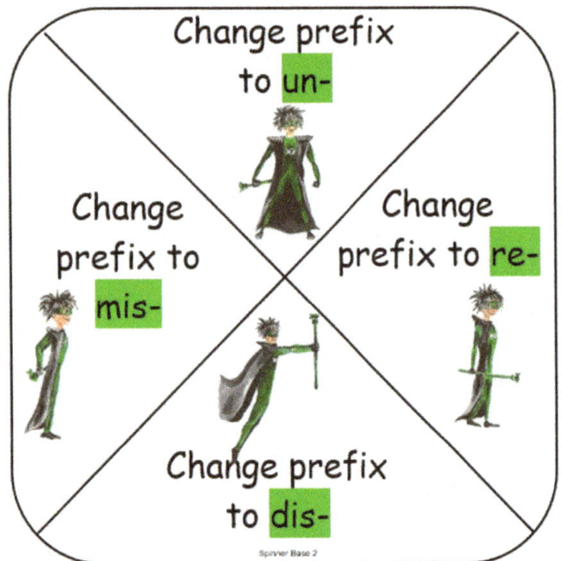

unreff	untock
unrop	unvap
relop	retick
redight	refarn
disfum	dispim
discoan	disvam

- **How to play:** Player 1 picks up a card and spins the spinner. S/he must follow the instructions on the spinner base and say the answer (no writing). Example: The word card is **unrop**. The spinner's instruction is change prefix to **re-**. The answer is **rerop**.
- **Easier version for weaker readers:** adult reads the card every time.

Spinner Game 5 (decomposition and production of nonsense words)

- **You will need:** Spinner Base 3 and Nonsense Word Cards set 1, 2, or 4.

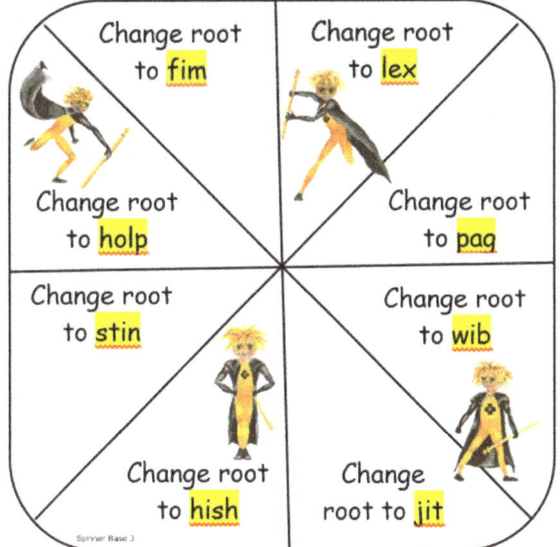

unreff	untock
unrop	unvap
relop	retick
redight	refarn
disfum	dispim
discoan	disvam

- **How to play:** Player 1 picks up a card and spins the spinner. Player 1 must follow the instructions on the spinner base and say the answer (no writing). Example: The word card is **kennest**. The spinner's instruction is change root to **fup-**. The answer is **fuppest**.
- **Easier version** for weaker readers: adult reads the card every time.
- **Harder version** to include more roots: use Nonsense Cards set 3 (alternative nonsense roots).

Spinner Game 6 (decomposition and production of nonsense words)

- **You will need:** Spinner Base 4 and Nonsense Word Cards set 4 (cut up).

unfoddy	unguns
unfashed	ungaxes
ungiddest	unhetty
unricking	unforlment
unhockness	untoshful
unfoatless	ungorkly

- **How to play:** Player 1 picks up a card and spins the spinner. S/he must follow the instructions on the spinner base and say the answer (no writing). Example: The word card is **unfashed**. The spinner's instruction is remove prefix and suffix. The answer is **fash**.
- **Easier version** for weaker readers: adult reads the card every time.
- **Harder version** to include more roots: use Nonsense Cards set 3 (alternative nonsense roots).

How to adapt the Spinner Games for Morphological Awareness for the whole class

All of these games can be played with teams instead of individuals. Teams can take turns to pick up a card and spin a spinner, either displayed on the visualiser or using an online spinner (there are numerous options available).

Alternatively, group your learners according to ability and give each group a different spinner and set of cards.

Voice Families

(games to support morphological awareness development and spelling)

For this game, if the learner is a weak reader, the adult reads all the words. Stronger readers may read the word when it is their turn.

- **You will need:** one or more voice recorders which have the capacity for at least ten very short recordings in total and a set of 20 blank cards. Before you play, on your voice recorder, pre-record between two and ten roots. On a set of blank cards, write up to 20 words that are built from these roots.
- **How to play:** shuffle the cards and place them face down on the table. Players take turns to turn over the top card, read it, then press a button on the voice recorder. If the word on the card that you are holding derives from the spoken root on the voice recorder, get a point. Continue playing until one player reaches a decided number of points. If the cards run out, simply shuffle them and place them back on the table face down. Example: your roots could be **form**, **place**, **port** and **grace**. You might write on your cards the following words: **formation**, **forming**, **reform**, **displaced**, **placement**, **replacing**, **portable**, **export**, **importation**, **report**, **speedily**, **speeding**, **graces**, **ungraceful**, **disgrace** and **gracious**.

Voice Families game with spelling

- **You will need:** for the spelling version of this game, choose roots and suffixes that you want your learners to practise spelling. For example, if you have taught the roots **race, light**, **fit**, you might record these on your voice recorders. Then on your cards you might write **racing**, **raced**, **racer**, **lighter**, **lightest**, **lighting**, **fits**, **unfit**, **fittest**.
- **How to play:** follow the same instructions for Voice Families but include spelling, as follows: Shuffle the cards. Player 1 picks up the top card and reads it to Player 2. Player 2 then presses a button on the voice recorder. If the root that Player 1 reads from the card derives from the root that is recorded on the voice recorder pressed by Player 2, Player 2 writes the word that was on the card. If the spelling is correct, Player 2 gets a point. Continue playing until one player reaches a decided number of points. If the cards run out, simply shuffle them and place them back on the table face down.

How to adapt the Voice Families game for the whole class

Option 1 – Human Voice Families: choose ten pupils to be the human voice recorders! Allocate each pupil with a root. Give the remaining pupils a list of words which are built from these roots – you could write this on the whiteboard. In pairs, they choose one of the words on the list and write it down. Then, ask one of your human voices to say their root. Each pair must decide if their written word can be made from this root. They get a point if it does. The winner is the first to get a decided number of points. For example, your ten pupils might be given the following roots: **help**, **form**, **teach**, **wait**, **ride**, **count**, **poison**, **port**, **sect**, **cycle**. The word list on the board might be **helper**, **formation**, **unteachable**, **waiter**, **riding**, **countless**, **poisonous**, **portable**, **section**, **bicycle**. Choose words linked to the class spellings or topic work.

Option 2 – Card Families: group your class in mixed ability groups of four ot six. Instead of using voice recorders, write (or type and print) the roots on to cards, as well as the words that are built from these roots. Photocopy these sets of cards for each group (or give each group some blank cards and word lists). Groups should have both sets of cards to each group in two separate piles. Allocate one reader per group. Players spread out both piles of cards face down on the table, making sure that the cards are kept in their two sets. Players take turns to pick up one card from both sets. If they have a match they get a point. Continue playing until one player has gained 4 points – or a bigger number if time allows.

Extension of Option 2 for more able pupils: pupils make the above card game themselves using morphemes that you have been learning.

Happy Families

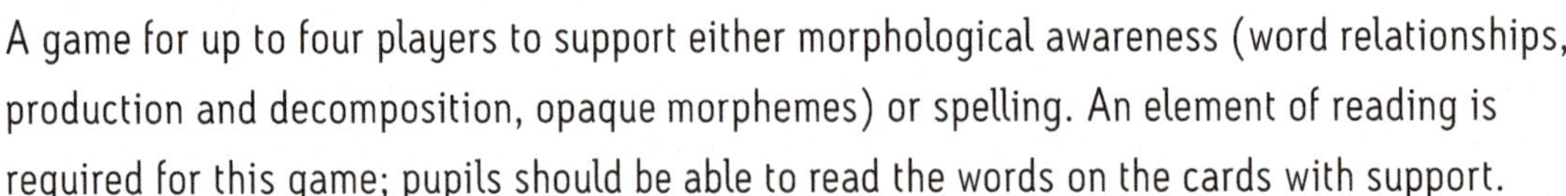

(games to support morphological awareness and spelling)
A game for up to four players to support either morphological awareness (word relationships, production and decomposition, opaque morphemes) or spelling. An element of reading is required for this game; pupils should be able to read the words on the cards with support.

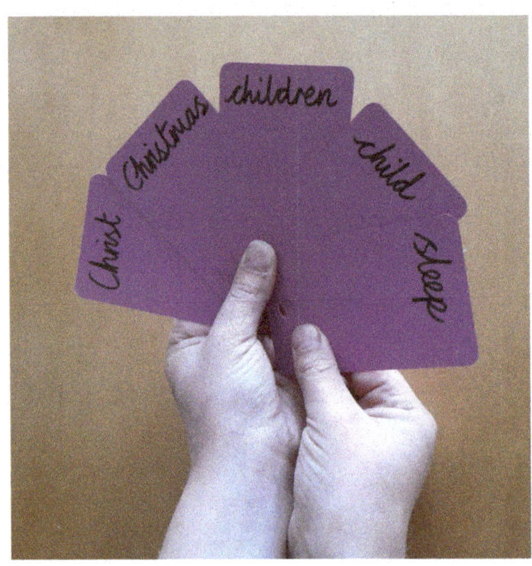

- **You will need:** in advance, prepare 12 cards on which are written words which are related – there should be three word cards for each family. Examples of groups of word families are below. These can be mixed and matched, and remember, they are just examples!

zip, unzip, zips, pick, picking, unpick box, boxes, boxing milk, milky, milking	tip, tipping, tipped fat, fatter, fattest help, helpful, unhelpful light, lighter, lighting
mobile, mobilise, mobility centimetre, centurion, century dissect, section, sector project, eject, trajectory	credible, incredible, credit scribe, script, inscribe interrupt, rupture, erupt flex, flexible, reflex
kindly, helpfully, thoughtlessly react, rewire, rewrite unwind, unsafe, unpack payment, placement, employment	subheading, submarine, subway interact, intercity, international autograph, autobiography, autopilot antisocial, antiseptic, antifreeze

- **How to play:** read all the cards to the learners before you play, or if your learners are able, ask them to read them. Shuffle all the cards. Deal out four cards each and put the remaining cards face down on the table. Players take turns to ask if the other player has a word related to one that you are holding.

For example:

Player 1: Morpha, do you have a word related to **tip**?
Morpha has **tipping**, so gives it to player 1.

If the other player does not have a card you have asked for, you may pick up a card from the pile on the table. If it is your turn and you have a set of three cards, you have a family; put them all down on the table. You can put down more than one family at one time. You can do this at the start of your turn, after getting a card from another player, or after picking up a card from the pile. The winner is the person with the most families when one person has lost all their cards, or when the pile on the table has run out.

- **To play the game with opaque morphemes:** choose words containing opaque morphemes. For example:

heal, **health**, **healthy**
child, **children**, **childish**
sleep, **slept**, **sleepy**
christ, **Christmas**, **Christian**

There are many more examples in Appendix 13, **Examples of phonologically opaque morphemes**.

Happy Families Game with Spelling

- **You will need:** the resources are the same, but choose only morphemes you have been teaching.
- **How to play:** the game is the same as Happy Families, but add the following spelling elements:
  - Learners write the words onto the cards before they begin
  - If a player tells another player s/he has a word that player asked for, the asking player must write it down before being shown the card. The card is then only handed over if it is spelled correctly. For example:

Player 1: Do you have a word related to **helpless**?
Player 2: Yes, I have **helping** (does not show the card).
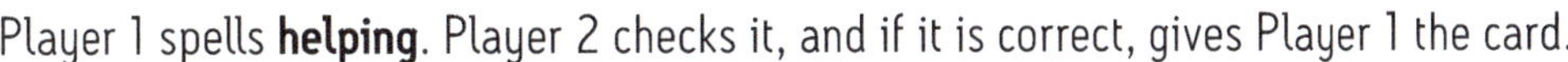
Player 1 spells **helping**. Player 2 checks it, and if it is correct, gives Player 1 the card.

How to adapt the Happy Families game for a whole class

Arrange your learners into groups of four. Give each group 12 blank cards and 12 words, three in each word family – choose some of the families listed above or make up your own. Pupils make the cards together first then play the game. You can either put your pupils in mixed ability groups and give them all the same words or differentiate the word families for ability groups.

Pairs Down

(games to support morphological awareness and spelling)

- **You will need:** in advance, prepare a set of at least 18 blank cards with words written on them (or at least 25 for three or more players). Examples of words are provided, but make sure they are appropriate for your learner. Use the Morph Mastery **Word Lists for Planning** (Appendix 7) or **Examples of phonologically opaque morphemes** (Appendix 13) for more choices of words. Make sure the pupil can read the words, or read the words out to the pupil as you play.
- **How to play:** the aim of the game is to put down as many pairs as you can. The pairs are different depending on which game you are playing.
  Deal out the word cards, three cards per player, and place the remaining word cards on a pile face down on the table. Take turns to pick up a word card from the pile. After picking up a card, if you have a pair, you may put it down on the table. At the end of your turn, put one of your cards to the bottom of the word pile: you can choose any card. The game ends when one player has no cards left. The winner is the person with the most pairs at the end.

Game 1: (morphological awareness) to recognise words containing the same root

Use pairs containing the same root. These should be chosen carefully according to the child's ability. Do not limit these words to the words you have taught for spelling, however, because this is a morphological awareness game. Examples of pairs are as follows:

wish – wishful
patch – patches
help – unhelpful
like – likeability

To make the game harder: include words that sound the same but do not have the same root, for example:

pillow – pillows
pill – pills
meat – meaty
meeting – met
tea – teabag
way – ways
weight – weights
waiting – waited

Game 2: (morphological awareness) to recognise words containing the same suffix/prefix

Use pairs of words containing the same suffix, or prefix, or both. For example:

helpless – careless
kindness – madness
react – repair
rewriting – repairing

Game 3: (morphological awareness) to decompose/produce words containing opaque morphemes

Use the **Opaque Morpheme Cards** resource (available on companion website), or choose your own words which contain opaque morphemes when they are affixed. Examples are below, or see **Examples of phonologically opaque morphemes** (Appendix 13).

say – said
bite – bit
write – wrote
heal – health
magic – magician
courage – courageous
decide – decision
collect – collection
rectangle – rectangular
circle – circular
produce – production
pirate – piracy

Game 4 (morphological awareness): to build words by adding an affix

The game is similar to Games 1, 2 and 3, but you will prepare only one set of cards (roots). Before play, the adult chooses one or more target affixes and writes them where they can be seen throughout the game, e.g. on the whiteboard.

Take turns to pick up a word card. You have a pair if you can add the target affix to your word to make a new word. For example, if your target affix is **-ed** and your word is **wait**, you have a pair; you can add **-ed** to both to make a word.

Game 5 (spelling): to apply spelling rules when adding an affix to a root word

This can be played to reinforce spelling rules, for example double the consonant when adding ***-ing, -ed (let – letting, fit – fitted)***.

Follow the instructions for Pairs Down Game 4. Use only one pile of cards (18 to 25 in total) and write the roots you have been teaching on them. Write down one or more targeted affixes somewhere visible (e.g. a whiteboard). As for Game 4, you have a "pair" if you can add one of the targeted affixes to a word in your hand. NB for this game you will not hold two cards in your hand for the pair; the second part of your pair is the affix written on the board.

Examples of words where spelling rules can be applied (can apply to affixes **-ed**, **-ing**, **-y**, **-ly**, **-est**, **-er**, **-ness**, **-less**, **-ful**):

fit, let, rip, tip, run, sit (double consonant)
chase, hate, poke, hike, lose, shake (drop e)
sticky, beauty, rust, mess, fuss, laz (y – i)

Adapting Pairs Down Game 5 for class:

Write down the affixes that you would like to target on the board (see examples above) and choose some roots that use these affixes (again, examples are above). Group your pupils into mixed ability groups.

Write down all the roots you chose (or ask the pupils to write them) on small pieces of paper or card and place them in a bag. Before each turn, every group must choose one of the affixes from the board and write it down. Then one group picks a root out of the bag (without looking) and reads it out. All groups must make a word and spell it correctly using their chosen affix and the root from the bag in order to get a point. Repeat play until all groups have had a turn then count up the points. The group with the most points is the winner.

Pairs

(a reading and spelling game to support correct use of the suffixes -es or -s)

- **You will need:** a set of blank cards (between 10 and 20).
- **How to play:** pupils write down a selection of the following words on the blank cards. Choose a selection from both lists.

  Words using -s suffix

  cats, dogs, bags, fans, fins, hats, huts, jugs, tans, logs, legs, mats, mugs, nets, pans, pits, pins, rags, rats, ribs, vets, vans, wigs, zips, shops, days, schools, friends, pens, toys, games, cups, ponds, books, boys, desks, digs, bats, bets, gets, hits, jogs, tips, licks, mops, pats, picks, quits, sits, sobs, kicks, spins, runs, cooks, plays, jumps, drags, drops, grabs, hugs, stops

  Words using -es suffix

  boxes, ashes, bushes, churches, foxes, brushes, dishes, kisses, patches, lunches, glasses, watches, fizzes, wishes, mixes, rushes, catches, buzzes, hisses, fixes, touches, washes

  If working with a group ask them to check each other's spellings. Shuffle the cards well, then split them into two piles and place the piles face down on the table. Players take turns to pick up two cards. If the word on both cards uses the same suffix, either **-s** or **-es**, they have a pair. For example, fox and hiss are a pair because they are both suffixed with **-es**.
- **Alternative version:** instead of placing the cards in two piles on the table, spread them out face down. Players pick any two cards, and if both words end in the same suffix they have a pair.
- **To make the game harder:** words are only pairs if they have the same affix **and** are both verbs or both nouns. For example:

box – fox (**-es**, nouns)

wish – rush (**-es**, verbs)

pot – boat (**-s**, nouns)

run – spin (**-s**, verbs)

Morph Connect

(a game for practising reading and spelling by combining morphemes)

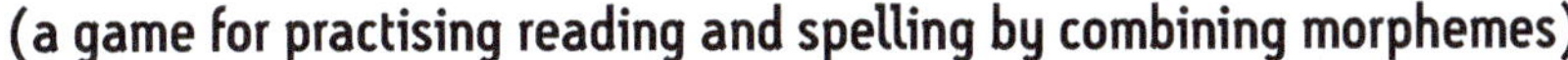

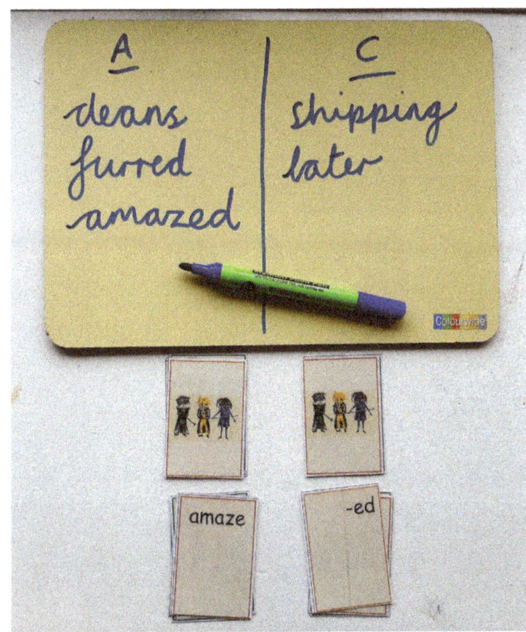

- **You will need:** Morpheme Cards for roots and affixes (**Appendix 17** – choose cards in advance that are either known by the learners, or are being taught/revised)
  Pencil & paper/whiteboards & pens
- **How to play:** decide if you are playing with suffixes and roots, prefixes and roots or, for a more experienced group, all three. Lay out, face down, a pile of Morpheme Cards for each; so if you have chosen roots and suffixes, as in the illustration above, you will have a pile of root cards and a pile of suffixes. In turn, players take one card from each pile and try to make a word. If they can make a word, write it. For more confident pupils, ask them to turn the cards back face down before the write. They get a point if it is a real word and correctly spelled.

How to adapt Morph Connect for the whole class

Option 1: On Your Feet!

Combine the game with physical exercise to make the game into a speed game. Divide the class into teams. Put the cards at the end of an obstacle race course – teams pick up two cards when they reach the end and play the game as above.

Option 2

Use two spinners or dice apps on an interactive whiteboard – put roots on one and affixes on another. Spin both spinners and pupils spell the word. Make it competitive by turn taking.

Option 3 (younger children)

Use bricks e.g. Unifix. Write your roots and affixes onto sticky labels and stick onto bricks. Separate the bricks into piles, bags or boxes. Pupils take one from each pile and attempt to make a word.

Morph Guess

(to rehearse spelling words containing affixes and root words)

All these games can be played as a whole class with no adaptions.

- **You will need:**
  Set of blank cards/pieces of paper
  A bag (not see-through)
  Paper and pencil/ mini whiteboard and pen for each pupil
  Whiteboard for writing words on and scoring (if playing with a small group or individual this can be a mini whiteboard)
  Morph Race Track or Craft Game Board (optional)
- **Scoring:** choose how many points you want to play to (if short of time, play to 2 points). The first player to reach this number of points is the winner.
  To add interest, if time allows, use the Morph Race Track Game or Craft Game Board instead of counting points.

Game 1: to rehearse spelling words containing one affix

- **How to play:**
  1. In advance, adult chooses one target affix and a list of four to eight words which contain the affix. Write the list of words on the whiteboard and also on individual cards/pieces of paper. Place the cards/paper in a bag
  2. Each player chooses one word from the list on the board and writes it on his/her piece of paper/ mini whiteboard
  3. Adult or one player picks a word from the bag and shows it to the pupil/group/class
  4. Get a point if the word picked out is the word you wrote down
- ***To make the game harder:*** hide the words on the board while pupils write them down.

Game 2: to rehearse spelling words containing one affix (harder version of game 1)

- **How to play:**
  1. In advance, adult writes one affix on the whiteboard and writes four to eight words containing that affix onto cards or pieces of paper. Put these in a bag
  2. Players write down one word from memory which contains the targeted affix
  3. Adult or one player picks a word out of the bag and shows it to the pupil/group/class
  4. Get a point if the word that was picked out is the word you wrote down
- ***To make the game harder:*** Choose some words which apply a spelling rule. If a player successfully applies the rule and the word is picked out, get two points.

Game 3: to rehearse spelling more than one affix (to be played when at least two affixes have been taught)

- **How to play:**
  1. In advance, adult writes a list of taught affixes on the board (maximum 8 affixes). Write onto cards or pieces of paper words containing these affixes – choose one word for each affix. Place these in a bag
  2. Players choose one affix from the list on the board and write it down
  3. Adult/one player picks a word from the bag and shows it to the pupil/group/class
  4. Players get a point if their affix is in the word

Game 4: to rehearse spelling words containing one targeted root

- **How to play:**
  1. In advance, write a list of four to eight words containing one targeted root on the board. The adult can do this, or prepare it together as a whole class or group. Write the words onto cards or pieces of paper and put them in a bag
  2. Players choose one word from the list and write it down
  3. Adult picks a word from the bag and shows it to the pupil/group/class
  4. Get a point if it is the word you wrote

Game 5: to rehearse spelling words containing one targeted root and one targeted affix

- **How to play:**
  1. In advance, write one targeted root and one targeted affix on the board. This can be done by the adult, or together as a whole class or group. Prepare a list of words containing either the root or the affix, or both (between four and eight words). Write the words on cards or pieces of paper
  2. From memory, pupils write down one word containing the root or the affix
  3. Adult picks a word from the bag and shows it to the pupil/group/class
  4. Get a point if it is the word you wrote down
- ***To make the game harder:*** include some words which apply a spelling rule. Players get an extra point if they successfully applied the rule and their word was chosen.

Morph Match & Spell

(a game to support word agility and spelling)

This game is very similar to Morph Match, but it involves spelling. You will be matching two spoken morphemes to make words, which you must then spell.

- **You will need:**
  1. Two sets of six voice recorders. You can either use two voice recorders with a capacity of six recordings each, for example two giant dice, or microphones with separate buttons, or 12 individual sound buttons or recordable microphones in two groups of six. Whichever option you choose, make sure you have two sets of six recordings. If only one set of six is available, use cards or tiles in place of the second voice recorder.
  2. Mini whiteboard and pen or pencil and paper
  3. (Optional) a race game track board – players can move along this instead of counting points if time allows
- **How to play:** in advance, on your voice recorders, record morpheme pairs: one taught root and one taught affix for each pair. For example, one pair could be **wish** and **-es**. You can choose to use some pairs that can be interchanged, for example **wish** and **-es** and **box** and **-ing**. Make sure one recorder from each pair is in each set. Players take turns to press two buttons, one from each set of voice recorders. If a word can be made with the root and affix they hear, the player writes the word and gets a point if it is spelled correctly.

  If you have been teaching spelling rules (e.g. double the consonant, drop the e, y → i), get two points if you can apply a rule and successfully write the word.

How to adapt Morph Match and Spell for the whole class

Option 1: play the game as a whole class with two sets of voice recorders – in teams, pupils take turns to choose two recordings and try to match them. They get a point if they can make a word and spell it.

Option 2: play the game in teams with human voice recorders! Split the class into 12 teams. Play Morph Match as above, but instead of recording your words or morphemes on voice recorders, each team has a morpheme to say. Choose one team who must pick two other teams to say their morphemes. Get a point if you have a pair and can spell the word.

Spin Words and Spin Words Trick Games

(games to support word agility (reading and spelling))

- **You will need:**
  1. A spinner and blank spinner base (bases can be personalised to the game and child; only include what has been taught) – see the resource list in Appendix 18.
     Morpheme cards or blank cards for writing words on (if applicable to your chosen game)
  2. (Optional) General race game board.

Spin Words: to support word building and spelling using known/taught morphemes

Choose between two and eight affixes that you wish to target and write these on the spaces on a blank spinner base. If you are choosing fewer than four affixes, you can double them up on the spinner base. Use a set of up to 20 Morpheme Cards (roots). The roots you choose should link with your targeted affixes.

- **How to play:** take turns to pick up a Morpheme Card and spin the spinner. If you can make a word with the root on your card and the affix on your spinner, write the word and get a point if correctly spelled. If time allows, you could use the Morph Race Track or Stealth Game Board. Instead of getting a point, players take a turn on the board every time they spell a word correctly.

  For example: target affixes are **un-**, **dis-**, **-ing**, **-er**. If you pick up Morpheme Card **fit** and spin **un-**, you can write the word **unfit** and have a point. However, if you pick up **rot** and spin **un-** you cannot make a word, so you don't get a point.

Spin Words Trick: to support word building and spelling using known/taught morphemes and applying spelling rules

- **How to play:** play **Spin Words,** but use words where rules could be applied when affixed. The spinner base can be personalised from a Blank Spinner Base, according to what you have taught and what the child needs to practise, or use the examples below. For each game, choose some Morpheme Cards for roots which where the spelling rule applies, and some where it doesn't.

- **-es or –s:** Use Spinner Base 6 and an appropriate set of root cards (e.g. **fix, run, hiss, pat**)

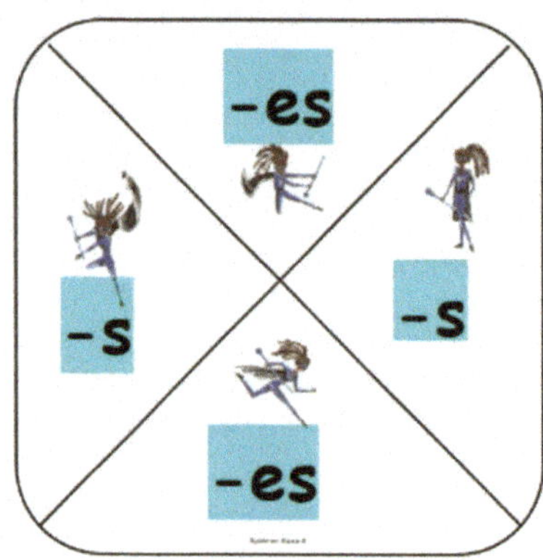

- **Double consonant rule:** Use Spinner Base 9 and an appropriate set of root cards (e.g. **fit**, **run**, **clean**, **light**). N.B. this spinner applies when **-est**, **-er**, **-ing,** and **-ed** have all been taught. If they have not been taught, or you want to target other affixes, use a blank Spinner Base Master and write your own chosen affixes.

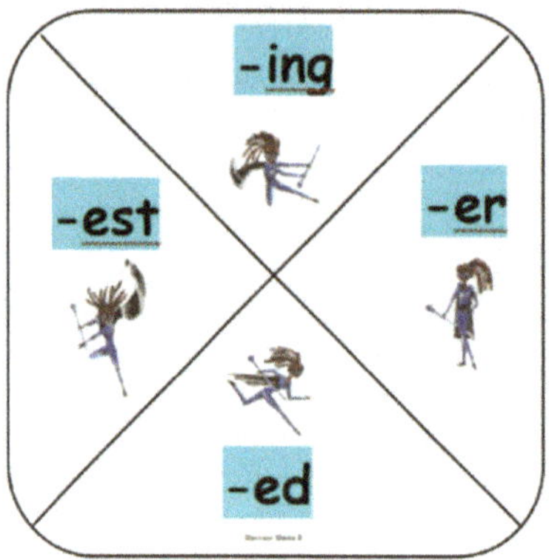

- **Drop e rule**
  Option 1: Use Spinner Base 13 and appropriate roots (verbs) e.g. like, wish, ride, sing
  Option 2: Use Spinner Base 9 and a set of appropriate word roots (e.g. like, drive, clean, light). N.B. this spinner applies when **-est**, **-er**, **-ing**, and **-ed** have all been taught. Write appropriate suffixes onto a blank spinner base master if these have not been taught.

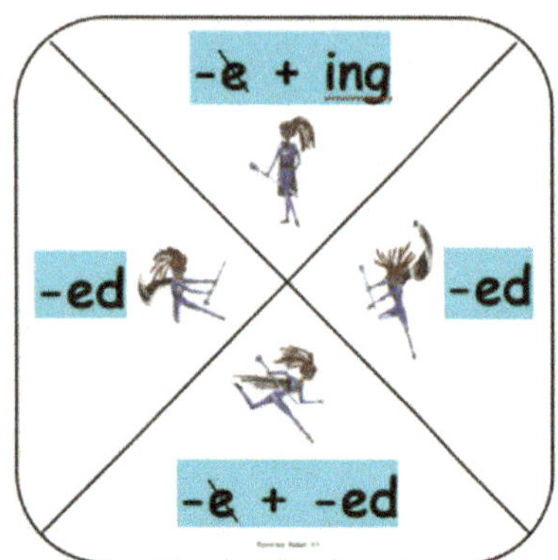

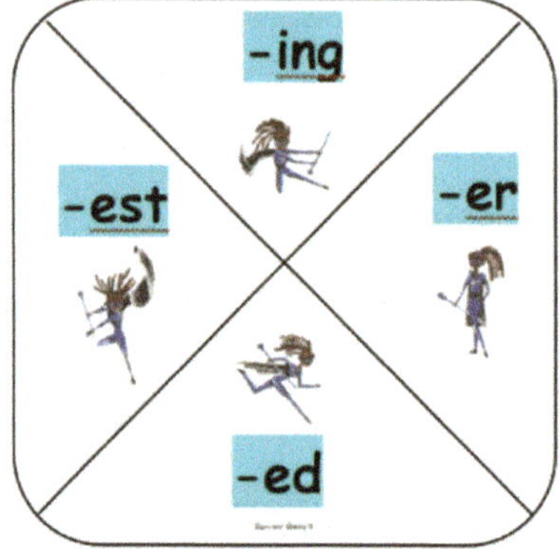

- **Y → i rule:** Use Spinner Base 16, or a personalised blank spinner base and a set of appropriate words, for example **try, copy, fry, tidy, happy**.

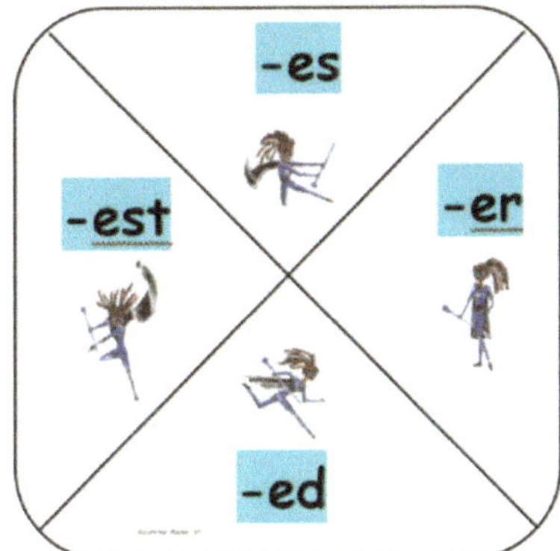

- **Scoring Spin Words Trick:**
  Option 1: Offer 1 point if the player can write a word, whether or not a rule is applied.
  Option 2: Offer an extra point if a rule is applied correctly in writing the word.
- **How to adapt Spin Words and Spin Words Trick to class**
  Option 1: set up your pupils in differentiated groups with blank cards and blank spinner base masters. Provide them with affixes according to their ability level and ask them to come up with their own roots to write on cards – or for less able learners give them the roots as well.
  Option 2: play as a whole class with one spinner – put the class into teams. Give each team a list of roots. They take turns to pick a root before you spin the spinner – get a point if they were correct and can write the word.
  Option 3: put the class into teams. Give each group a spinner and blank spinner base master (four boxes). Ask them to write different suffixes into the boxes on the spinner base – give them a choice of suffixes, they must pick two and write each suffix twice.
  The adult then picks out one Morpheme Card from a set of roots. Each team spins their spinner. Any team who can write a word correctly from the root and affix on their spinner gets a point.

Spinner Match and Spinner Match Trick Games

(games to support spelling and applying spelling rules)

Learners will need to be confident with at least two affixes to play these games.

- **You will need:**
  1. Two spinners and **Blank Spinner Bases** (available from companion website and at the end of this chapter – bases can be personalised to the game and child; only include what has been taught) – see resource list
  2. Morpheme cards (if applicable to your chosen game)
  3. (Optional) General race game board, e.g. **Craft** or **Morph Race Track**– if using move along the board instead of getting a point. This can add interest but takes longer.
- **Scoring:** offer 1 point (or turn on the game board) if the player can write a word. If playing Spinner Match Trick, get an extra point (or turn) if a spelling rule is applied correctly in writing the word.

Spinner Match

- **How to play:** choose between two and eight roots and affixes that can be made into words. Use two spinners with blank bases. On one spinner write your taught/known roots. On the other, write your taught/known affixes. Double up some of the roots and/or affixes on the spinners if you are using fewer than four.
  Take turns to spin both spinners. If you can make a word and write it with the correct spelling, get a point or have a turn on a game board.
  For example: use roots **stick**, **clean**, **agree**, **light** and affixes **un-**, **dis-**, **-ing**, **-er**. If you spin **clean** and **un-**, you can write the word **unclean** and have a point/turn. However, if you spin **agree** and **un-** you cannot make a word, so you don't get a point/turn.

Spinner Match Trick

This game supports spelling or word building using known/taught morphemes and applying spelling rules.

- **How to play:** play **Spinner Match,** but use words where rules must be applied when they are affixed (for example, **run** requires the double consonant rule when it is affixed with **-er**, **-y** or **-ing**: **runner**, **runny**, **running**). The spinner bases are likely to need to be personalised according to what you have taught and what the child needs to practice. Here are some examples using the Spinner Base Masters:
  - **-es or -s:** Use Spinner Bases 6 and 7 (or use a blank spinner instead of spinner 7 according to what you have taught)

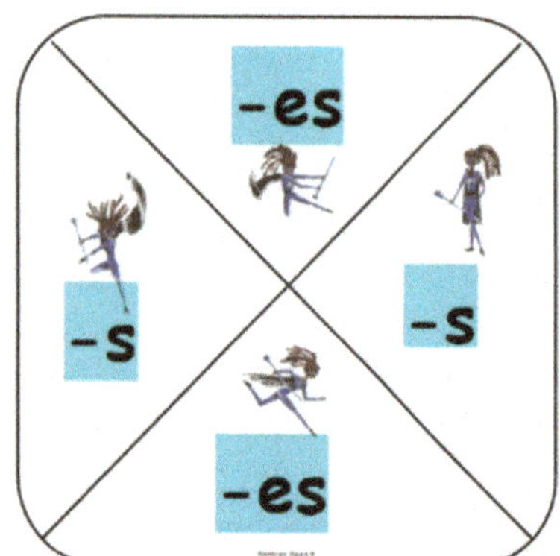

- **Double consonant rule:** Use Spinner Bases 8 and 9.

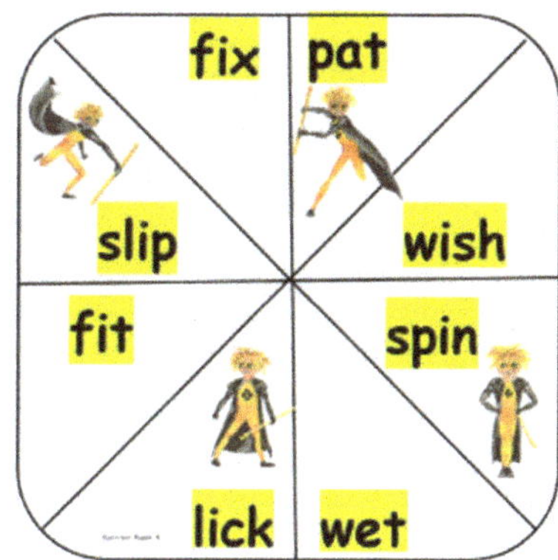

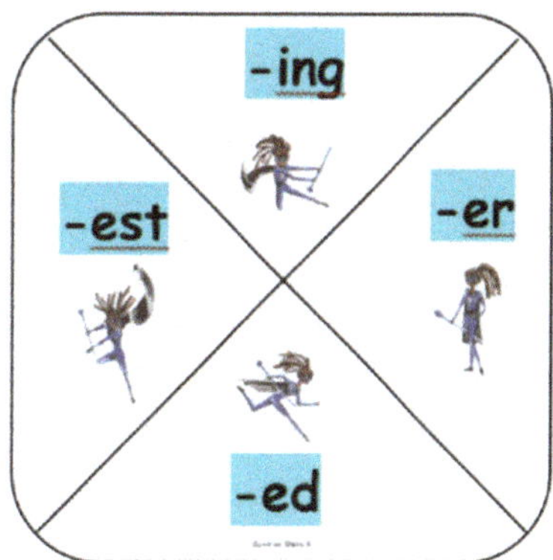

- **y-i rule:** Use Spinner Bases 10 and 11.

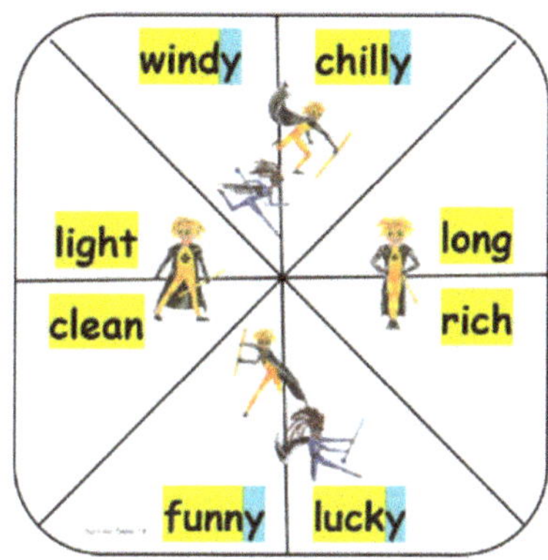

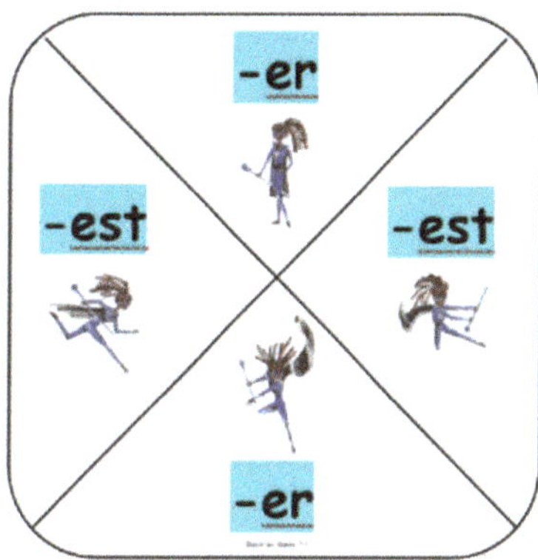

- **Drop e rule:** Use Spinner Bases 12 and 9. N.B. these spinners apply when **-est**, **-er**, **-ing** and **-ed** have all been taught.

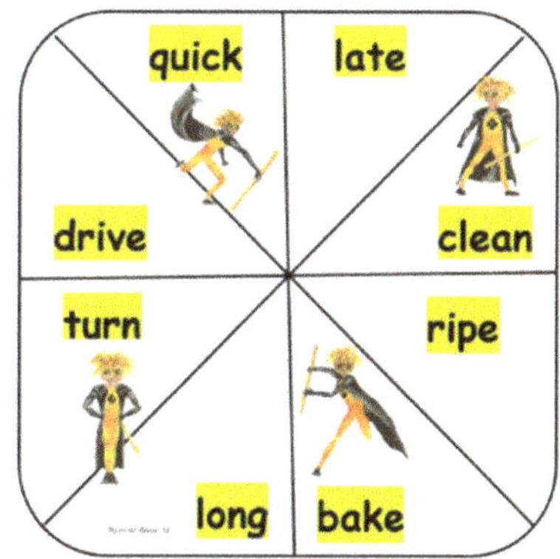

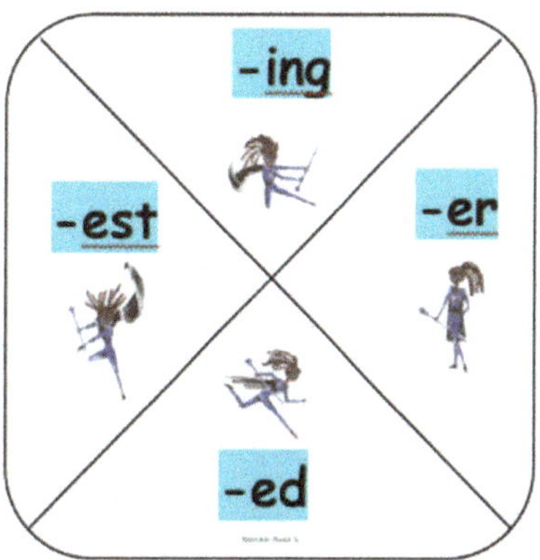

How to adapt Spinner Match and Spinner Match Trick for the whole class

Option 1

If you have enough spinners, you could play the game in groups. Differentiate the targeted words and affixes according to your groups' ability. Alternatively use a dice maker app on a tablet, or sticky labels to write the words and affixes onto dice – each group can use two dice instead of spinners.

Option 2

Put your class into six teams – three teams are Team A, and three teams are Team R. Provide a choice of affixes for Team A, written on the whiteboard. Provide a choice of roots, also written on the whiteboard, for Team R.

When everyone is ready, say "Write". Team A must choose and write down an affix. Each Team R must write a root down. Show the other team what you have written.

When everyone has done this, the adult says "Go". Team A must choose a Team R to run to. If another Team A gets to your chosen team, you must find a different Team R to match with. If both the root and affix for the matched teams can make a word, each player must write the word, and a point is awarded.

Repeat in the same manner.

The first team to reach a given number of points is the winner.

Stealth

(games to practise reading and spelling multi-morphemic words)

- **You will need:**
  1. Photocopied stealth stronghold grid (one for each player):

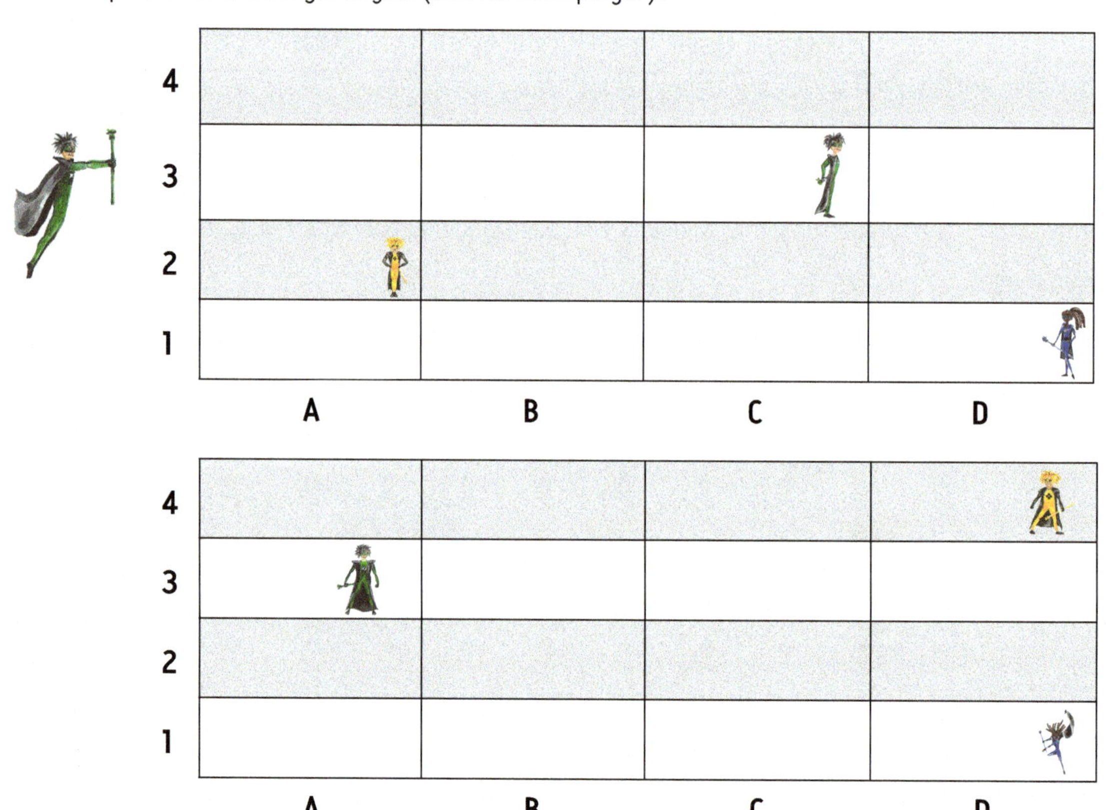

2. Small whiteboard and pen/pencil and paper
3. A4 ring binder or similar to act as a barrier between players

- **How to play:** the idea of the game is to locate your opponent's strongholds and master them. Do this by finding words on their (hidden) grid.
  1. Adult and pupil each take a stealth stronghold grid
  2. Stand up the A4 ring binder between the two grids so that neither player can see their opponent's grid
  3. Adult dictates words or morphemes (depending on which game you are playing) and both the adult and the pupil write each morpheme or word into any rectangle on their grid
  4. Player 1 starts by saying a grid reference, e.g. A3, to which player 2 will say **miss** if the rectangle is blank or **hit** if the rectangle has a morpheme or word written in it. If it is a **miss**, player 2 then takes their turn. If it is a **hit**, player 2 reads out the morpheme for player 1 to spell on their white board/ paper, and player 2 puts a line or cross through this word or morpheme on his/her grid to show that it has been hit. Player 1 writes a mark, e.g. a tick, in the box with the same grid reference. This indicates that s/he has already asked about that box, so s/he won't ask it again.
  5. Player 2 then takes their turn, repeating step 4
  6. Depending on the game you are playing, the game ends when either:

     One player has written down a set number of words (number decided in advance, minimum 2). The first to achieve this number is the winner

     Only one player has words or morphemes on his/her grid that have not been hit. This player is the winner.

Game 1: to practise word building and spelling using known morphemes

- **How to play:** in advance, adult chooses four to eight morphemes, a mix of roots and affixes (those that have been taught) These morphemes are used on all players' grids. For example:

4	***-es***			***fit***
3				
2			***-s***	
1		***wish***		
	A	**B**	**C**	**D**

If a player gets a "hit", write down the morpheme on the whiteboard or paper. As soon as any player has two morphemes that can join together to make a word, they write that word. Continue playing the game until one player has written two (or more, depending on your time and number of morphemes played with) whole words. This player is the winner.

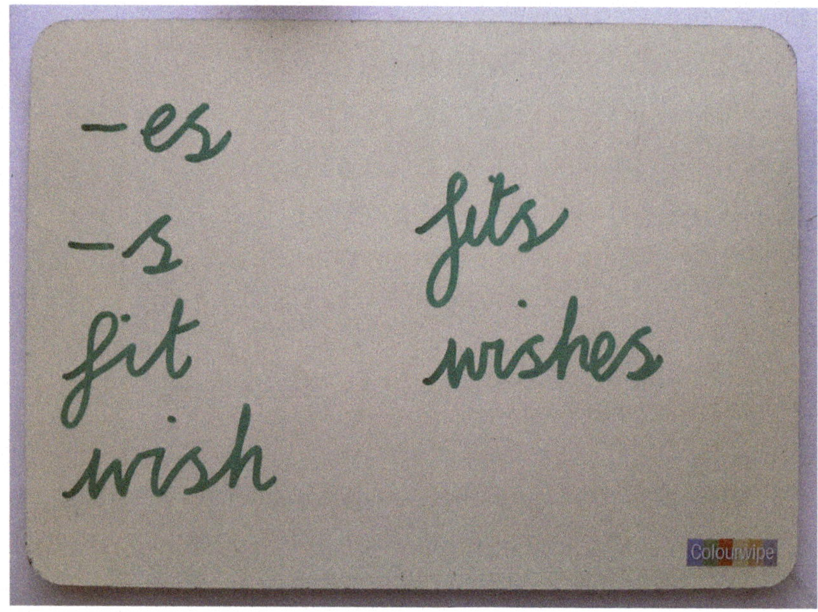

- **Variation of Stealth Game 1 for teaching spelling rules:** players get one point for writing a whole word and two points for writing a word where a spelling rule is applied. The first player to reach 5 points (for example, this can be varied as time allows) is the winner.

Game 2: to practise reading and spelling words containing taught morphemes

- **How to play:** play the game in exactly the same way as Game 1, except that on steps 3 and 4 you are writing whole words. If it is a hit there is no word building involved – just write the word that you have hit. The winner is the person who hits all the other player's strongholds first, or if time is limited the first person to hit two or three strongholds.

Game 3: to practise word building and spelling words where a rule is applied

- **How to play:**
  - **-es or -s rule:** Play in the same way but apply **-es** or **-s** rule. Sample words could be **fox**, **wish**, **run**, **sit**

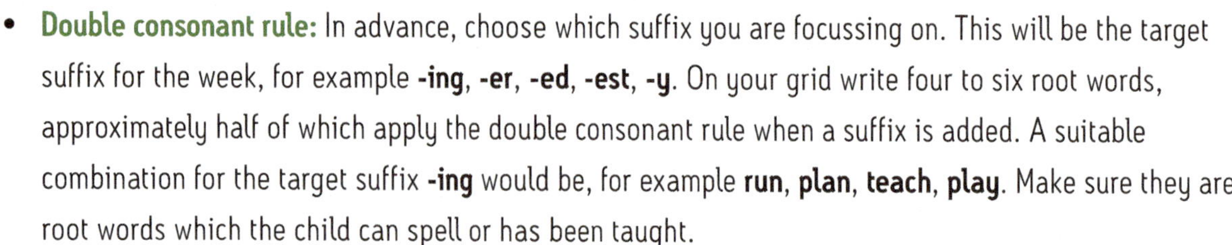

  - **Double consonant rule:** In advance, choose which suffix you are focussing on. This will be the target suffix for the week, for example **-ing**, **-er**, **-ed**, **-est**, **-y**. On your grid write four to six root words, approximately half of which apply the double consonant rule when a suffix is added. A suitable combination for the target suffix **-ing** would be, for example **run**, **plan**, **teach**, **play**. Make sure they are root words which the child can spell or has been taught.

    Play Stealth. Each time a player hits, s/he adds the chosen target suffix to the root that was hit. If s/he can make a word, write it down and score a point if it is spelled correctly. If s/he doubled the consonant in order to make a word, get two points.

    For example, if **play** is hit, and the target suffix is **-er**, write **player** and score one point. If **run** is hit, with the same suffix, write **runner** and score two points.

- **Drop e rule:** Play the game in the same way as for double consonant rule but apply drop e rule instead. Sample word roots could be, for example, **make, smile, drive, teach, wait, help.**
- **y - i rule:** Play the game in the same way as for double consonant rule but apply y - i rule instead. Sample word roots could be, for example, **cry, try, sticky, runny.**

How to adapt Stealth for the whole class

Stealth games are easy to set up because they need very few resources. Put the class into pairs with word and affix lists to play the games – differentiate the spellings. Alternatively play groups against one another.

Word Morph

(an extended word building card game (reading and/or spelling))

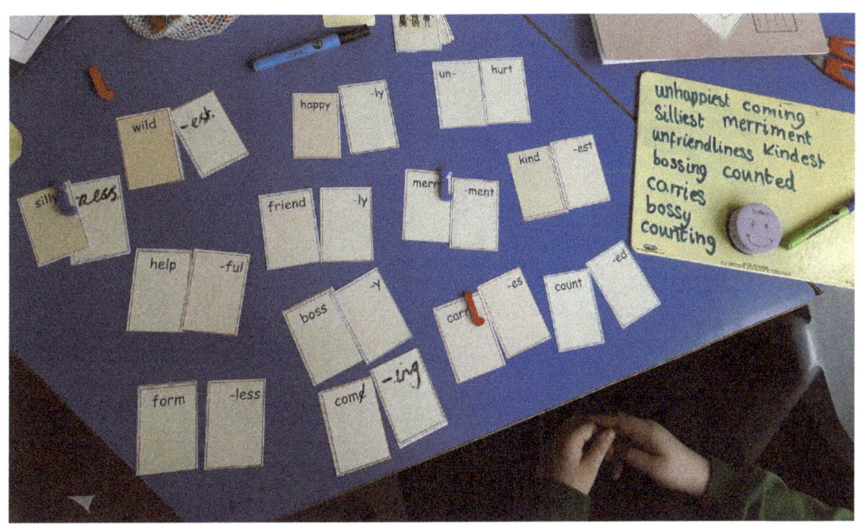

- **You will need:**
  Morpheme cards (**Appendix 17** – affixes and root words) – between 20 and 50
  Interactive whiteboard spinner (for whole class version)
  Paper or mini whiteboard and pen
  A set of tactile letters
- **How to play:** the object of the game is to put all your cards down on the table.
  Shuffle the cards and deal out five cards each. Put the remaining cards in a pile on the table, face down. Player 1 picks up one card from the pile. If s/he can make any words from the morphemes on her cards, she puts those cards down together on the table face up, then writes the word. There is no limit to how many words s/he can make, but a card can only be used in one word at any time. Player 2 repeats the same process.
  As the game continues, it will become possible to swap cards that are already on the table to make new words. For example, if player 1 holds the cards **-es** and **rain**, and the two cards **box** and **-ing** have already

been put together on the table to make **boxing**, the player may separate these two and put down **-es** and **fit** to make **boxes** and **raining**. Cards may only be taken to make new words if they can be replaced with another card; it is against the rules to leave cards alone on the table. Every time a new words is made, the player who made it must write it down, correctly spelled.

If a word is created where a spelling rule is applied by doubling a consonant or changing a **y** to **i**, for example **fitting**, **flies**, indicate this by placing a tactile letter on the cards in the appropriate place. If the drop e rule is applied, place the suffix card over the e on the root so that it is now showing.

If a player can't go, s/he must pick up a card from the pile.

The winner is the first person to lose all their cards **or**, if the pile of cards runs out first, the person with the least cards in his/her hand.

- **Alternative scoring if using spelling rules:** play for points. Every time a player writes down a word s/he has made, score one point, or two points if s/he applied a spelling rule. The winner is the person with the most points when all the cards are on the table. Or to speed the game up, the winner is the first to a decided number of points.

How to adapt Word Morph for the whole class

Use an interactive white board spinner with a different affix on each section and the Morpheme cards (roots). Deal out the morpheme cards between teams: five cards for each team. Teams take turns to spin the spinner. If a word can be made with the result of the spinner and one of the morpheme cards that a team holds, the team puts put down that card and write the word on the board. Repeat until one team loses all their cards; this team is the winning team.

- **Variation:** play the spelling rules variation above, where each team scores a point for every word they can spell and 2 points if they apply a spelling rule. The winning team has the most points at the end of the game.

Wordcraft

(an extended word building game to practice building multi-morphemic words)

- **You will need:**
  Spinner Base 14 or 15
  Morpheme Cards (suffixes, prefixes, roots) ***or*** blank cards for words to be written on
- **How to play:** *the end point (first to 5 points) can change depending on the time allocated – change the number of points as appropriate or play with a race game board.*

Game 1: if more than one prefix, root and suffix has been taught

- **You will need:** in advance, write between eight and 20 multi- morphemic words on blank cards. If playing with an individual or small group, use only words containing morphemes that have been taught.
- **How to play:** use Spinner Base 14. Player 1 picks up a word card and spins the spinner. If player 1 can write a new word based on the instruction on the spinner, s/he gets a point. For example, if the word s/he picked up is **shipment**, and the instruction on the spinner is ***change*** suffix, s/he could write **ships**. If s/he can write a new word based on the instruction on the spinner and also apply a spelling rule (e.g. double the consonant, for example in **shipping**), s/he gets two points. The first to 5 points is the winner.

Game 2: if more than one root and more than one suffix has been taught

- **You will need:** Spinner Base 15. Use the same resources as in Game 1, but add to the table a pile of Morpheme Cards for roots and suffixes, in two separate piles, face down.
- **How to play:** pick up a word card (prepared in advance, as in Game 1), and spin the spinner. If the instruction is to remove the suffix, just write the new word. If it is to change a root or suffix, pick up a card from the appropriate pile and change the root or suffix to the one on the card, then write the word. If you can't make a word, you don't get a point.
  For example, if the word on the card you pick up is **shipment**, and the spinner tells you to change the root, pick up one of the root Morpheme Cards from the relevant pile. If the root on this card says **pay**, you can make **payment**. If, however, your root is **run**, you cannot make a word so you do not get a point.

Game 3: if more than one prefix, root and suffix has been taught

- **How to play:** play Game 2 but use Spinner Base 14. In addition to your root and suffix Morpheme Cards, use a pile of prefix cards. You will have three piles of Morpheme Cards, face down.

How to adapt Wordcraft for the whole class

Play the same game but with the following adaptions. Give pupils a word list instead of cards. Put the chosen spinner under a visualiser, or use an online spinner for the interactive whiteboard. Pupils choose one of the words from the list and write it down. Adult spins the spinner. If pupils can do what the spinner says, they write the word and get a point. Check with a partner. Repeat until the first player reaches a set number of points, depending on how much time you have.

Resources for games

A list of general resources can be found in Appendix 18. You will also find other resources needed for games in the appendices and on the website www.routledge.com/cw/speechmark, for example **Morpheme Cards** (Appendix 14), **Examples of phonologically opaque morphemes** (Appendix 13) and the Morph Mastery **Word Lists** for each year group (Appendix 7).

Where resources are not shown in full, they can all be downloaded from the website www.routledge.com/cw/speechmark. The first page is shown here to help you see what the resource looks like.

Morph Race Track Game

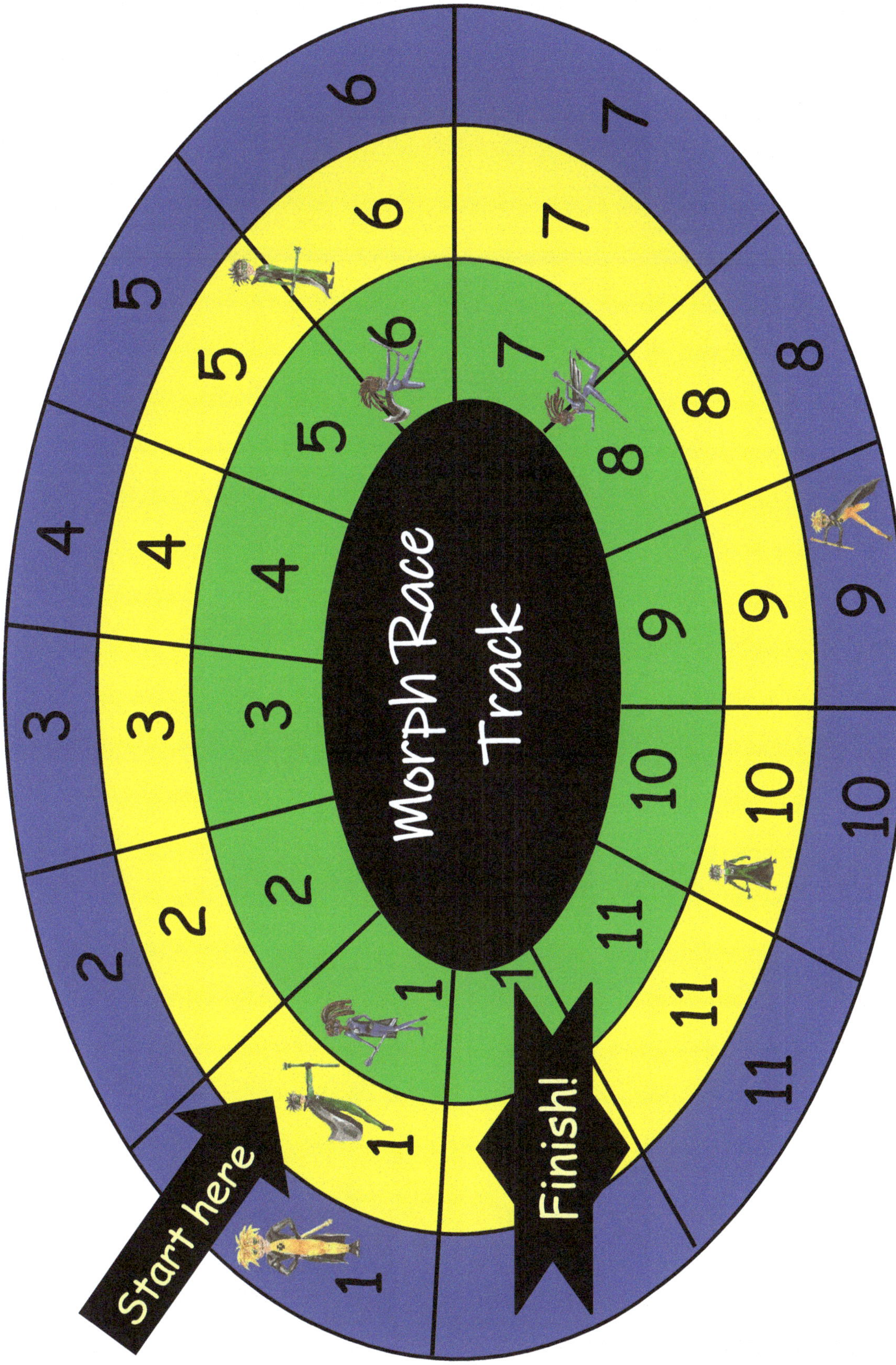

Morph Race Track

Start here

Finish!

1 2 3 4 5 6 7 8 9 10 11

1 2 3 4 5 6 7 8 9 10 11

1 2 3 4 5 6 7 8 9 10 11

Craft Board Game

The Craft Board Game can be used as a general race track game board for any of the games to make them fun and competitive.

Morph Mastery

Craft

A general board game which can be used for overlearning and practising skills. Players may take a turn if s/he can correctly answer a question which targets the skill to be practised.

The object of the game

The first to reach the end is the winner. But beware; there are many twists and turns!

You will need

Dice

Counters (1 for each player)

Word cards or similar, depending on what skill is being practised

How to play

Players take turns to answer a question targeting a key skill (for example, this might be spelling a word or adding an affix).

?f correct, roll the dice and move on that number of spaces (called ?bnes). ?f you land on a numbered square, sinking sand or a shooting star, follow the instructions for that ?bne.

Craft Game Instructions

1. Find a secret message in rice! Roll the dice. If you roll:

1, 2, Rice disturbed – message destroyed! Miss 3 turns.

3, 4 Crack the code – but yesterday's news. Stay where you are

5, 6 Crack the code - find the enemy's stronghold. Take 2 more turns!

2. Throw a star! Roll the dice. If you roll:

1, 2, 3 Star lands in your own stronghold. Move backwards 5 zones.

4, 5, 6 Star exposes enemy stronghold. Move forwards 5 zones.

3. Enemy Stake-out! Roll the dice. If you roll:

1 The enemy blows you up! Return to the start!

2,3, 4 Confuse the enemy with fire! □ave another turn!

5, 6 Enemy steals away! Move back 5 zones

4. Find secret passage! Go 10 zones forward.

5. Chirping Cricket! Roll the dice. If you roll:

1,2,3 Cricket dies. Wait 1 turn

4, 5 Your footsteps are masked by chirping. Take another turn.

6 Mission accomplished. Move forward 7 zones.

6. Sceptre! Roll the dice. If you roll:

1,2 Expose a secret enemy clan! Move on 5 zones.

3,4 Block a morph passage! Move on 3 zones.

5, 6 Land in bog – lost sceptre. Move back 8 zones.

7. Splat! Fall in a hidden trap. Back to START

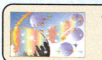

Shooting Star! Move forward 6 zones

Sinking Sand! Throw the dice. If you roll:

1,2,3 Mission aborted! Go back to START

4,5,6 Access a world of tunnels and create a stronghold! Go 6 fields forward.

CRAFT

start

1

2

3

4

5

6

7

end

Spinner Base Masters

For a list of where to find spinners and other resources, see Appendix 18.

Spinner Base 1

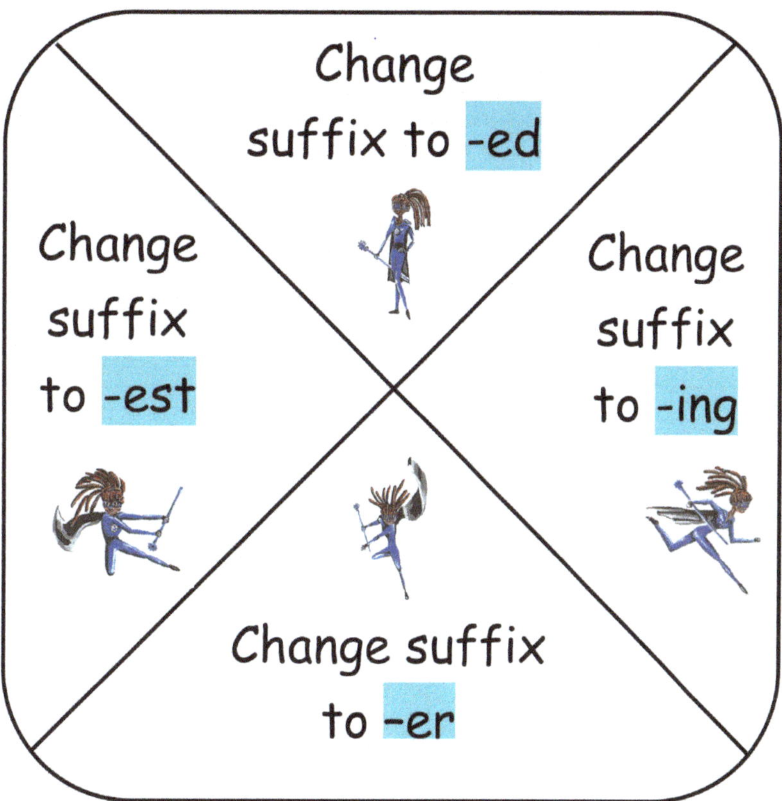

Spinner Base 2

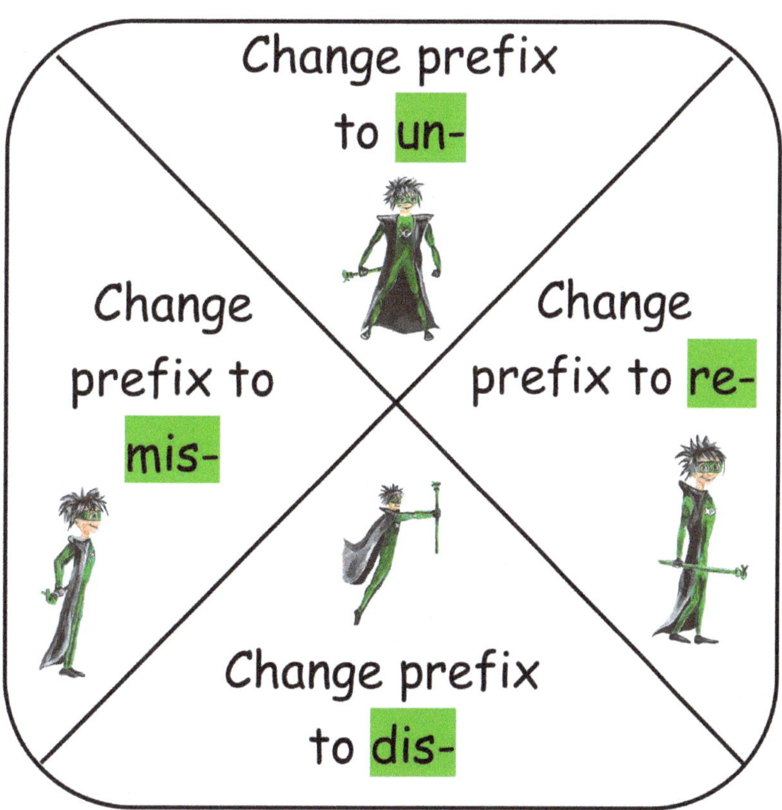

Spinner Base 3

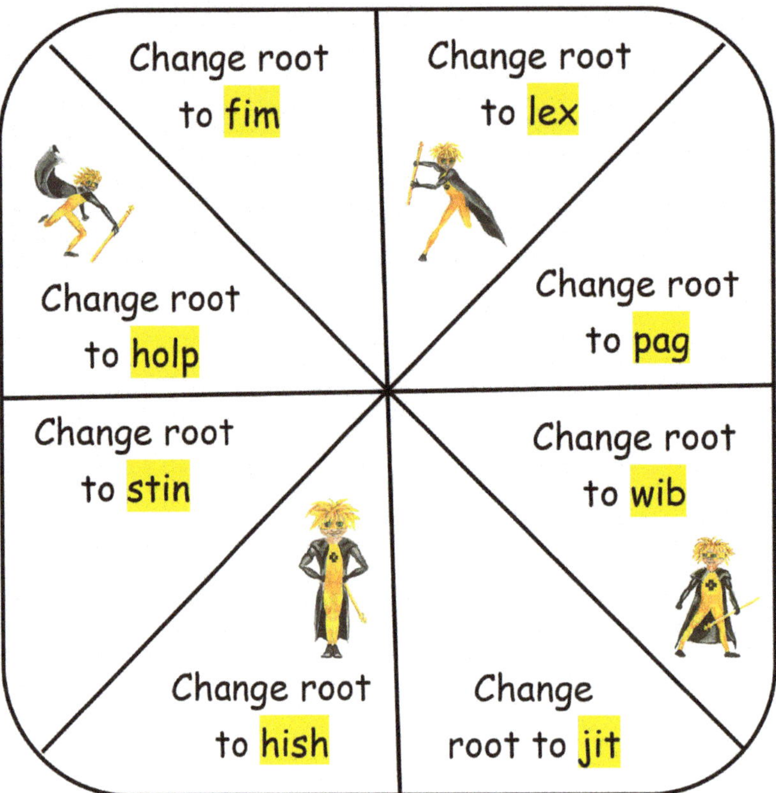

Spinner Base 4

Spinner Base 5

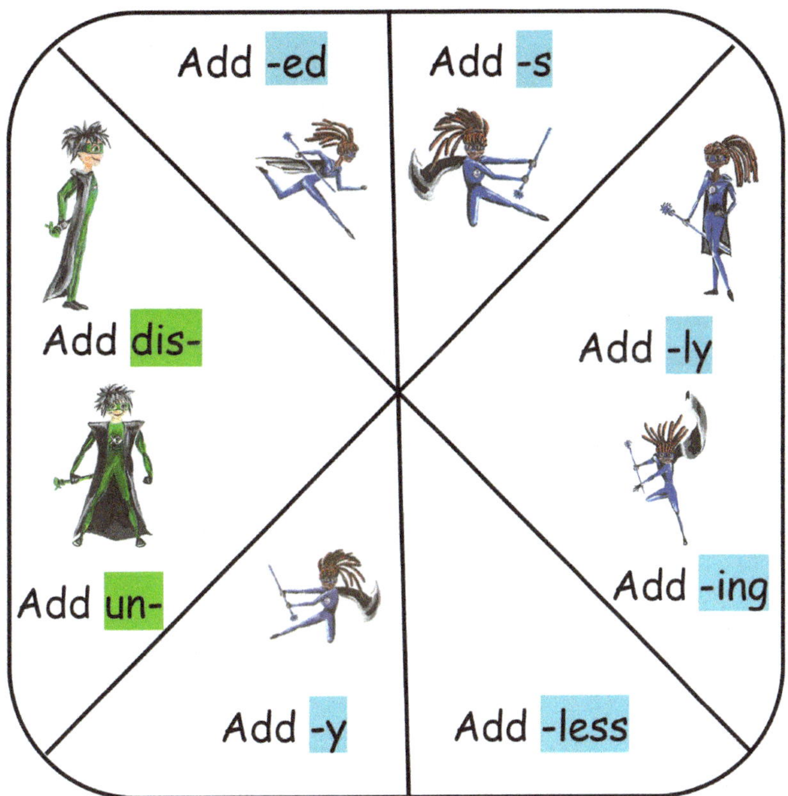

Spinner Base 6

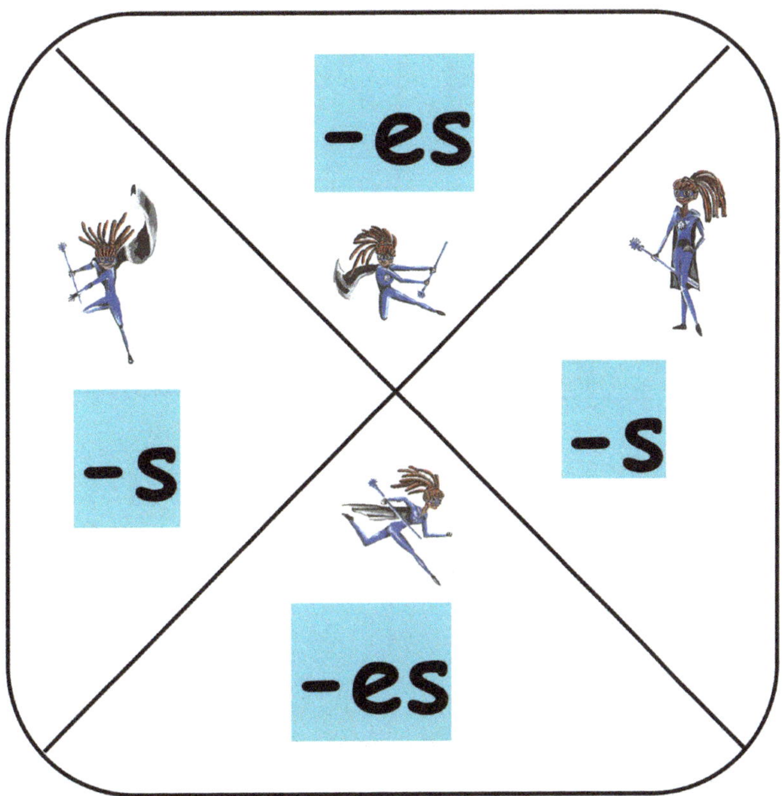

Spinner Base 7

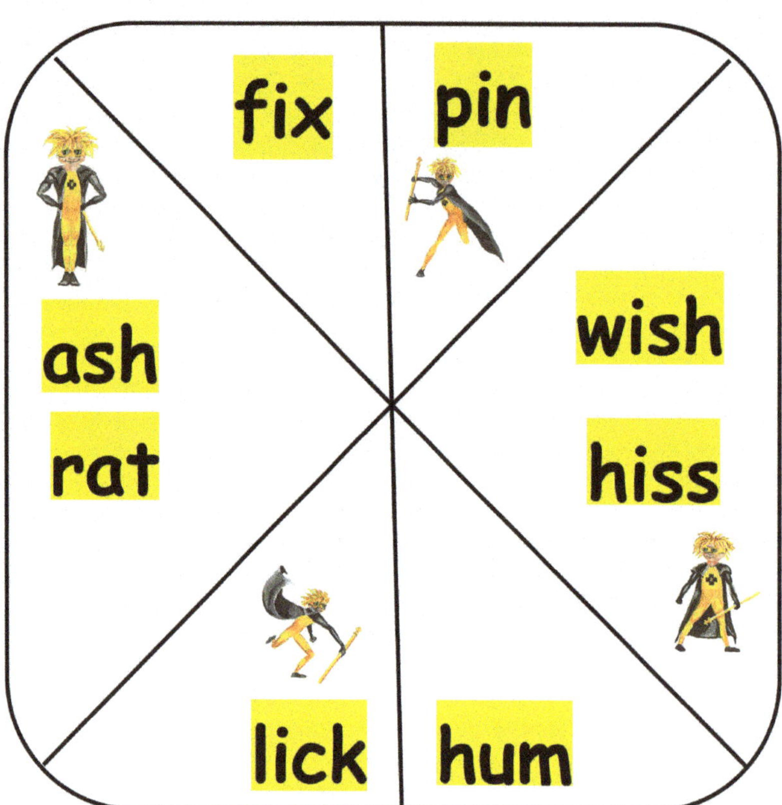

Spinner Base 8

Spinner Base 9

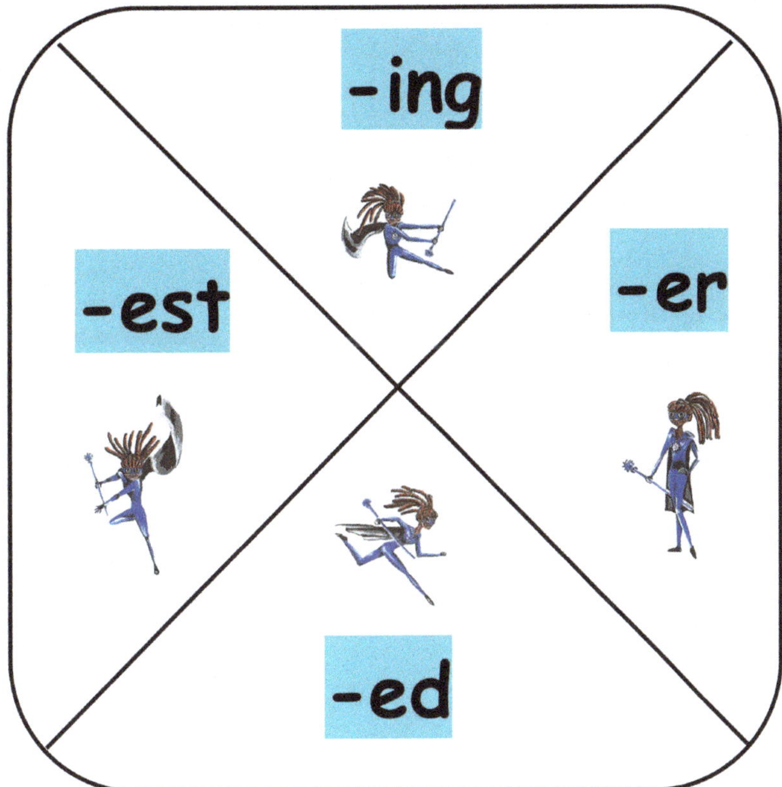

Spinner Base 10

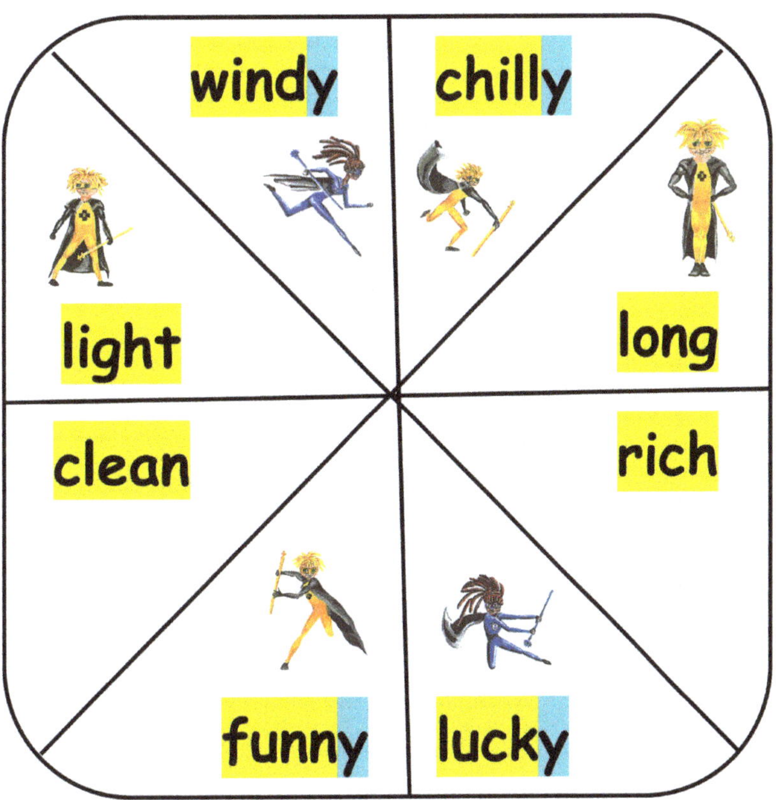

Spinner Base 11

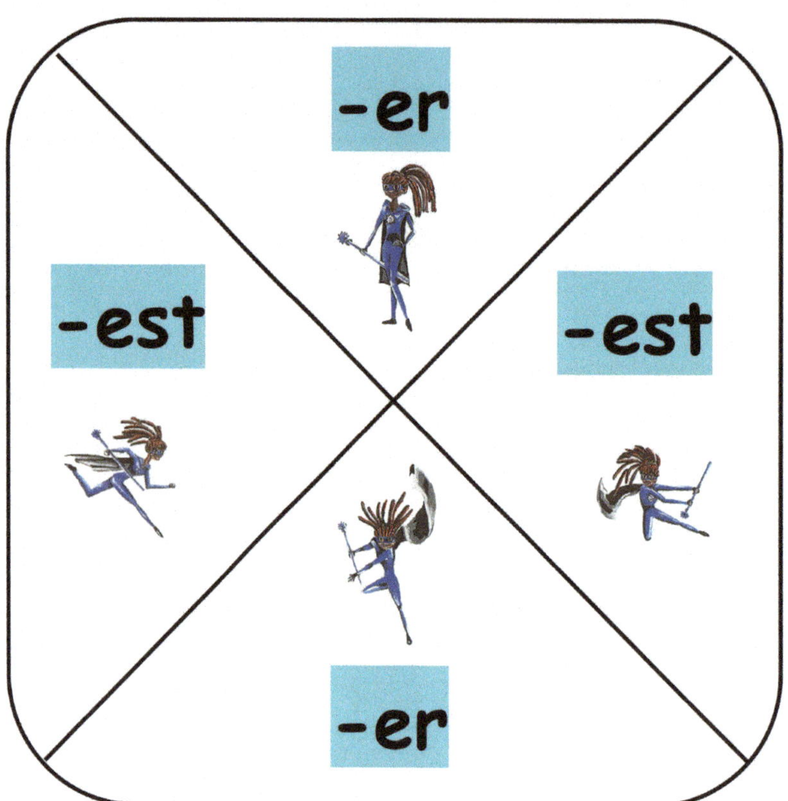

Spinner Base 12

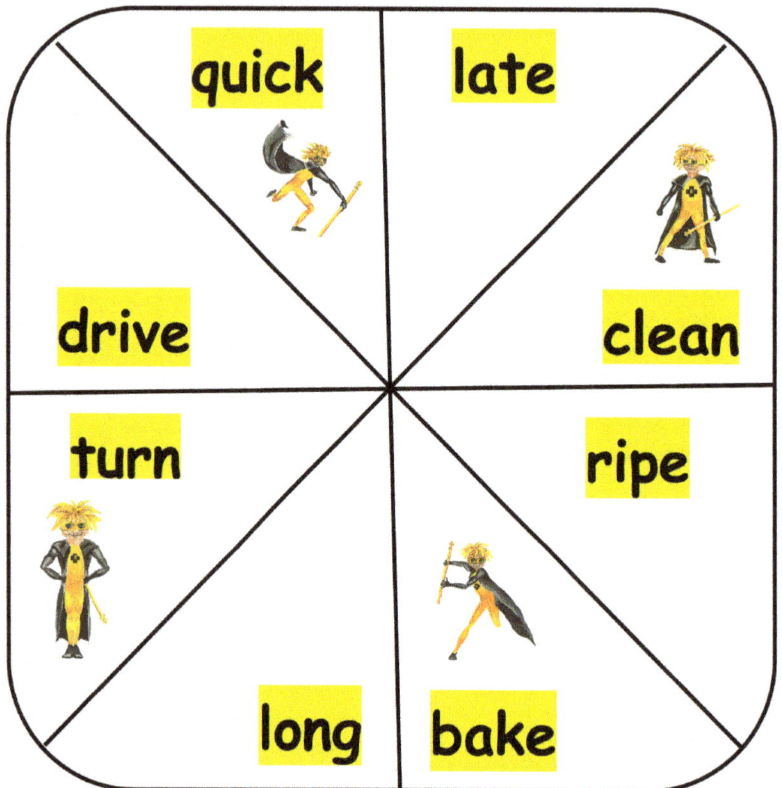

Spinner Base 13

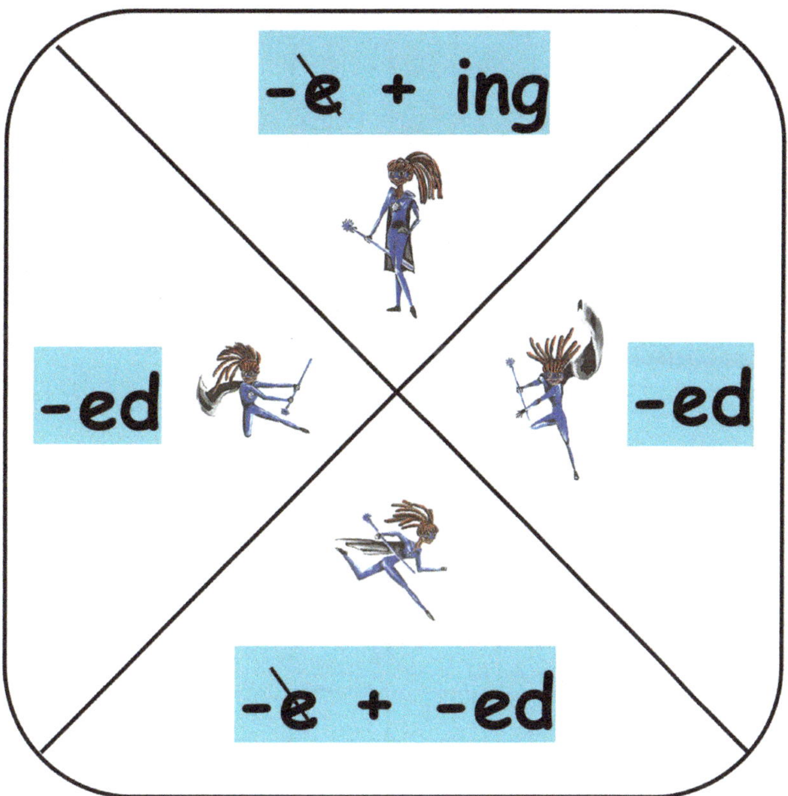

Spinner Base 14

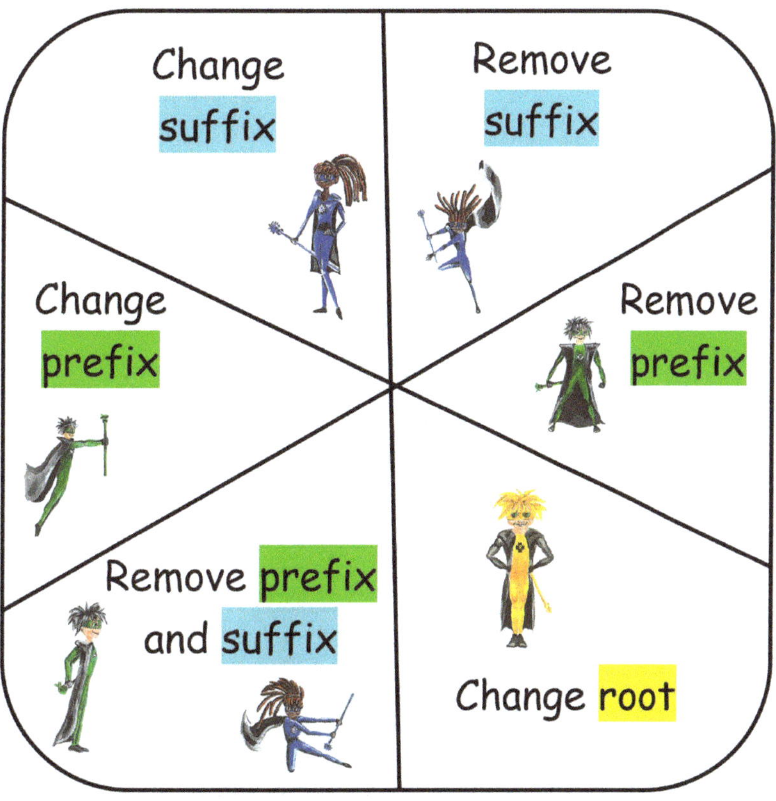

Spinner Base 15

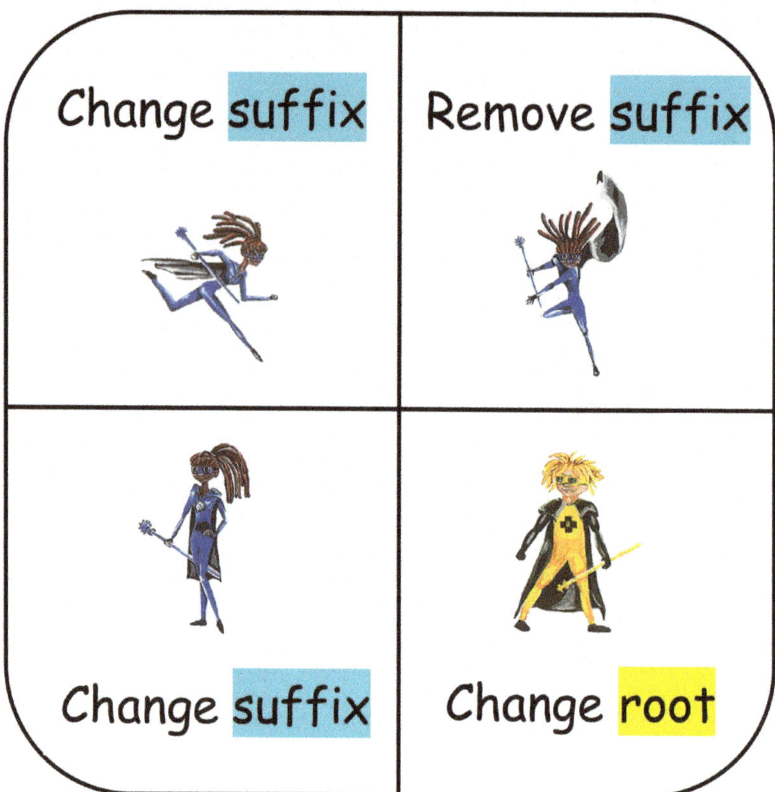

Spinner Base 16

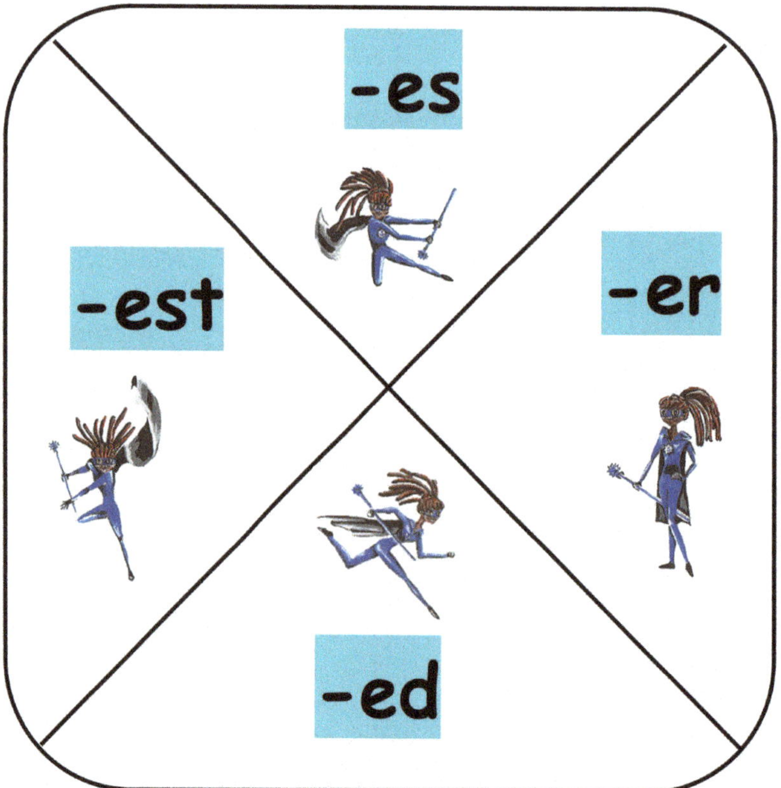

Blank Spinner Base Masters:
If you need more options on your base, you can either adapt this base by drawing more lines to create your desired number of boxes, or print a different one, available on the companion website.

Real Word Cards

(Page 1: whole file downloadable from www.routledge.com/cw/speechmark)

disliked	unties
unhappiness	reacted
unzips	untying
distrusted	mishits
remaking	refills
replaying	reliving

Nonsense Word Cards Set 1

(Page 1: whole file downloadable from www.routledge.com/cw/speechmark)

pons	gegs
fuds	beffs
teshes	puxes
wosses	nisses
lenging	roating
hicking	saiting

Opaque Morpheme Cards

(Page 1: whole file downloadable from www.routledge.com/cw/speechmark)

build	built
buy	bought
creep	crept
draw	drew
drink	drank

Photocopiable Stealth Stronghold Grids

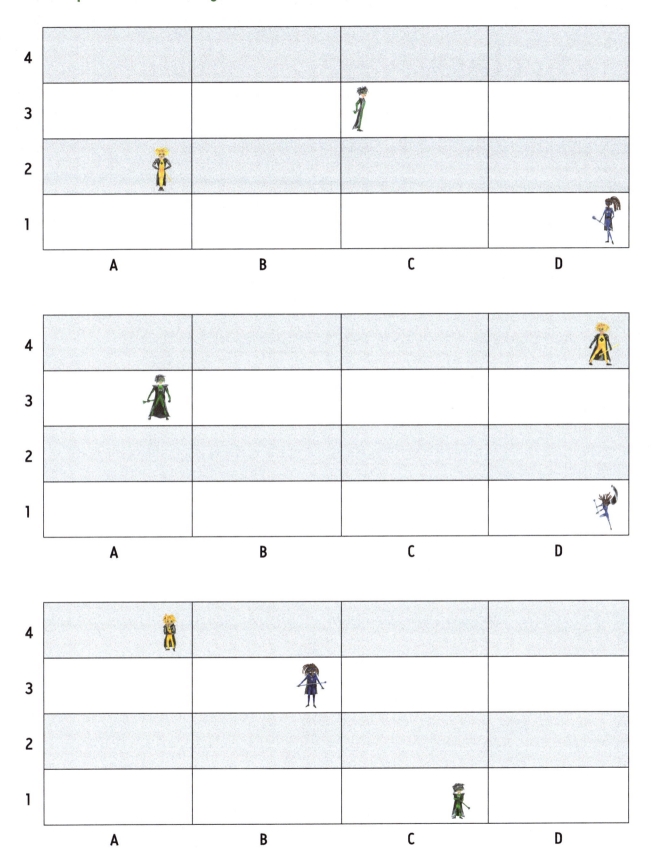

4				
3				
2				
1				
	A	B	C	D

4				
3				
2				
1				
	A	B	C	D

4				
3				
2				
1				
	A	B	C	D

11. Using Morph Mastery in class

Fundamentally, the three foundational skills in Morph Mastery are extremely relevant in whole class teaching. These are detailed in Chapter 3, as follows:

1. Word Agility

This is playing games and conducting experiments with word structures and meanings. Word agility involves constructing, deconstructing, comparing and transforming words.

2. Word Mastery

This is the study of words and their parts. It is asking questions about words and the morphemes within them. We discuss what happens to words if we deconstruct them or build them again with different morphemes. We talk about their meaning and how their morphemes contribute to this.

3. Word Espionage

Morph Masters are spies when reading and writing text. We actively look out for morphemes in text and use morphemes to check for meanings of words within texts. We think about what we know about morphemes to help us understand the words we find and to create new words.

By training pupils in these three core skills, we are developing their confidence in the meaning and potential of words. We are enabling them to become active thinkers, problem solvers and language transformers. This active thinking, or metacognition, supports many areas of the English curriculum.

Practically speaking, most of Morph Mastery is applicable in a class setting; you just need to know where to look in the manual. This chapter serves to signpost you in the right direction. Here are ten practical routes.

1 Word Mastery: investigate words and word play

The Word Mastery cards (Figure 11.1) can be used for any words. Pupils can also create their own questions and make additional Word Mastery Cards.

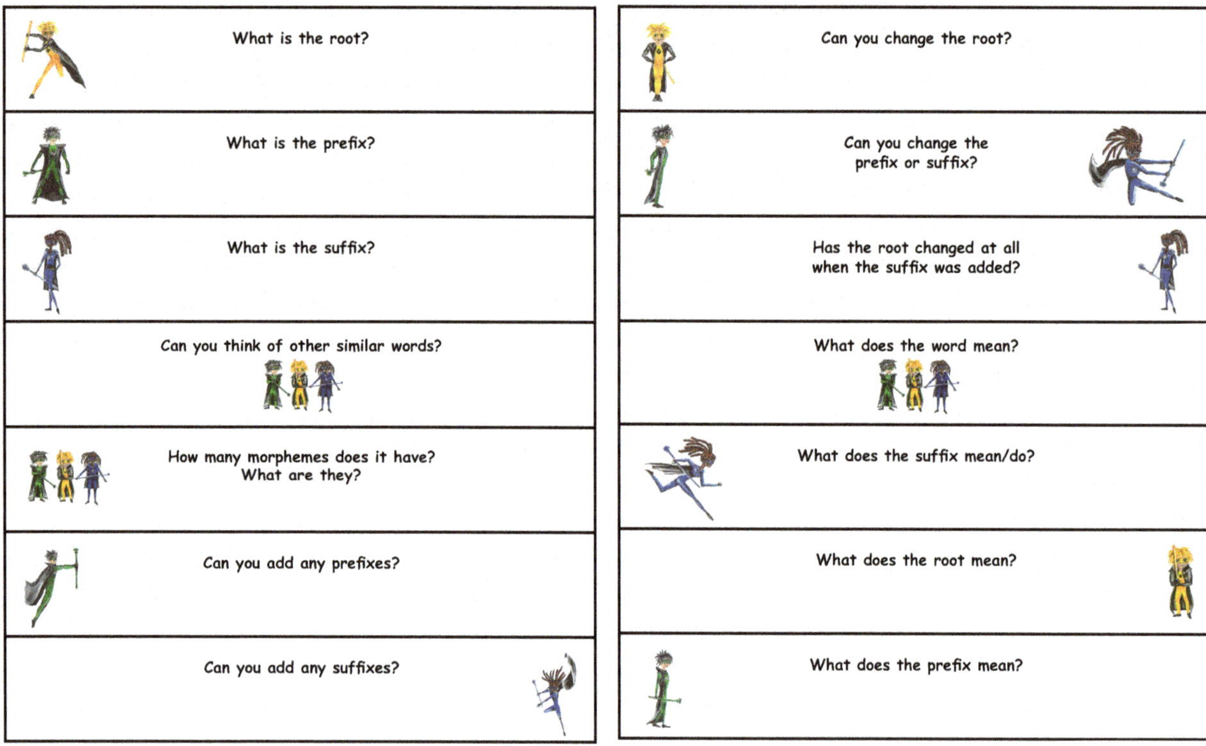

What is the root?
What is the prefix?
What is the suffix?
Can you think of other similar words?
How many morphemes does it have? What are they?
Can you add any prefixes?
Can you add any suffixes?
Can you change the root?
Can you change the prefix or suffix?
Has the root changed at all when the suffix was added?
What does the word mean?
What does the suffix mean/do?
What does the root mean?
What does the prefix mean?

Figure 11.1 Word Mastery Questions

Pupils can be encouraged to investigate words in many ways. Some suggestions are:

- Use morphology to find links between words. For example: how are **unkindness**, **unkindly** and **unkinder** all related? In what ways are they different? How do their differences affect the meaning and function? Discuss this in terms of their morphemes, as follows.
  - They all share the same root and prefix. The suffix is different, and each is a different word form: **-ness** makes **unkind** into a noun, **-ly** makes it into an adverb and **-er** makes it into a comparative.
- This type of investigation can be differentiated by outcome or by task; use different sets of words.
  - Use morphology to establish meanings of words. For example, where does the word **contradict** come from? (**dict** means to say or tell. **contra-** means against).
- Use morphology to understand and explain spellings of words. For example, pose the following questions (answers provided in brackets):
  - Why do we spell **misspell** with a double **s** but **mistake** with only one **s? (mis-** + **spell** = **misspell**, **mis** + **take** = **mistake)**
  - Why does **people** have an **o** in it? (It derives from the Latin **populus** and is related to the word **popu-lation)**
  - Why is it **jumped** not **jumpt? (jump** + **-ed** = **jumped)**
  - Why **business** not **bizness**? **(business** is a noun that comes from **busy**. **Busy** is the root, **-ness** is the suffix. The y → i rule is applied)
  - Why do we double the l in **really** when it is single in **dearly? (real** + **-ly** = **really, dear** + **-ly** = **dearly)**

There are multiple possibilities for these types of questions. When pupils analyse words in this way they make sense of spellings which otherwise seem arbitrary, and they gain skills that can be applied to vocabulary development.

2 Word Agility: play the spelling games

Most of the games that target Word Agility (reading and spelling) translate well into the whole class. They are all detailed in Chapter 10.

3 Vocabulary: play the morphological awareness games

Use the Morphological Awareness games to teach vocabulary. They are all detailed in Chapter 10. These games encourage investigation and deeper understanding of words.

4 Use the characters, colour coding and handshake

4.1 Characters: The three characters, Prefa, Root and Sufa, are appealing to pupils and can be used in class in a variety of ways. Pupils enjoy becoming familiar with them, their colours, symbols and sceptres, using the Meet the Masters page (Figure 11.2). Teach the pupils which character stands for which part of a word and refer to them when working on spellings, grammar and vocabulary. Display the characters and ask pupils to talk about their role when you discuss words.

Figure 11.2 Meet the Masters

Each character holds a sceptre which they use to transform words. Pupils can act out the character with their own makeshift sceptre to change words in spelling and vocabulary activities. They can also use their pencils/pens as sceptres when editing.

4.2 Morph colour coding: Colour is a powerful tool for memory and learning. The three colours (green for prefixes, yellow for roots, and blue for suffixes) can be used across the school to enable pupils to learn about parts of words and analyse them for themselves.

4.3 "The Morph" handshake: The Morph handshake (Figure 11.3) is popular with pupils and can be used in many word-based contexts. Details of how it applies to words can be found in Figure 9.17 in Chapter 9 (page 82) Use it when learning spellings, vocabulary and grammar, or even when editing writing.

- **Step 1 The Fish (Prefa):**
  Two hands approach each other like swimming fish

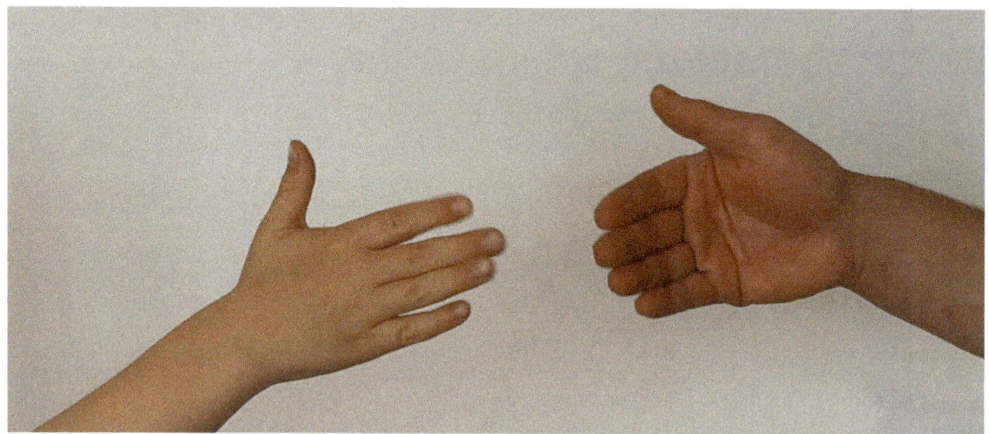

- **Step 2 The Cross (Root):**
  Both thumbs interlink to make a cross shape

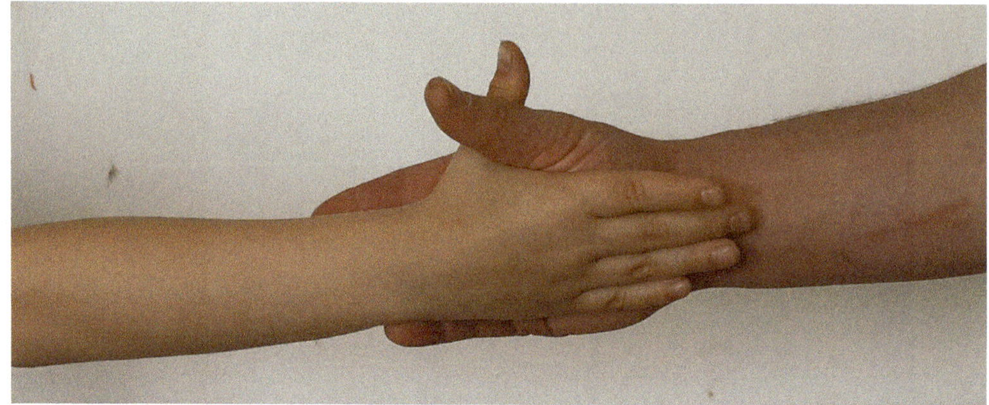

- **Step 3 The Star (Sufa):**
  The fingers wiggle and wave like twinkling stars

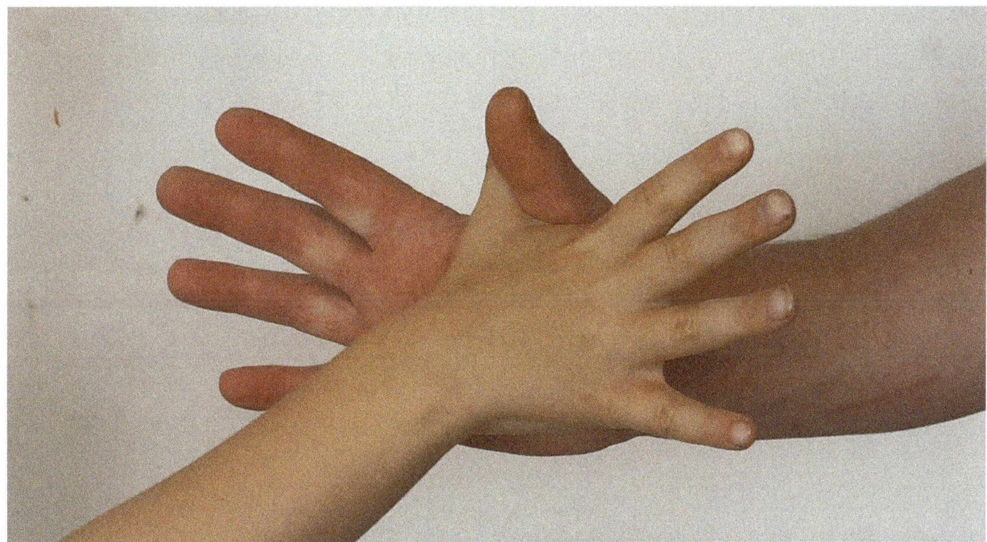

Figure 11.3 The Morph handshake

5 Conduct Word Espionage

Both types of **Word Espionage** that are used in Morph Mastery the intervention (reading texts and editing pupils' writing, detailed in Chapter 9) already link to class work because they use text from class. These techniques of spying out, highlighting and discussing morphemes within text can be used in class lessons as well, as follows.

- **Word Espionage: Reading.** Pupils of all abilities can conduct **Word Espionage** when reading. Espionage can be done with differentiated texts, individual texts or whole class texts and it can relate to grammar, spelling or vocabulary. Known morphemes can be spied out within text. Pupils could be asked to spy out interesting morphemes and write them down for discussion. They could be asked to spy out words with unfamiliar roots for the class to investigate. For example:
  - Search for morphemes which make words into nouns (eg **-ness, -ment**), comparatives **(-er**) or types of verbs (**-ed, -s, -es, -ing)**
  - Find words which follow the spelling rule you've been learning, e.g. double consonant – **dropped, clapped**
  - Spy out for words which share the same root/prefix/suffix, or words which have a particular root/prefix/suffix
  - Look for words which have more than 2/3/4 morphemes
- **Word Espionage: Editing Written Text.** Morph Masters use coloured highlighters to show prefixes, roots and suffixes (remembering the Morph colour code). This is extremely useful for editing; it supports

vocabulary and grammar as well as spelling. For example, in Figure 11.4, the learner had written ***I am writing to inform you that the government are aware*** . . . When conducting word espionage for editing, the learner highlighted **gover** in yellow, then noticed that the root should be **govern**, knowing that it has an **n** at the end of it, which you don't hear in the word **government.** She then noticed the noun maker suffix **-ment**, and was prompted to consider whether it should be followed by **is** or **are**.

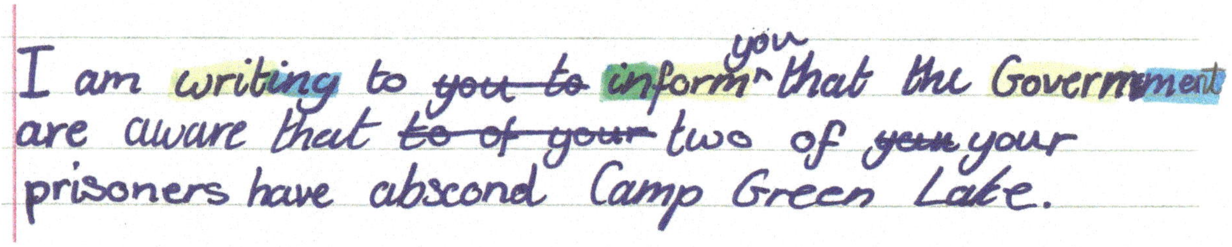

Figure 11.4

In the Figure 11.5, highlighting the morphemes helped the learner to correct her own spelling mistakes. She realised that unspeakable comes from the word **speak**, which she knows how to spell. When she broke down the word **unknown** into its components she realised that she had omitted the **k** in **know**.

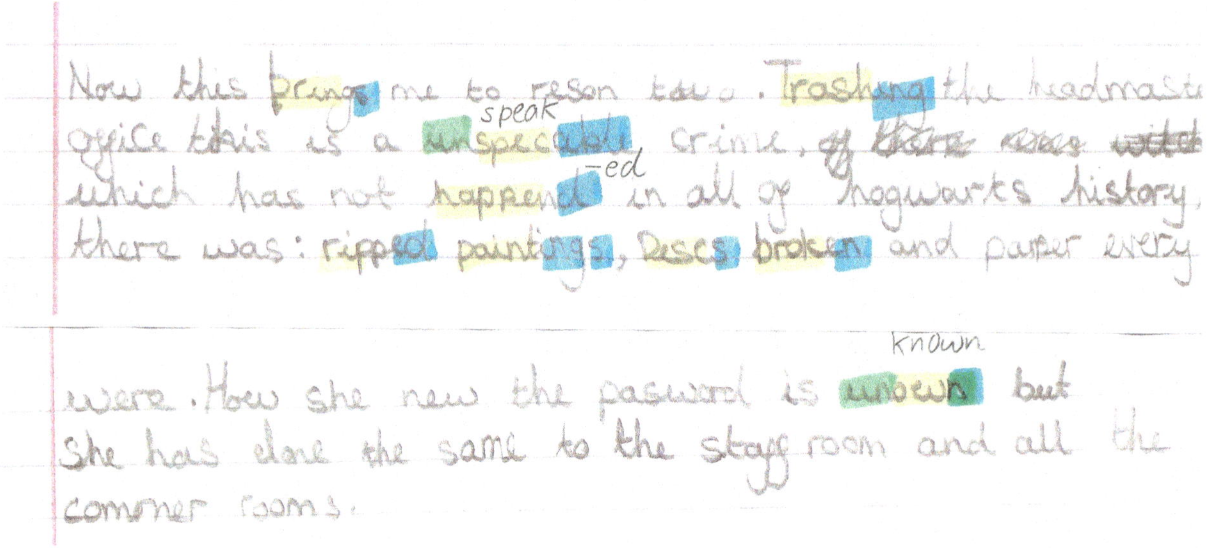

Figure 11.5

6 Use portals

The concept of the portal (detailed in Chapter 9 on page 83–85, 90, and 100–1) is incredibly simple, but it is both appealing and instructive. It helps learners to break words down into morphemes, and to investigate their relatives. In addition, the portal is a very useful visual tool for learning spelling rules.

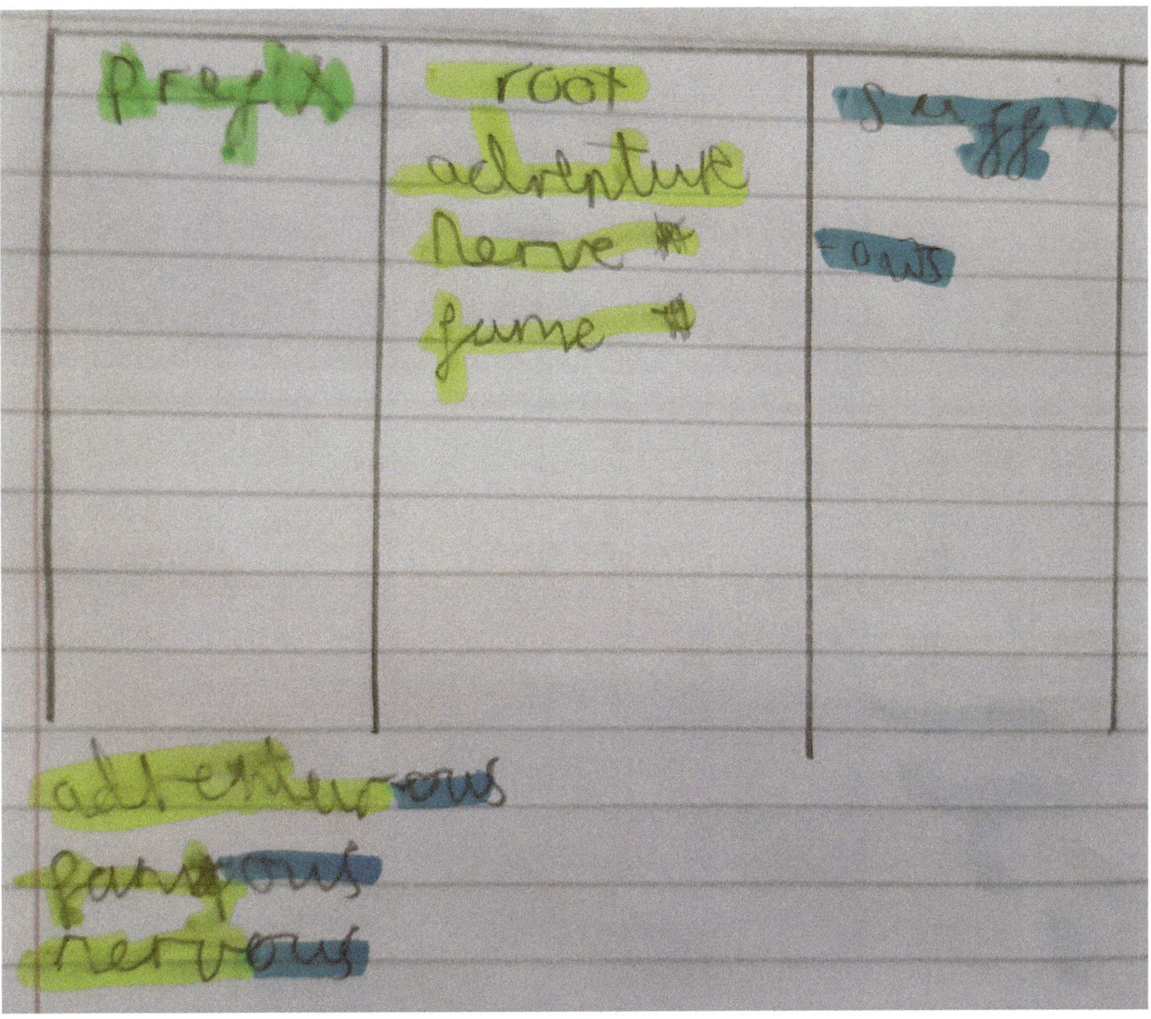

Figure 11.6

The portal in Figure 11.6 shows how the **-ous** suffix has been used with the drop e rule. There are more examples in Chapter 9.

7 Use morphology to teach grammar

One reason why pupils find grammar so difficult is that it can seem dry and arbitrary. A Morph Mastery approach to teaching grammar brings meaning and a multi-sensory dimension. There are generally two types of morphemes: those that have a grammatical function (for example **-ed**, **-ness**, **-ly**, **-er**) and those that change meaning (for example **un-**, **pre-**, **auto**). Many of the suffixes listed in the **Word Lists for planning** have a grammatical function and can be used to teach grammar. For example, Figure 11.7 shows the Year 2 **Word Lists** for the noun maker suffixes **-ment** and **-ness**. Pupils can enjoy the experience of playing with some of these words, writing them in a portal, changing the suffix to see what difference it makes, playing the **Word Agility** games, using the **Word Mastery** cards to explore the words, and using colour coding and a handshake to represent them.

Year 2	**Rule 1: No change to the root** **If a suffix starts with a consonant, it is added to the root word without any change in the spelling of the root word.**	
	-ment ***pay, ship, move, place***	**-ness** ***mad, rude, fit, kind, happy,* empty, silly**
	Noun maker	**Noun maker**
	movement placement enjoyment employment management replacement payment shipment amazement	rudeness fitness kindness greatness darkness fairness hardness madness softness gladness flatness neatness sadness strictness shyness loudness
	-ful	**-less**

Figure 11.7

8 Use the Suggested Teaching Sequence and Word Lists for planning

The **Suggested Teaching Sequence** for affixes with roots and **Word Lists** for planning (found in Appendix 6 and 7) are really useful planning documents for spelling, grammar and vocabulary. Both are linked with the English Curriculum (2014). The first page of each of the **Word Lists** is illustrated in Figure 11.8, 11.9, 11.10 & 11.11, while the **Suggested Teaching Sequence** is illustrated in Figure 11.12.

Year 1 & 2[1,*]

Words in bold have phonics and/or spelling rules that relate to that year group or below. Words in red are common exception words for that year group. *Highlighted words in italics* have more possibilities for word building and are in the suggested teaching sequence for word roots, with further word lists below for playing games and spelling lists.

Year 1	**-s** ***cat, dog, tan, zip***	**_es** ***fix, wish,* box, mix, rush, hiss**
	Plural maker (noun)	**Plural maker (noun)**
	cats dogs bags fans fins hats huts jugs tans logs legs mats mugs nets pans pits pins rags rats ribs vets vans wigs zips shops days schools friends pens toys games cups ponds books boys desks	boxes ashes bushes churches foxes brushes dishes kisses patches lunches glasses watches

Figure 11.8

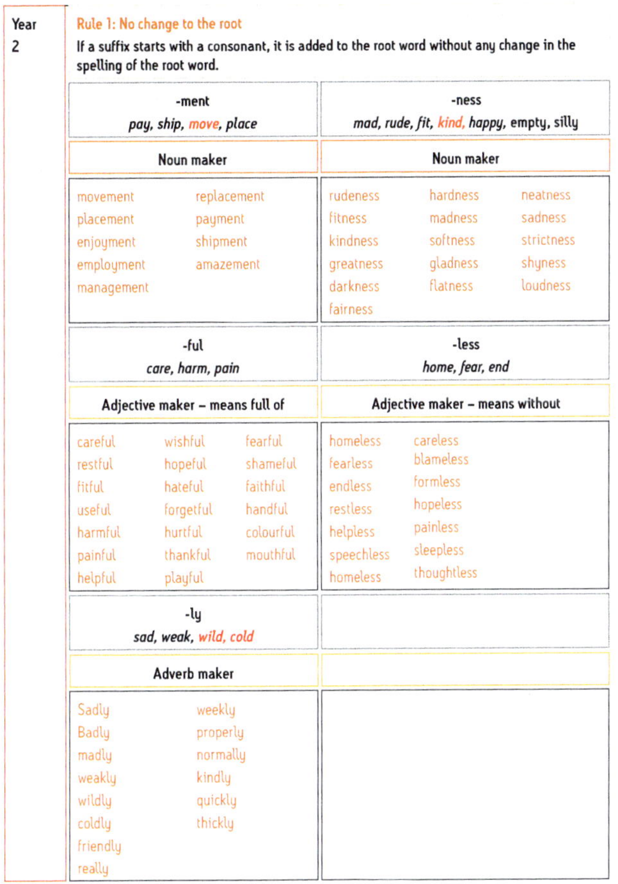

Year 2	Rule 1: No change to the root **If a suffix starts with a consonant, it is added to the root word without any change in the spelling of the root word.**	
	-ment ***pay, ship, move, place***	**-ness** ***mad, rude, fit, kind, happy,* empty, silly**
	Noun maker	**Noun maker**
	movement placement enjoyment employment management replacement payment shipment amazement	rudeness fitness kindness greatness darkness fairness hardness madness softness gladness flatness neatness sadness strictness shyness loudness
	-ful ***care, harm, pain***	**-less** ***home, fear, end***
	Adjective maker – means full of	**Adjective maker – means without**
	careful restful fitful useful harmful painful helpful wishful hopeful hateful forgetful hurtful thankful playful fearful shameful faithful handful colourful mouthful	homeless fearless endless restless helpless speechless homeless careless blameless formless hopeless painless sleepless thoughtless
	-ly ***sad, weak, wild, cold***	
	Adverb maker	
	Sadly Badly madly weakly wildly coldly friendly really weekly properly normally kindly quickly thickly	

Figure 11.9

Year 3 & 4[1]

Words in bold have phonics and/or spelling rules that relate to that year group or below. Words in red are on the list of 100 words in the National Curriculum that children in England are expected to be able to spell by the end of Year 4. *Highlighted words in italics* have more possibilities for word building and are in the suggested teaching sequence for word roots, with further word lists below for playing games and spelling lists.

Year 3 & 4		
	dis- ***connect, continue,* agree, like, trust**	**mis-** ***spell, calculate,* behave, fire, use**
	Opposite, not	**Opposite, not**
	disagree disobey discover dislike dishonest dishearten dislodge disown displease disqualify disappear disconnect disinfect disembark disapprove discomfort distrust discontinue	misunderstand misspell misdeed misbehave miscalculate misplace miscount misfire misfortune mishear misinform misread mistake misfortune misguide mislead misprint mistrust misuse
	re- ***visit, appear,* make, place, act, call, bound**	
	Again	**Back**
	remake redo regrow replace reawaken react relive revisit rewrite refresh reappear redecorate rebuild recycle refill reform replay	retreat recede return recall reflect rebound

Figure 11.10

Year 5 & 6[1]

Words in bold have phonics and/or spelling rules that relate to that year group or below. Words in red are on the list of 100 words in the National Curriculum that children in England are expected to be able to spell by the end of Year 6. *Highlighted words in italics* have more possibilities for word building and are in the suggested teaching sequence for word roots, with further word lists below for playing games and spelling lists.

Year 5 & 6		
	-cious (c + ious) *grace, space*, malice	-tious (t + ious) *caution*, superstition
	Adjective maker (when the root ends in ce – remove the e)	Adjective maker (when the root ends in n – remove the n)
	vicious, gracious, spacious, officious, malicious	rebellious, repetitious, superstitious, cautious, infectious, nutritious
	-cial *face*, office, prejudice, race	-tial *part, essence*, existence, evidence
	Adjective maker (when the root ends in ace or a short vowel sound followed by ce – remove the e)	Adjective maker (when the root ends in nce or t)
	facial, prejudicial, beneficial, official, artificial, racial, commercial, financial, sacrificial	existential, partial, essential, confidential, evidential, substantial, inferential, torrential, sequential
	Exception: Spatial	
	-ant *observe, expect*, tolerate, hesitate	-ance *attend, resist*, defy, guide
	Adjective maker (when the root ends in t or ate – remove ate. Often made from roots that can also be used with -ation)	Noun maker Used when related adjective ends in -ant Refers to action, state or quality
	observant, participant, hesitant, tolerant, abundant, distant, dominant, expectant, pregnant, buoyant	hesitance, tolerance, resistance, brilliance, attendance, ignorance, elegance, arrogance, alliance, defiance, distance, guidance

Figure 11.11

Figure 11.12

If planning for older and more able pupils, the **Latin and Greek meanings and derivatives** chart (Appendix 15) is extremely useful for finding origins of words at a glance and selecting words for pupils to explore (see Point 10 below).

9 Use the assessments to identify gaps in spelling

Some of the schools involved in the pilot reported that they used the **Knowledge of Morphemes** reading and spelling assessments (detailed in Chapter 6 and Appendix 2 and 3) with pupils who were not weak enough to need the full intervention, but still had some spelling difficulties. They found the assessments very useful. These curriculum-based assessments can be used to uncover spelling gaps, and help to plan material for booster spelling groups, especially with pupils who have grasped phonics but are struggling to make progress.

10 Provide for greater depth in word exploration

As pupils progress with their knowledge of words, there will be even more interesting word relationships and morphemes to find. The **Latin and Greek meanings and derivatives** chart in Appendix 15 (Figure 11.13) offers some meanings for Greek and Latin morphemes and their derivatives.

LATIN ROOTS		
Root	**Meaning**	**Derivatives**
anni, annu	year	annual, anniversary, biannual
aud	hear	audible, auditory, audio, audit, audition
cede, cess	to go or surrender	access, excess, precede, interceded, recede success, process
cise	cut	concise, decide, incisor, precise, scissors
conus	cone	conical, cone, conifer
cred	believe	credit, credible, creed, accredited, discredit
dict	say or tell	contradict, dictate, diction, dictionary, verdict
duct	lead	abduct, conduct, deduction, induction, reduction, production
fact, fect	do or make	affect, infect, defect, refectory, fact, factory, confectionery, artefact
fer	to bear or yield	confer, defer, differ, different, ferry, fertile, infer, offer, prefer, refer, suffer, transfer
fid, fide	trust or faith	confide, confident, fidelity, federal, infidelity, bona fide, diffident, perfidious, defy
fin	finish, end	final, infinity, define, refine, confine, finite
flect, flex	to bend or curve	flex, deflect, reflect, flexion, reflex, flexible
grat	a favour	grateful, gracious, grace, gratitude, graceful
form	shape	inform, formation, reform, deformed, unformed, uniform, conform, perform, formulate, formula, transform
fortis	strong	fort, comfort, fortune
fuse	pour	infuse, refuse, defuse, fusion
ject	throw	eject, abject, dejected, inject, interject, object, project, subject, trajectory

GREEK COMBINING FORMS (These can be used as prefixes, suffixes or roots. Where marked with -, they are usually used as prefixes, e.g. auto-. Sometimes suffixes are added to these combining forms.)		
Morpheme	**Meaning**	**Derivatives**
ast	star	astrology, astronomy, asteroid, astronaut, asterix
auto-	self	autism, autobiography, automatic, autograph, autopsy, automatic, automobile
bio	life	antibiotic, biography, biology, bionic
cycl	wheel or circle	cycle, cyclist, bicycle, unicycle, cyclone, recycle, tricycle
di-	two	digraph, dioxide
dyn	power, force	dynamo, dynamic, dynamite, dynasty
dys-	bad or difficult	dyslexia, dyscalculia, dysfunctional, dysentery
eco	house or home	economy, ecology, economic, ecological
geo-	earth	geography, geology, geometry, geothermal
giga-	billion	gigabyte, gigahertz, gigametre
graph	written or drawn	autograph, choreography, graphic, graph, graphite, grapheme, bibliography
hemi-, demi-, semi-	half	hemisphere, semicircle, semi-final, semicolon, semiconscious
hect-	hundred	hectare
hept-	seven	heptagon, heptathlon
hex-	six	hexagon, hexameter
kilo-	thousand	kilogram, kilometre, kilowatt
kritikos	judge or decide	critic, critical, criticise, criteria, critique
mega-	million, large, great	megabyte, megawatt, megaphone
mono-	one	monocle, monochrome, monocycle, monopoly, monarch, monastery, monosyllabic, monotony
para-	beside, position	parallel, parachute, paralysed, paraphernalia, paradox, paralegal, paramedic
pent-	five	pentagon, pentathlon
photo	light	photograph, photogenic, photosensitive
poly-	many	monopoly, polygon, monopolize

Figure 11.13

This chart can be used as a resource for teachers in a variety of ways. One way is to give pupils a group of words and ask them to find the relationship between them. It could be the root that is the same in all the words, as in **prepare**, **parent**, **pare**, **compare**. Or it could be the prefix, for example **interact**, **interrupt**, **interject**, **interview**. Pupils could also be asked to find the origin and derivatives from a word. For example, if pupils are asked to find the root of the word **concise**, they could use a dictionary to discover that **cise** is Latin for cut, while **con-** means with. They might then explore other related words, for example **scissors**, **incisors**, **decide**, **incision**. Another way to use the chart is to give pupils a Latin root and ask them to find some derivatives. For example, the root **voke** (meaning call or name) could lead them to find **advocate**, **vocation** and **vocabulary,** and explore their meanings.

For these activities, pupils will need access to a good dictionary which provides the origins (etymology) of words. There are some online versions of these, for example www.dictionary.com.

In Appendix 16 and on the website **www.routledge.com/cw/speechmark** you'll also find versions of the Morpheme Cards with indicators for Latin and Greek. These are the same as the Morpheme Cards, but they provide colour coding to indicate the roots' origin. They are named **Morpheme Cards Roots Year 3 & 4 with Latin and Greek**, and **Morpheme Cards Roots Year 5 & 6 with Latin and Greek.** Examples of these are shown in Figure 11.14.

agree	obey	cover
like	honest	heart
lodge	own	please

vice	grace	space
sist	malice	rebel
repeat	stit	caution

fect	nutrit	face
judic	benefit	fic
race	merc	finance

Figure 11.14

In addition, you will find the resource **Morpheme Cards Prefix and Suffix with additional Latin and Greek** in Appendix 16 (Figure 11.15).

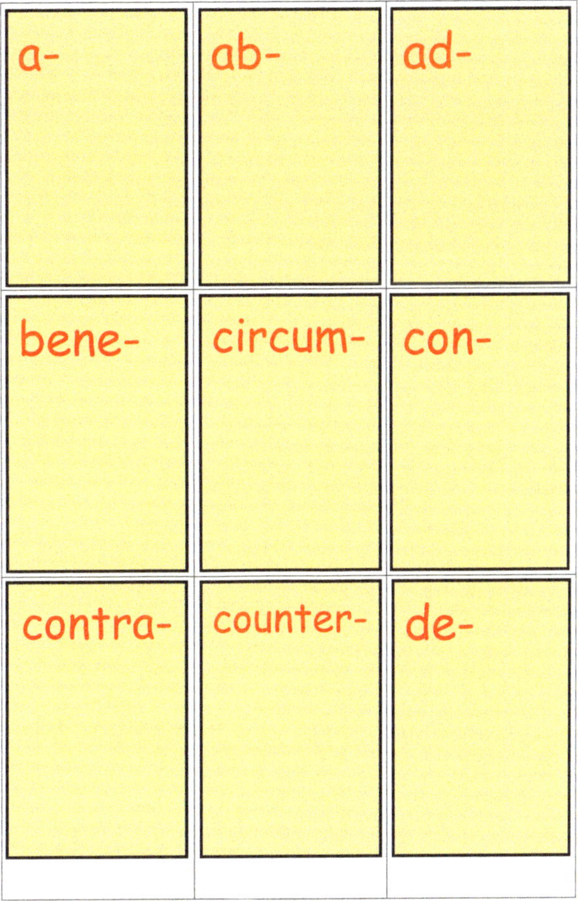

Figure 11.15

All these cards enable learners to dig a little deeper to find the origins of words whilst playing games, which enhances vocabulary and metacognition. On these cards, the words with Latin origins are red, while the words with Greek origins are underlined. Words with Old English and other origins are black. Using these cards in your planning and within the games will support pupils' greater depth in understanding words and in learning to spell them.

The possibilities for using Morph Mastery are endless... enjoy exploring them. If you remember the key foundation skills of **Word Mastery**, **Word Agility** and **Word Espionage**, you can't go wrong!

12. What next?

In Chapter 6, Morph Mastery the intervention was outlined within the framework of the ***Assess-Plan-Do-Review*** cycle from the UK Special Education Needs and Disability (SEND) Code of Practice: 0–25 Years (Government of UK 2015). Figure 12.1 illustrates this. This chapter addresses the question: What next?

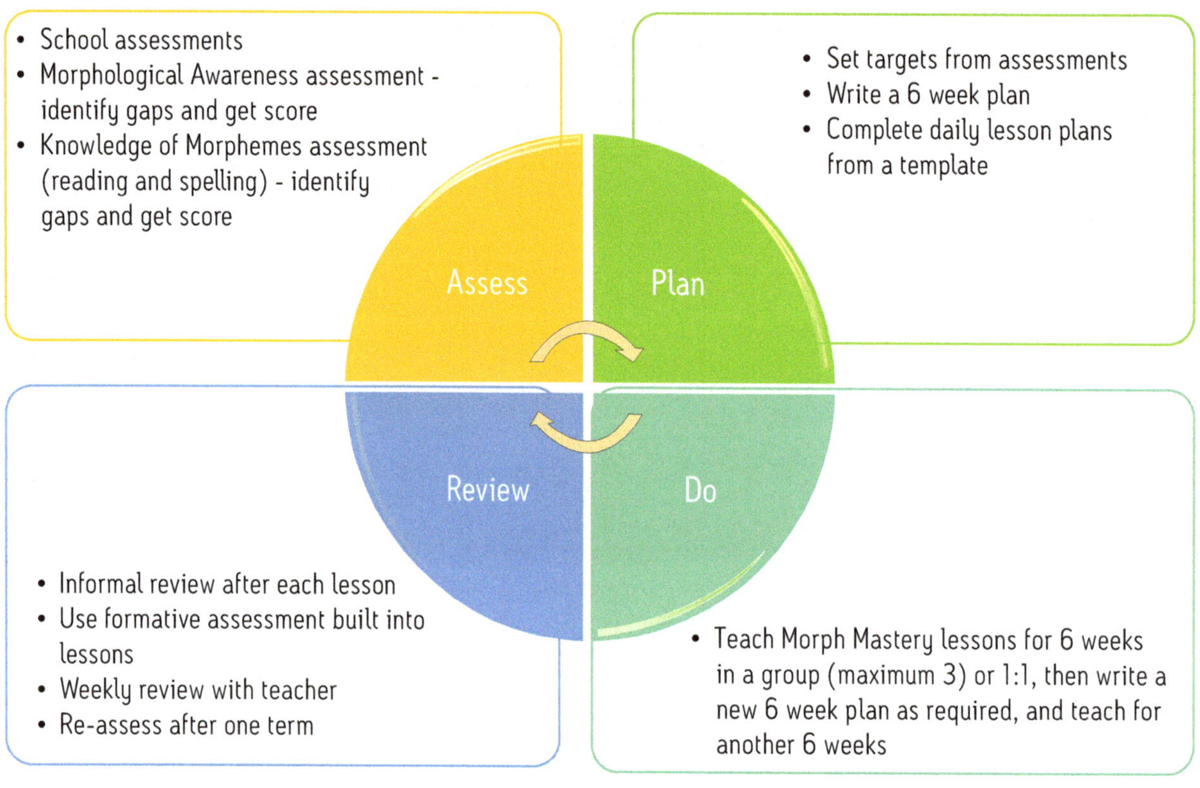

Figure 12.1

Figure 12.2 is a flow chart which could be used to answer this question. If the learners are making good progress there is no need to change anything, unless intervention is no longer required. If progress is inadequate, use the flow chart to consider why. This should lead to one of three actions:

1. Make changes to the intervention to make it more effective
2. Discontinue the intervention and try something different
3. Seek specialist advice

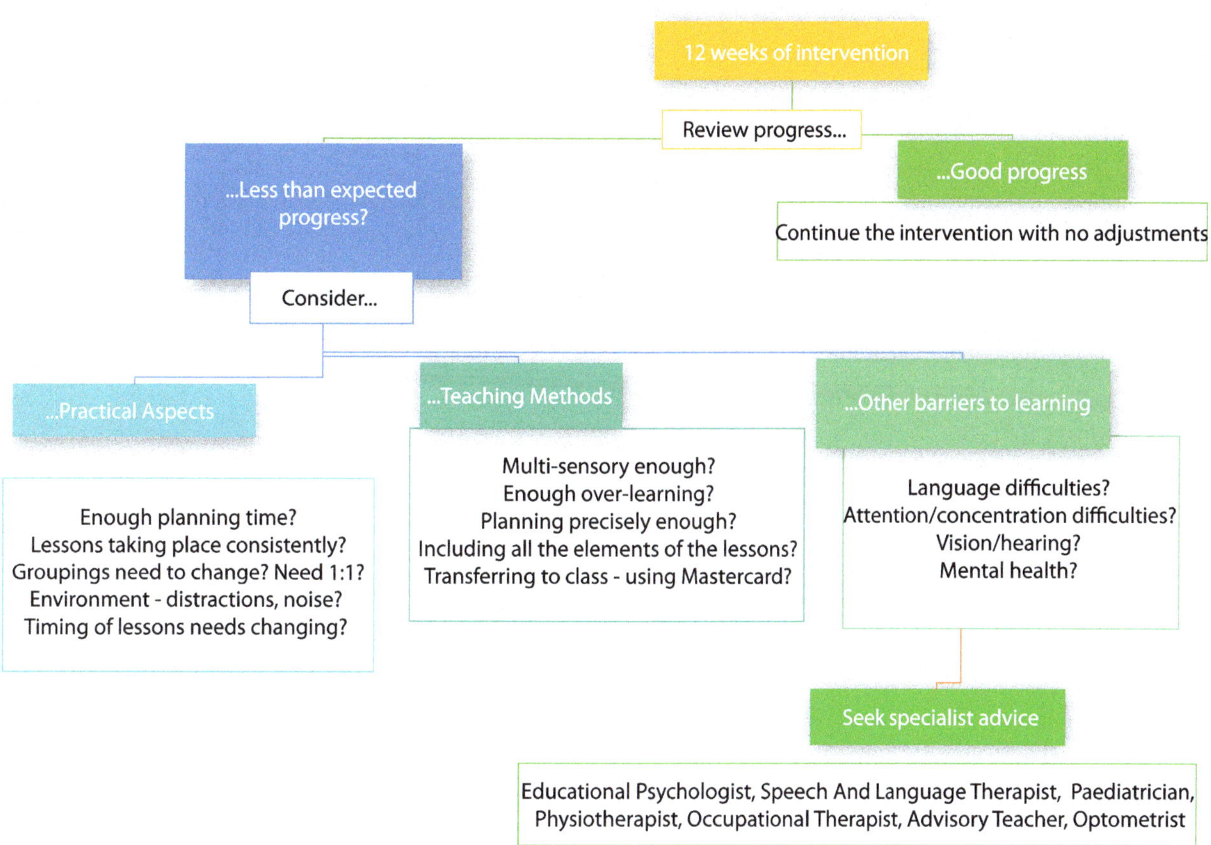

Figure 12.2

In most cases, where the intervention does not work as well as expected, there are practical factors causing this. Sometimes the adult delivering the intervention is pulled away for other tasks, sometimes learners are taught within groups that are too large to be effective and sometimes timetabling is unhelpful, for example lessons when learners are tired or hungry. Sometimes the adult simply doesn't have any time to plan. In some cases the teaching methods are not multi-sensory enough, and sometimes the need for overlearning is forgotten, or the planning has not been precise enough. In all of these cases, simple changes can serve as a catalyst to progress.

However, it is important to acknowledge when **either** the support of an outside agency is needed, **or** the intervention is not right for the learner at this time. If this is the case, your assessment and review cycle should enable you to identify these. If the intervention does not seem right for the learner, consider whether s/he needs any of the following:

- Speech and language intervention
- Basic phonics intervention

- Behavioural/emotional support
- Motor skills/ handwriting intervention
- Attention, concentration and sensory integration support

This chapter has demonstrated the importance of the **Assess-Plan-Do-Review** cycle in meeting the changing needs of your learners. The final, and most important factor to consider, is the need for practitioners to work together, as has been illustrated. The best teaching assistant in the world is unlikely to be effective without the support and evaluation of the class teacher and/or SENCO.

References and bibliography

Ayto, J (2013), *Oxford School Dictionary of Word Origins*, Oxford University Press, Oxford

Beck, I, McKeown, M & Kucan, L (2002), *Bringing Words to Life: Robust Vocabulary Instruction*, Guildford Press, New York

Berthiaume, R, Daigle, D, & Desrochers, A (2020), *Morphological Processing and Literacy Development, Current Issues and Research*, Routledge, London

Breadmore, H, Vardy, J, Cunningham, A, Kwok, R & Carroll, J (2019), *Literacy Development: Evidence Review*. London, Education Endowment Foundation. https://educationendowmentfoundation.org.uk/public/files/Literacy_Development_Evidence_Review.pdf (accessed June 2020)

Carstairs-McCarthy, Andrew (2002), *An Introduction to English Morphology*, Edinburgh University Press, Edinburgh

Cresswell, J (2010), *Oxford Dictionary of Word Origins*, Oxford University Press, Oxford

Crystal, D (2013), *Spell it out*, Profile Books, London

Draze, D & O'Shaugnessy, S (2005), *Red Hot Root Words, Mastering Vocabulary with Prefixes, Suffixes and Root Words*, Prufrock Press, Texas

Goldup, W (2010), How Words Work Morphological strategies, *Dyslexia Review* Spring 2010, Volume 21 Number 2, Dyslexia Action, www.dyslexiaaction.org.uk

Henry, M.K (2010), *Unlocking Literacy, Effective Decoding and Spelling Instruction*, 2nd Edition, Paul H Brookes Publishing Co, Baltimore

Nunes, T & Bryant, P (2006), *Improving Literacy by Teaching Morphemes*, Routledge, Abingdon

Parsons, S & Branagan, A (2014), *Word Aware, Teaching Vocabulary across the day, across the curriculum*, Speechmark, Routledge, London

Quigley, A & Coleman, R (2019), *Improving Literacy in Secondary Schools*, London, Education Endowment Foundation. https://educationendowmentfoundation.org.uk/public/files/Publications/Literacy/EEF_KS3_KS4_LITERACY_GUIDANCE.pdf (accessed June 2020)

Wechsler, D (2018), *Wechsler Individual Achievement Test – Third UK Edition for Teachers*, Pearson, London

Web references

Apel, K., Diehm, E., and Apel, L. (2013) Using Multiple Measures of Morphological Awareness to Assess its Relation to Reading, *Top Lang Disorders* (Online) Vol. 33 (1) pp. 42–56. http://alliedhealth.ceconnection.com (accessed February 2021)

Bowers, P (2006), Adding Transparency to Morphologically Opaque Words Through Instruction, *Wordswork kingston.com*. https://www.researchgate.net/publication/228384609_ (accessed June 2020)

Bowers, P, Deacon, H & Kirby, J. (2010), The Effects of Morphological Instruction on Literacy Skills: A Systematic Review of the Literature, *Review of Educational Research* Vol. 80 https://www.researchgate.net/publication/249797979_ (accessed June 2020)

Brooks, G (2016), *What works for children and young people with literacy difficulties? The effectiveness of intervention schemes*, 5th Ed http://www.interventionsforliteracy.org.uk/wp-content/uploads/2017/11/What-Works-5th-edition-Rev-Oct-2016.pdf (accessed June 2020)

Carroll, J & Breadmore, H (2017), *Morphological Processing in Children with Phonological Difficulties*, https://www.nuffieldfoundation.org/project/morphological-processing-in-children-with-phonologi cal-difficulties (accessed June 2020)

Carrol, J & Breadmore, H (2018), *Not All Phonological Awareness Deficits Are Created Equal: Evidence From a Comparison Between Children With Otitis Media and Poor Readers*, https://pubmed.ncbi.nlm.nih.gov/28880490/ (accessed June 2020)

Carrol, J & Breadmore, H (2018), *Sublexical and syntactic processing during reading: evidence from eye movements of typically developing and dyslexic readers*, https://pureportal.coventry.ac.uk/en/publica tions/sublexical-and-syntactic-processing-during-reading-evidence-from- (accessed June 2020)

Cooke, G (2012), *Making Sense of Spelling*, https://www.youtube.com/watch?v=OmbuwZKOlr8 (accessed June 2020)

Cunningham, AJ & Carroll, J (2012), *Early Predictors of Phonological and Morphological Awareness and the Link with Reading: Evidence from Children with Different Patterns of Early Deficit, Applied Psycholinguistics*, https://www.researchgate.net/publication/290181543 (accessed June 2020)

Deacon, S, Kieffer, M, & Laroche, A (2014), *The Relation Between Morphological Awareness and Reading Comprehension: Evidence From Mediation and Longitudinal Models*, https://www.researchgate.net/pub lication/266262949_ (accessed June 2020)

Department for Education and Skills (2004), *A Framework for Understanding Dyslexia*, https://framework.thedyslexia-spldtrust.org.uk/resources/framework-understanding-dyslexia (accessed June 2020)

Government of UK (2015), *Special Educational Needs and Disability Code of Practice*, https://www.gov.uk/government/publications/send-code-of-practice-0-to-25 (accessed June 2020)

Kirby, J et al (2012), *Children's morphological awareness and reading ability*, https://www.researchgate.net/publication/225753256_ _ (accessed June 2020)

Levesque, K, Kiefter, J, & Deacon, H (2017), *Morphological Awareness And Reading Comprehension Examining Mediating Factors*, https://www.researchgate.net/publication/314390398_

McCutchen, D, Herrera, B, Evans, S, Stull, S, & Lotus, S (2014), *Putting Words to Work: Effects of Morphological Instruction on Children's Writing*, https://www.researchgate.net/publication/259201387

Tsesmeli, S & Seymour, P (2009), *The Effects of Training of Morphological Structure on Spelling Derived Words by Dyslexic Adolescents*, https://pubmed.ncbi.nlm.nih.gov/19026109/

Nicholls, H et al (2017), Implicit and explicit morphological awareness: insights from developmental trajectories and implications for future research, https://www.researchgate.net/publication/317940960 (accessed June 2020)

The National Curriculum

Government of UK (2014), *English Programmes of Study*, https://www.gov.uk/government/publications/national-curriculum-in-england-english-programmes-of-study (accessed June 2020)

Government of UK (2014), *Glossary for the Programmes of Study for English (non-statutory)*, https://assets.publishing.service.gov.uk/government/uploads/system/uploads/attachment_data/file/244216/English_Glossary.pdf (accessed June 2020)

Government of UK (2014), *English Appendix 1: Spelling*, https://assets.publishing.service.gov.uk/government/uploads/system/uploads/attachment_data/file/239784/English_Appendix_1_-_Spelling.pdf (accessed June 2020)

Government of UK (2014), *English Appendix 2: Vocabulary, Grammar and Punctuation*, https://assets.publishing.service.gov.uk/government/uploads/system/uploads/attachment_data/file/335190/English_Appendix_2_-_Vocabulary_grammar_and_punctuation.pdf (accessed June 2020)

Websites

www.dictionary.com

www.bdadyslexia.org

www.patoss-dyslexia.org

www.thedyslexia-spldtrust.org.uk

Appendices

Appendix 1 to 17 are all photocopiable resources. Colour photocopying is strongly recommended. Examples are given in these appendices but the full resources can all be found on the companion website www.routledge.com/cw/speechmark.

1. Morphological Awareness Assessment

<table>
<tr><td colspan="6">Pupil's name:</td><td colspan="3">DOB:</td></tr>
<tr><td colspan="6">Completed by:</td><td colspan="3">Date:</td></tr>
<tr><td colspan="3">TRANSPARENT MORPHEMES score: /16</td><td colspan="3">OPAQUE MORPHEMES score /12</td><td rowspan="3">WORD RELATIONSHIPS score /11</td><td rowspan="3">PSEUDOWORDS score /11</td><td rowspan="3">TOTAL Score /50</td></tr>
<tr><td>Words</td><td>P /4</td><td>D /4</td><td>Words</td><td>P /3</td><td>D /3</td></tr>
<tr><td>Sentences</td><td>P /4</td><td>D /4</td><td>Sentences</td><td>P /3</td><td>D /3</td></tr>
<tr><td colspan="3">Comment</td><td colspan="3">Comment</td><td>Comment</td><td>Comment</td><td>General comments</td></tr>
<tr><td colspan="6">Strengths</td><td colspan="3">Weaknesses</td></tr>
</table>

Guidelines and terminology for assessment

TRANSPARENT MORPHEMES are morphemes where the root word does not change its sound when affixed, e.g. **like** becomes **dislike**.

OPAQUE (PHONOLOGICALLY COMPLEX) MORPHEMES are morphemes where the root word is not heard or its sound is changed when it is affixed, e.g. **catch** becomes **caught**.

WORD RELATIONSHIPS involve the morphological relationship between words. Specifically, for this assessment, it concerns whether they have the same root.

PSEUDO-WORDS are made up, or nonsense words.

PRODUCTION tasks require a pupil to add a morpheme to a word or say a word.

DECOMPOSITION tasks require a pupil to remove a morpheme from a word or reduce its morphemes.

Some tasks are "**WORD**" tasks. Others are "**SENTENCE**" tasks. Sentence tasks may place additional load on working memory. In order to alleviate this, pictures are provided at the end of the assessment.

All instructions are given with each task. The answers are in orange. The words the adult says are in green.

What you need: Blank copy of the assessment, a pencil, and the pictures for transparent morpheme sentence tasks cut up.

Discontinue rule: Administer all of the transparent and opaque morphemes sections. Discontinue the word relationships and pseudowords sections if the learner makes 4 consecutive errors.

Scoring: Score 1 point for each correct answer and write it in the boxes at the end of each section. Transfer these scores to the scoring box on above and calculate a total score out of 50.

TRANSPARENT MORPHEMES
(where the root word does not change its sound when affixed)

1. Words: Production

The pupil listens to two words. The second word is the first word with an added affix. The pupil is then given a different word and asked to say an affixed version of it.

Say: *I am going to say two words. Listen to how the first word is changed to make the second word. Ready?* ***High: highest***. *What words did I say?* (if the child doesn't know, repeat them). *Did you hear how the first word changed?* If the child doesn't know: *I added* ***-est***. *Now you try. I will say the first two again to remind you what to do.* ***High, highest, kind...*** *What comes next?* (If the child doesn't know, say ***High, highest, kind, kindest***. *I added* ***-est*** *to* ***kind.)*** *So you had these words:* ***High, highest, kind, kindest.*** *Now try these.*

For each question there is an example pair of words and a test word. The adult says the example pair, pauses then says the test word. The pupil must say the missing word (answer in orange)

a) **long: longer**
   short: __________ (shorter)

b) **happy: happiness**
   kind: _________ (kindness)

c) **appear: disappear**
   trust: __________ (distrust)

d) **fit: unfit**

e) **friendliness: _______ (unfriendliness)**

Transparent morphemes production score (words)	/4
Comments	

2. Words: Decomposition

The pupil is asked to listen to two words. The first word is followed by the same word with its affix taken away. The pupil is then given a new word and asked to take the same affix away.

Say: *I am going to say two words. Listen to how the first word is changed to make the second word. Ready?* ***Bendy: bend.*** *What words did I say? Did you hear how the first word changed? I took off the* ***-y.*** *Now you try. I will say the first two again to remind you what to do.* ***Bendy: bend, Smelly....*** *What comes next?* (If the child doesn't know, say ***Bendy: bend, smelly: smell.*** *I took away the* ***–y*** *from* ***smelly.)*** *So you had these words:* ***Bendy: bend. Smelly: smell.*** *Now try these.*

The adult says the first two words (in black), pauses, then says the third word. The pupil must say the missing word (answer in orange).

1. **unkind: kind**
   unfair: ________ (fair)
2. **careless: care**
   endless: __________ (end)
3. **happiness: happy**
   laziness: __________ (lazy)
4. **poisonous: poison**
   famous: ___________ (fame)

Transparent morphemes decomposition score (words)	/4
Comments	

3. Sentences: Production

The pupil is asked to listen to two sentences. In the second, one of the words is affixed. The pupil then hears a new sentence and is asked to complete the sentence in the same way. Pictures of each sentence are available to support working memory difficulties. These can be found at the back of the assessment and should be shown to the pupil on separate cards.

Say: *I am going to say two sentences. Then I will give you a sentence to finish off yourself. Listen to the first sentence.* ***I am kind****. Now the second.* ***You are kinder****. Can you say both those sentences back to me? Which words did I change? Yes,* ***kind*** *changed to* ***kinder****. Now listen to the next sentences and see if you can finish off the last one.* ***I am bossy. You are bossier.*** *What word did I leave out?* **(If the child doesn't know say *bossier*)** *So you said,* ***I am kind. You are kinder. I am bossy. You are bossier****. Now try these ones.*

For each question there is an example pair of sentences and a test pair, where the last one is not complete. Adult says the example pair, pauses then says the test pair. Show the pupil the pictures (available on separate cards). The pupil must say the missing word from the last sentence (in orange). Do not show the pupil the written sentence.

a) I play with Billy. Billy plays with me.
I sit with Rachel. Rachel _____ with me. (sits)

b) He works on a farm. He is a farmer.
She works in a bakery. She is a ______. (baker)

c) First I pack my bag, later I will unpack it.
First I tie my laces, later I will __________ them. (untie)

d) Please can you run that race again? That's a rerun.
Please can you write that text again?
That's a _________ (rewrite)

Transparent morphemes production score (sentences)	/4
Comments	

4. Sentences: Decomposition

The pupil is asked to listen to two sentences. In the second, an affix is taken away from one of the words. The pupil then hears a new sentence and is asked to change the sentence in the same way. Pictures of each sentence are available to support working memory difficulties. These can be found at the back of the assessment and should be shown to the pupil on separate cards.

> *Say: I am going to say two sentences. Then I will give you a sentence for you to change yourself in the same way. Listen to the first sentence.* ***He washes his clothes****. Now the second.* ***I wash mine****. Can you say both those sentences back to me? Which words did I change? Yes,* ***he washes*** *changed to* ***I wash****. Now listen to the next sentences and see if you can finish off the last one.* ***She watches TV. I _______ TV****. What word did I leave out? (watch). (*If the child doesn't know *say* ***watch****) So that's* ***He washes his clothes. I wash mine. She watches TV. I watch TV.*** *Now try these ones.*

For each question there is an example pair of sentences and a test pair, where the last one is not complete. Adult says the example pair, pauses then says the test pair. Show the pupil the pictures (available on separate cards). The pupil must say the missing word from the last sentence (in orange). Do not show the pupil the written sentence.

a. **There are too many matches. I want just one match.**
   There are too many lunches.
   I want just one _________. (lunch)

b. **I like jumping. Can you jump?**
   I like singing. Can you _____________. (sing)

c. **When you are forgetful it means you forget.**
   When you are helpful it means you ______. (help)

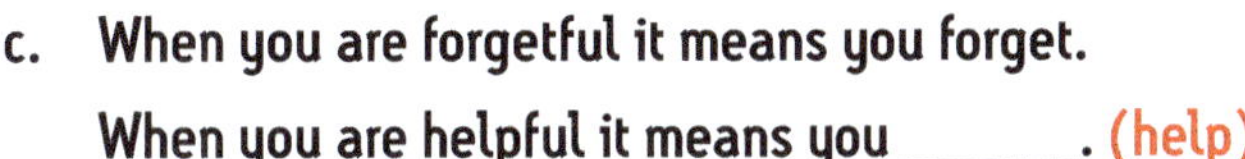

d. **Dislike is when you don't like something.**
   Distrust is when you _________ something. (don't trust)

Transparent morphemes decomposition score (sentences)	/4
Comments	

OPAQUE (PHONOLOGICALLY COMPLEX) MORPHEMES
(where the root word is not heard or its sound is changed when it is affixed):

1. Words: Production

The pupil is asked to listen to two words. The second word is the first word in a different form. The pupil is then given a different word and asked to generate the same form of that word.

> **Say**: *I am going to say two words. Listen to how the first word is changed to make the second word.* ***Drink: drank***. *What words did I say? Did you hear how the first word changed? Now you try. I will say the first two again to remind you what to do.* ***Drink, drank, hide...*** *What comes next? (*If the child doesn't know, say ***Drink, drank, hide, hid.)*** *So you had these words:* ***Drink, drank, hide, hid.*** *Now try these.*

For each question there is an example pair of words and a test word. Adult says the example pair, pauses then says the test word. Pupil must say the missing word (in orange)

a. **Eat: ate. Come: __________** (came)
b. **Circle: circular, rectangle: ______________** (rectangular)
c. **King: kingdom, wise: ____________** (wisdom)

Opaque morphemes production score (words)	/3
Comments	

2. Words: Decomposition

The pupil listens to two words; the second word is the first in its root form. The pupil is then given a different word and asked to generate the root form of that word.

Say: I am going to say two words. Listen to how the first word is changed to make the second word. ***Say: said.*** *What words did I say? Did you hear how the first word changed? Now you try. Here is your word. I will say the first two again to remind you what to do.* ***Say: said. Write...*** *What comes next? (*If the child doesn't know, say ***Say: said. Write: wrote)*** *So you had these words:* ***Say: said. Write: wrote.*** *Now try these.*

For each question there is an example pair of words and a test word. Adult says the example pair, pauses then says the test word. Pupil must say the missing word (in orange)

a. **Built: build, brought: __________ (bring)**
b. **Production: produce, presentation: __________ (present)**
c. **Exclusion: exclude, decision: ____________ (decide)**

Opaque morphemes production score (words)	/3
Comments	

3. Sentences: Production

The pupil is asked to listen to a target word followed by an incomplete sentence, where the missing word is a changed version of the target word. The pupil is asked to generate the word which completes the sentence.

Say: I am going to say a word. Then I will give you a sentence to finish off yourself by adding one word. Ready? Listen to my word. ***Child****. Now can you finish this sentence. The clue is in the word,* ***child. I have four...*** *What word have I missed out? Yes, children.* ***Child. I have four children.*** *Now try these.*

OPAQUE (PHONOLOGICALLY COMPLEX) MORPHEMES

For each question the adult says a word and an incomplete sentence. The pupil must say the missing word (in orange).

a. **Magic. He performs magic. He is a ________. (magician)**
b. **Wise. A wise person is known to have _________. (wisdom)**
c. **Know. When you know a lot, you have a lot of ____________. (knowledge)**

Opaque morphemes production score (sentences)	/3
Comments	

4. Sentences: Decomposition

The pupil is asked to listen to a target word followed by an incomplete sentence, where the missing word is the root of the target word. The pupil is asked to generate the word to complete the sentence.

Say: I am going to say a word. Then I will give you a sentence to finish off yourself with one word. Ready? Listen to the word. ***Woke****. Now can you finish this sentence. The clue is in the word,* ***woke. What time did you...*** *? What word have I missed out? Yes,* ***wake. Woke. What time did you wake?***

For each question the adult says a word and an incomplete sentence. The pupil must say the missing word (in orange).

1. **Meant. What did the teacher ___________? (mean)**
2. **Decision. What did you _______? (decide)**
3. **Creation. The model took the girls a long time to _________. (create)**

Opaque morphemes decomposition score (sentences)	/3
Comments	

OPAQUE (PHONOLOGICALLY COMPLEX) MORPHEMES

WORD RELATIONSHIPS

In this task the pupil is asked to say if two words have the same root.

> Say: *In this one, I am going to say two words. I will ask you if they come from the same root. The root is the bit of the word where its meaning comes from. Here is an example.* ***Sing*** *and* ***singing*** *come from the same root,* ***sing****. Now try these.* ***Heal*** *and* ***healthy****. Do they words come from the same root? Yes, because* ***heal*** *is about having good health, or being* ***healthy****.*

The adult says the two words then asks if they come from the same root. Answers in orange. Pupil's answer is written in the box.

1. **Wish & wishfulness? (yes)**
2. **Pillow & pill? (no)**
3. **Pay & repay? (yes)** 
4. **Touch & touchy? (yes)**
5. **Match & mat? (no)**
6. **Moth & mother? (no)**
7. **Cook & cookery? (yes)**
8. **Mailbag & female? (no)**
9. **International & nation? (yes)** 
10. **Export & supportive? (yes)**
11. **Detention & Punishment? (no)**

Word relationships score (sentences)	/11
Comments	

PSEUDOWORDS (an advanced task)

Pupils are asked to change forms of nonsense words following morphological rules.

> Say. *In this task, you will be given some sentences using nonsense words. I will give you the word in two sentences then ask you to finish a third sentence off. Try this one for practice. Ready?* ***This is a jax. If you give me another jax, what will I have?*** **(jaxes)**. Now try these.

1. The man knows how to spag. He likes spagging. He did it yesterday. What did he do yesterday? ________________ (spagged)

2. I like to trurp. Trurping is great fun. I did it yesterday. All day tomorrow I will be ______ (trurping).

3. Sally likes to ketch her clothes. What does she do to her clothes? (ketches)

4. This is a lig book. That is a lig book. But this one is more lig. It is _______. (ligger)

5. My mum is not at all grimp, and my sister is grimper, but my dad is even more grimp. He is the _________. (grimpest)

6. Every day this man has been meeping his garden. Yesterday he mept it. Today he will do the same thing. What will he do today? (meep his garden)

7. She walked chiddily and chattered with chiddiness. She felt very _______ (chiddy).

8. I am feeling very wompy. I talk wompily and laugh with ________ (womp/wompiness).

9. In school we are working on shonment. We are learning to (shon).

10. You are so unpug. I wish you would be more _______ (pug).

11. Someone who has no grat is _________ (gratless).

Pseudo words score (sentences)	/11
Comments	

PSEUDOWORDS

Pictures for sentence tasks

3. Transparent Morphemes Production

3a.		
3b.		
3c.		
3d.		

4. Transparent Morphemes Decomposition

4a		
4b		
4c		
4d		

2. Knowledge of Morphemes

Reading and Spelling Assessment (Adult Record Sheet)

COMPANION WEBSITE

This is an assessment of spelling and reading of suffixes and prefixes from the National Curriculum (2014) from Year 1 to 4. There are separate pupil sheets for the pupil to read from. To score, award one mark per item, and allow a mark if the suffix/prefix and rule (if relevant) are correctly read or spelled, even if the whole word is not correct. If more than ten spelling errors are made in one set of words, complete the set and score it, but do not continue to the next sets and score 0 for any sets that are not administered.

Knowledge of Morphemes Assessment Adult Record Sheet

Summary	Pupil's Name:			Date:	
	Year 1	Year 2	Year 3 & 4	Year 5 & 6	Total Score
Score: Read	/10	/24	/23	/18	/75
Score: Spell	/10	/24	/23	/18	/75

Morphemes to target through teaching: (Highlight/circle if unknown)	
Year 1	**-s** (plural), **-s** (3rd person), **-es**, **-ing**, **-ed** (past tense), **-ed** (added syllable), **-er**, **-est**, **-y**, **un-**
Year 2	**Rule 1) No change to root: -ment, -ness, -ful, -less, -ly** **Rule 2) y →i: -es, -ed, -er, -est, -ness, -ful, -less, -ly** **Rule 3) drop e: –ing, -es, -ed, -er, -est, -y** **Rule 4) double final consonant: –ing, -ed, -er, -est, -y**
Year 3 & 4	**dis-**, **mis-**, **re-**, **in-**, **il-**, **im-**, **ir-**, **sub-**, **super-**, **inter-**, **anti-**, **auto-**, **-ation**, **-ation** (drop e), **-ly** (le → ly), **-ly** (ic →ically), **-ous**, **-ous** (drop e), **-ous** (our → or) **-tion** (t + **-ion**), **-sion** (s + **-ion**), ssion (ss + **-ion**), **-cian** (c + ian)
Year 5 & 6	**-cious**, **-tious**, **-tial**, **-cial**, **-ant**, **-ance**, **-ent**, **-ence**, **-ancy**, **-ency**, **-able**, **-ible**, **-able** (drop e), **-ible** (drop e), **-ability**, **-ibility**, **-ably**, **-ibly**

Year 1

Affix	Meaning/function/rule	Test word	Pupil response: read	Pupil response: spell
-s	Noun plural	cats		
-s	3rd person singular	sits		
-es	Adds a syllable /iz/ when noun plural or verb 3rd person	fixes		
-ing	Verb present continuous tense	jumping		
-ed	Verb past tense	helped		
-ed	Verb past tense when adds extra syllable /id/	hunted		
-er	Makes root word into comparative	burner		
-est	Superlative	quickest		
-y	Makes root into adjective	crispy		
un-	Opposite (not)	unzip		

Summary: highlight if unknown	
Read:	Spell:
-s (plural)	-s (plural)
-s (3rd person)	-s (3rd person)
-es	-es
-ing	-ing
-ed	-ed
-ed (added syllable)	-ed (added syllable)
-er	-er
-est	-est
-y	-y
un-	un-
Total /10	Total /10

Year 2 (Page 1 of 2)

Affix	Meaning/function/rule	Test word	Pupil response: read	Pupil response: spell
-ment	Makes root word into a noun	**shipment**		
-ness	Makes root word into a noun	**fitness**		
-ful	Makes root word into adjective	**wishful**		
-less	Makes root word into an adjective	**restless**		
-ly	Makes root word into adverb	**sadly**		
-es	If root ends in **y** change to **i**	**cries**		
-ed	If root ends in **y** change to **i**	**dried**		
-er	If root ends in **y** change to **i**	**luckier**		
-est	If root ends in **y** (ee sound) change to i	**runniest**		
-ness		**bendiness**		
-ful	If root ends in **y** change to i	**plentiful**		
-less		**penniless**		
-ly		**angrily**		

Summary: highlight if unknown	
Read:	Spell:
-ment	-ment
-ness	-ness
-ful	-ful
-less	-less
-ly	-ly
-es (y → i)	-es (y → i)
-ed (y → i)	-ed (y → i)
-er (y → i)	-er (y → i)
-est (y → i)	-est (y → i)
-ness (y → i)	-ness (y → i)
-ful (y → i)	-ful (y → i)
-less (y → i)	-less (y → i)
-ly (y → i)	-ly (y → i)

Year 2 (page 2 of 2)

Affix	Meaning/function/rule	Test word	Pupil response: read	Pupil response: spell
-ing	If the root has a consonant before the final **e**, drop it if the suffix begins with a vowel or **-y**	liking		
-es		roses		
-ed		saved		
-er		nicer		
-est		latest		
-y		shiny		
-ing	Double the final consonant in one syllable root words ending in a single consonant to keep the vowel short	letting		
-ed		popped		
-er		runner		
-est		saddest		
-y		nutty		

Summary: highlight if unknown	
Read:	Spell:
-ing (drop e)	-ing (drop e)
-es (drop e)	-es (drop e)
-ed (drop e)	-ed (drop e)
-er (drop e)	-er (drop e)
-est (drop e)	-est (drop e)
-y (drop e)	-y (drop e)
-ing (double consonant)	-ing (double consonant)
-ed (double consonant)	-ed (double consonant)
-er (double consonant)	-er (double consonant)
-est (double consonant)	-est (double consonant)
-y (double consonant)	-y (double consonant)
Total /24	Total /24

COMPANION WEBSITE

Year 3 & 4 (Page 1 of 2)

Affix	Meaning/function/rule	Test word	Pupil response: read	Pupil response: spell
dis-	Opposite/not	**dislike**		
mis-	Opposite/not	**misprint**		
re-	Again/back	**react**		
in-	Not	**insane**		
il-	Not (when root starts with l)	**illegal**		
im-	Not (when root starts with m or p)	**improper**		
ir-	Not (when root starts with r)	**irregular**		
sub-	Under	**submarine**		
super-	above	**superman**		
inter-	Between, among	**interact**		
anti-	against	**antifreeze**		
auto-	Self, own	**autograph**		
-ation	Noun maker	**formation**		
-ation	Verb maker: If the root has a consonant before the final e drop the e	**sensation**		
-ly	Adverb maker (if the root ends in -le drop the e)	**gently**		
-ly	Adverb maker (if the root ends in -ic add al before the -ly)	**frantically**		

Summary: highlight if unknown	
Read:	**Spell:**
dis-	dis-
mis-	mis-
re-	re-
in-	in-
il-	il-
im-	im-
ir-	ir-
sub-	sub-
super-	super-
inter-	inter-
anti-	anti-
auto-	auto-
-ation	-ation
-ation (drop e)	-ation (drop e)
-ly (le → ly)	-ly (le → ly)
-ly (-ic → ically)	-ly (-ic → ically)

Year 3 & 4 (page 2 of 2)

Affix	Meaning/function/rule	Test word	Pupil response: read	Pupil response: spell
-ous	Adjective maker	**poisonous**		
-ous	Adjective maker: If the root has a consonant before the final e drop the e	**famous**		
-ous	Noun maker (if the root ends in -our, drop the u)	**humorous**		
-tion	Noun maker (use if the root ends in t or te)	**action**		
-sion	Noun maker (use if the root ends in d, de or se)	**erosion**		
-ssion	Noun maker (use if the root ends in ss or mit)	**procession**		
-cian	Noun maker (use if the root ends in c or s)	**musician**		

Summary: highlight if unknown	
Read:	**Spell:**
-ous	-ous
-ous (drop e)	-ous (drop e)
-ous (our → or)	-ous (our → or)
-tion	-tion
-sion	-sion
-ssion	-ssion
-cian	-cian
Total /23	Total /23

Year 5 & 6 (Page 1 of 2)

Affix	Meaning/function/rule	Test word	Pupil response: read	Pupil response: spell
-cious	Adjective maker (when the root ends in **ce** – drop **e**)	**spacious**		
-tious	Adjective maker (when the root ends in **n** – drop **n**)	**infectious**		
-tial	Adjective maker (when the root ends in **nce** or **t**)	**partial**		
-cial	Adjective maker (when the root ends in **ace** or a short vowel + **ce** – drop the **e**)	**facial**		
-ant	Adjective maker (when the root ends in **t** or **ate**, drop **ate**)	**observant**		
-ance	Noun maker	**brilliance**		
-ent	Adjective maker	**urgent**		
-ence	**Noun maker**	**silence**		
-ancy	Noun maker	**pregnancy**		
-ency	Noun maker	**emergency**		

Summary: highlight if unknown	
Read:	**Spell:**
-cious	-cious
-tious	-tious
-tial	-tial
-cial	-cial
-ant	-ant
-ance	-ance
-ent	-ent
-ence	-ence
-ancy	-ancy
-ency	-ency

Year 5 & 6 (page 2 of 2)

Affix	Meaning/function/rule	Test word	Pupil response: read	Pupil response: spell
-able	Adjective maker (primarily used with Anglo Saxon roots)	readable		
-ible	Adjective maker (primarily used with Latin roots)	flexible		
-able	Adjective maker (drop the final e)	likable		
-ible	Adjective maker (drop the final e)	sensible		
-ability	Noun maker	notability		
-ibility	Noun maker	reversibility		
-ably	Adverb maker	reasonably		
-ibly	Adverb maker	incredibly		

Summary: highlight if unknown	
Read:	Spell:
-able	-able
-ible	-ible
-able	-able
-ible	-ible
-ability	-ability
-ibility	-ibility
-ably	-ably
-ibly	-ibly
Total /18	Total /18

3. Knowledge of Morphemes Assessment

Pupil Word Lists

cats

sits

fixes

jumping

helped

hunted

burner

quickest

crispy

unzip

shipment	angrily
fitness	liking
wishful	roses
restless	saved
sadly	nicer
cries	latest
dried	shiny
luckier	letting
runniest	popped
bendiness	runner
plentiful	saddest
penniless	nutty

dislike

misprint

react

insane

illegal

improper

irregular

submarine

superman

interact

antifreeze

autograph

formation

sensation

gently

frantically

poisonous

famous

humorous

action

erosion

procession

musician

spacious

infectious

partial

facial

observant

brilliance

urgent

silence

pregnancy

emergency

readable

flexible

likable

sensible

notability

reversibility

reasonably

incredibly

4. Assessment Summary Sheet

Pupil's name:	Year group:	Date:	Weeks of intervention:	Working within phonics phase:
Morphological awareness Total Score /50	Transparent morphemes Areas of difficulty: Score /16	Opaque morphemes Areas of difficulty: Score /12	Word relationships Comments: Score /11	Pseudowords Comments: Score /11
Morphemic knowledge total score:			Reading /75	Spelling /75

Year 1 scores: Reading /10 Spelling /10	Difficulty with (highlight if the pupil has a difficulty in either spelling, reading or both): **-s, (plural) -s (3rd person), -es, -ing, -ed (past tense),** **-ed (added syllable) -er, -est, -y, -un**
Year 2 scores: Reading /24 Spelling /24	Difficulty with (highlight if the pupil has a difficulty in either spelling, reading or both): **Rule 1) No change to root: -ment, -ness, -ful, -less, -ly** **Rule 2) y →i: -es, -ed, -er, -est, -ness, -ful, -less, -ly** **Rule 3) drop e: –ing, es, -ed, -er, -est, -y** **Rule 4) double final consonant: –ing, -ed, -er, -est, -y**
Year 3 & 4 scores: Reading /23 Spelling /23	Difficulty with (highlight if the pupil has a difficulty in either spelling, reading or both): **dis-, mis-, re-, in-, il-, im-, ir-,** **sub-, super-, inter-, anti-, auto-** **-ation, -ation (drop e), -ly (le → ly), -ly (ic →ically),** **-ous, -ous (drop e), -ous (our → or)** **-tion (t + -ion), -sion (s + -ion), ssion (ss + -ion), -cian (c + ian)**
Year 5 & 6 scores: Reading /18 Spelling /18	Difficulty with (highlight if the pupil has a difficulty in either spelling, reading or both): **-cious, -tious, -tial, -cial,** **-ant, -ent, -ance, -ence, -ancy, -ency** **-able, -ible, -able (drop e), -ible (drop e)** **-abiliy, -ibility, -ably, -ibly**

5. The Six-week Plan

Pupil name(s): **Date:**

Shaded cells to be completed after the lessons

Week no.	Morphological Awareness Focus & games:	Morphemes		Sentence for dictation	Word chosen for Word Mastery (Day 2)	Notes (after the lessons)
		Day 1: root + words (choose 1 root and 2–12 words)	Day 2: affix + words (choose 1 affix and 3–12 words)			

6. Suggested Teaching Sequence

Affixes with roots

Optional: choose as appropriate for the pupil(s). These have been chosen for potential flexibility with word play as the programme continues. Words in red are listed in the National Curriculum as common exception words for that year group (Year 1 & 2) or 100 words that children are expected to spell by the end of that year group (Year 3 & 4, Year 5 & 6).

Y1

-s cat, dog, tan, zip
-es fix, wish
-ing train, mark, cook
-ed lock, form
-ed (extra syllable) wait, rest
-er, count, help, strong
-est rich, clean, light
-y jump, fuss, stick
un- fair, fold, pack

Y2

-ment pay, ship, move, place
-ness fit, mad, kind, happy
-ful care, harm, pain
-less home, fear, end
-ly sad, weak, wild, cold
y → i rule (-es, -ed, -er, -est, -ness, -ful, -less, -ly) try, cry, dry, copy, happy, tidy, dizzy
drop e rule (-ing, -es, -ed, -er, -est, -y) like, make, smile, hope, hate, drive, bike, safe, close, nice, smoke, laze,
double consonant rule (-ing, -ed, -er, -est, -y) run, win, grab, drop, sit, plan, wet, hot, fun, nut, fur

Y3 & 4

dis- connect, continue

mis- spell, calculate

re- visit, appear

in- correct, direct

il- legal

ir- regular, relevant

im – perfect, possible

sub- scribe, merge

super- market, star

inter- act, -rupt

anti- freeze

auto- graph

-ation inform, commend

-ation (drop e) create, educate

-ly (le → ly) idle, simple

-ly (ic → ically) basic

-ous danger, poison

-ous (drop e) fame, adventure

-ous (our → or) humour

-tion elect, act

-sion tense, comprehend, decide

-ssion admit, possess

-cian music, electric

Y5 & 6

-cious grace, space

-tious caution

-cial face, office

-tial part, essence

-ant observe, expect

- ent depend, exist

- ance attend, (re)sist (stand)

-ence indulge, compete

-ancy hesitate, expect

-ency fluent, urgent

-able port (carry), enjoy

-ible struct (build), flex

-able (drop e) love, excite

-ible (drop e) sense, force

-ability read

-ibility cred (believe)

-ably reason, note

-ibly leg (read)

7. Word Lists for planning

Year 1 & 2[1,*]

Words in bold have phonics and/or spelling rules that relate to that year group or below. Words in red are common exception words for that year group. *Highlighted words in italics* have more possibilities for word building and are in the suggested teaching sequence for word roots, with further word lists below for playing games and spelling lists.

Year 1	-s ***cat, dog, tan, zip***		_es ***fix, wish,* box, mix, rush, hiss**
	Plural maker (noun)		**Plural maker (noun)**
	cats	rats	boxes
	dogs	ribs	ashes
	bags	vets	bushes
	fans	vans	churches
	fins	wigs	foxes
	hats	zips	brushes
	huts	shops	dishes
	jugs	days	kisses
	tans	schools	patches
	logs	friends	lunches
	legs	pens	glasses
	mats	toys	watches
	mugs	games	
	nets	cups	
	pans	ponds	
	pits	books	
	pins	boys	
	rags	desks	

	Verb tense		Verb tense
	digs	sits	fizzes
	bats	sobs	wishes
	bets	kicks	mixes
	gets	spins	rushes
	hits	runs	catches
	jogs	cooks	buzzes
	tips	plays	hisses
	licks	jumps	fixes
	mops	drags	touches
	pats	drops	washes
	picks	grabs	
	quits	hugs	
		stops	

Year 1	-ing *train, mark, cook*, sleep, help	
	Verb tense	
	fishing	spending
	picking	going
	licking	leading
	jumping	looking
	cooking	meeting
	training	saying
	marking	trying
	cooking	playing
	sleeping	crying
	wishing	spying
	jumping	trying
	helping	frying
	seeing	
	doing	

-ed (no added syllable) *lock, form*, dream, turn, wish	
Verb tense	
fixed	looked
kicked	dreamed
locked	turned
licked	jumped
pushed	cooked
formed	played
	pulled

-ed (when an extra syllable is created after t) *wait, rest*, treat	
treated	sorted
rested	waited
hunted	floated
wanted	tinted
hinted	tested
rented	

-er *count, help, strong,* lead, think	-est *rich, clean, light,* long, cold, tall
Noun maker	
counter helper leader thinker reader teacher	
farmer trainer burner feeler dreamer kinder	
Comparative maker	**Superlative maker**
stronger longer quicker colder taller richer faster weaker hunter cleaner	richest cleanest lightest longest coldest tallest strongest quickest
-y *jump, fuss, stick,* smell, crisp	un- *fair, fold, pack,* fit, stick
Adjective maker	**Opposite, not**
jumpy fussy sticky smelly mucky rocky fizzy crispy bendy hilly windy bossy	unfair unfold unpack unfit unstick unhappy unlock unwell unseen undo unzip untidy unable unkind unlucky

Year 2

Rule 1: No change to the root

If a suffix starts with a consonant, it is added to the root word without any change in the spelling of the root word.

-ment *pay, ship, move, place*	**-ness** *mad, rude, fit, kind, happy,* empty, silly
Noun maker	**Noun maker**
movement, replacement placement, payment enjoyment, shipment employment, amazement management	rudeness, hardness, neatness fitness, madness, sadness kindness, softness, strictness greatness, gladness, shyness darkness, flatness, loudness fairness
-ful *care, harm, pain*	**-less** *home, fear, end*
Adjective maker – means full of	**Adjective maker – means without**
careful, wishful, fearful restful, hopeful, shameful fitful, hateful, faithful useful, forgetful, handful harmful, hurtful, colourful painful, thankful, mouthful helpful, playful	homeless, careless fearless, blameless endless, formless restless, hopeless helpless, painless speechless, sleepless homeless, thoughtless
-ly *sad, weak, wild, cold*	
Adverb maker	
Sadly, weekly Badly, properly madly, normally weakly, kindly wildly, quickly coldly, thickly friendly really	

Year 2

Rule 2 (y → i)

When there is a consonant before the y at the end of the root word, change the y to i before adding –es, -ed, -er, -est, -ment, -ness, -ful, less, -ly

-es *copy, dry,* city	-ly *dry,* angry, crazy, lazy
Plural maker (noun)	**Adverb maker**
tries, cries, flies, babies, copies, replies, puppies jellies, berries, fries, parties, lollies, cities, parties, lorries ***Some of these words are also used as verbs.***	drily, angrily, crazily, lazily, speedily happily, luckily, merrily, funnily
-es *try, cry*	-ed *dry, copy*
Verb tense	**Verb tense**
flies, carries, copies, replies, tries cries, relies, fries, dries	dried, replied, carried, copied tried, cried, relied, fried
-er *happy, tidy*	-est *Dizzy,* luck(y), craz(y)
Noun maker	
copier, carrier	
Comparative maker	**Superlative maker**
chillier, funnier, crazier, luckier, sunnier runnier, lazier, windier, happier, tidier muddier, skinnier, luckier, dizzier	happiest, chilliest, funniest, craziest, luckiest sunniest, runniest, laziest, windiest, muddiest dizziest, skinniest, tidiest, dizziest

<table>
<tr><td rowspan="3"></td><td>-ment*,
merry</td><td>-ness
Happy, busy</td></tr>
<tr><td>Noun maker</td><td>Noun maker</td></tr>
<tr><td>merriment</td><td>tidiness, happiness, emptiness, business, silliness, laziness, prettiness, loveliness, nastiness, bossiness, bendiness</td></tr>
<tr><td rowspan="11">Year 2</td><td colspan="2">Rule 2 (y ➔ i) continued</td></tr>
<tr><td>-ful*,
beauty</td><td>-less*
penny</td></tr>
<tr><td>Adjective maker – means full of</td><td>Adjective maker – means without</td></tr>
<tr><td>beautiful
plentiful</td><td>penniless
merciless</td></tr>
<tr><td colspan="2">Rule 3: Drop e
If the root word has a consonant before the final e, drop the final e if the suffix begins with a vowel or -y before adding -ing, -ed, -er, -est, -y, -es</td></tr>
<tr><td>-ing
like, make, ride, bake</td><td>-ed
smile, hope, hate</td></tr>
<tr><td>Verb tense</td><td>Verb tense</td></tr>
<tr><td>liking, proving, making, coming, driving, baking, smiling, biking, hiking, hoping, taking, hating, joking, poking, waking, riding, coming, raising, writing, deciding, caring, staring</td><td>smiled, hoped, hated, decided, hiked, liked, baked, biked, joked, poked, raised, cared, proved, stared</td></tr>
</table>

-er *drive, bike, safe,* rude, ripe	-est *Close, nice,* late
Noun	
driver, biker, hiker, rider, baker, joker, smiler, dancer, miner, diner	
Comparative maker	**Superlative maker**
ruder, riper, nicer, closer, safer, later	nicest, latest, closest, ripest, rudest, safest

Rule 3 (drop e) continued

-y *smoke, laze,* shine, stone	-es *Laze,* Face, pace
Adjective maker	**Plural maker**
smoky, lazy, shiny, stony, greasy, hazy, bony, scary, flaky, slimy, shaky, crazy, lazy	Faces, Paces, Roses, phrases, Noses, Poses, Prizes, braces, Sizes, Doses, Laces, Traces
	Third person verb
	races, paces, poses, doses, loses, traces, chases, lazes, closes

<table>
<tr><td rowspan="9">Year 2</td><td colspan="2">Rule 4: Double Consonant
Double the final consonant in one syllable root words ending in a single consonant to keep the vowel short before adding –ing, -ed, -er, -est, -y</td></tr>
<tr><td>-ing
run, win, spin</td><td>-ed
grab, drop, clap, rub</td></tr>
<tr><td>Verb tense</td><td>Verb tense</td></tr>
<tr><td>running, clapping, sitting, winning, shopping, dragging, spinning, planning, grabbing, humming, rubbing, hugging, dropping, slipping, stopping, patting, fitting, letting, hopping, tripping, swimming, shutting, betting, chatting</td><td>grabbed, planned, dropped, fitted, clapped, dragged, rubbed, hugged, patted, shopped, hummed, stopped, dropped, hopped, chatted</td></tr>
<tr><td>-er
sit, plan
Noun maker
winner, shutter, planner, spinner, runner, swimmer, stopper, grabber, robber, dropper, rubber, sitter</td><td>-est
wet, hot</td></tr>
<tr><td colspan="2">Rule 4 (double consonant) continued</td></tr>
<tr><td>Comparative maker</td><td>Superlative maker</td></tr>
<tr><td>sadder, wetter, fatter, fitter, bigger, redder, hotter, flatter, thinner</td><td>wettest, biggest, hottest, thinnest, saddest, fittest, fattest, reddest, flattest</td></tr>
</table>

	-y *fun, nut, fur*	
	Adjective maker	
	funny sunny nutty skinny furry floppy runny foggy fatty muddy	

Endnotes

1. You can also use the 2014 English Curriculum Appendix 1 Spelling word list to find examples of further words for each year group.

* There are few words in these lists. Teach ***-ment, -ful and -less (y ➔ i)*** alongside ***-ment, -ful and -less*** *(no change to the root)*.

Year 3 & 4[1]

Words in bold have phonics and/or spelling rules that relate to that year group or below. Words in red are on the list of 100 words in the National Curriculum that children in England are expected to be able to spell by the end of Year 4. *Highlighted words in italics* have more possibilities for word building and are in the suggested teaching sequence for word roots, with further word lists below for playing games and spelling lists.

Year 3 & 4	dis- *connect*, *continue*, agree, like, trust	mis- *spell*, *calculate*, behave, fire, use
	Opposite, not	Opposite, not
	disagree, disobey, discover, dislike, dishonest, dishearten, dislodge, disown, displease, disqualify, disappear, disconnect, disinfect, disembark, disapprove, discomfort, distrust, discontinue	misunderstand, misspell, misdeed, misbehave, miscalculate, misplace, miscount, misfire, misfortune, mishear, misinform, misread, mistake, misfortune, misguide, mislead, misprint, mistrust, misuse
	re- *visit*, *appear*, make, place, act, call, bound	
	Again	Back
	remake, redo, regrow, replace, reawaken, react, relive, revisit, rewrite, refresh, reappear, redecorate, rebuild, recycle, refill, reform, replay	retreat, recede, return, recall, reflect, rebound

	in- *correct, direct,* **sane, capable**	**il-** *legal,* **logical**
	Not	**Not (when root starts wih 'l')**
	inactive incorrect insane inadequate incompetent inconsistent incredible indifferent indigestion indirect inequality (noun) indefinite injustice (noun) insatiable instability inevitable infallible incompatible independent incapable	illegal illogical illuminate illegible
	im- *perfect, possible,* **patient**	**ir- (not)** *regular, relevant,* **rational**
	Not (when root starts with 'm' or 'p')	**Not (when root starts with 'r')**
	impatient imperfect immature immortal immobile immoral impartial improper impossible immovable (can also be spelt immoveable) impermeable improbable	irregular irrelevant irrational irresponsible irrevocable irresistible
	sub- *scribe, merge,* **plot, title**	**inter-** *act, -rupt,* **view, city**
	Under	**Between, among**
	subheading submarine submerge subscribe subplot subterranean subway subtitle subhuman subnormal subdivide	interact intercity international interview interrelated interrupt interlock interchange intermediate interpersonal

	super- *market, star,* man, natural	anti- *freeze,* climax
	Above	**Against**
	supermarket superman superstar superimpose superintendent supernatural supersonic	anticlockwise antiseptic antisocial antibiotic antifreeze anticlimax
	auto- *graph,* biography	
	Self, own	
	autobiography autograph automobile autopilot	
	-ation *Inform, commend,* expect, present	-ation (drop e rule) *create, educate,* sense, invite
	Noun maker	**Noun maker** Where the root ends in a consonant followed by e, drop the e
	information expectation deportation temptation recommendation presentation	invitation celebration admiration education dictation creation adoration sensation preparation frustration condensation exploration inspiration medication investigation preservation rotation relation suffocation imagination
	-ly (le ➔ ly) *idle, simple,* bubble, able	-ly (ic ➔ ically) *basic,* frantic, critic, tragic
	Adverb or adjective maker Where the root ends in -le, change the e to a y	**Adverb or adjective maker** Where the root ends in -ic, add -ally
	gently simply pimply purply idly wobbly sprinkly bubbly fiddly ripply wriggly ably	frantically simplistically basically typically poetically critically tragically exotically ironically numerically mechanically

-ous *danger, poison,* ruin, thunder		-ous (drop e rule) *fame, adventure,* nerve, fibre
Adjective maker (no rule)		Adjective maker Where the root ends in a consonant followed by an e, drop the e
poisonous dangerous mountainous ruinous	thunderous scandalous villainous coniferous murderous	famous adventurous nervous fibrous

-ous (our ➔ or rule) *Humour*		
Adjective maker Where the root contains -our spelling pattern, it is changed to -or		
humorous glamorous	rigorous vigorous	

-tion (t + ion) *elect, act,* edit, collect, adopt		-sion (s + ion) *tense, comprehend, decide*
Noun maker (meaning act of, state of or result of) Use if root ends in t or te		Noun maker (meaning act of, state of or result of) Use if root ends in d, de or se
adoption distraction edition election insertion prediction reflection refraction collection hesitation completion	objection construction election exception extraction interruption instruction obstruction action injection opposition separation	tension expansion comprehension extension erosion intrusion expansion invasion exclusion infusion decide

	-ssion (ss + ion) ***admit, possess, confess, permit***		-cian (c + ian) ***music, electric,* magic**	
	Noun maker (meaning act of, state of or result of) **Use if root ends in -ss or -mit**		**Noun maker (meaning one having a skill, job or ability of the root)** **Use if root ends in c or s**	
	depression	progression	musician	magician
	confession	recession	electrician	optician
	admission	regression	politician	physician
	expression	discussion	mathematician	
	possession	permission		
	procession	submission		

End Note

1. You can also use the 2014 English Curriculum Appendix 1 Spelling word list to find examples of further words for each year group.

Year 5 & 6[1]

Words in bold have phonics and/or spelling rules that relate to that year group or below. Words in red are on the list of 100 words in the National Curriculum that children in England are expected to be able to spell by the end of Year 6. *Highlighted words in italics* have more possibilities for word building and are in the suggested teaching sequence for word roots, with further word lists below for playing games and spelling lists.

Year 5 & 6		
	-cious (c + ious) ***grace, space,*** **malice**	**-tious (t + ious)** ***caution,*** **superstition**
	Adjective maker (when the root ends in ce – remove the e)	**Adjective maker (when the root ends in n – remove the n)**
	vicious gracious spacious officious malicious	rebellious repetitious superstitious cautious infectious nutritious
	-cial ***face,*** **office, prejudice, race**	**-tial** ***part, essence,*** **existence, evidence**
	Adjective maker (when the root ends in ace or a short vowel sound followed by ce – remove the e)	**Adjective maker (when the root ends in nce or t)**
	facial prejudicial beneficial official artificial racial commercial financial sacrificial	existential partial essential confidential evidential substantial inferential torrential sequential
	Exception: Spatial	
	-ant ***observe, expect,*** **tolerate, hesitate**	**-ance** ***attend, resist,*** **defy, guide**
	Adjective maker (when the root ends in t or ate – remove ate. **Often made from roots that can also be used with -ation)**	**Noun maker** **Used when related adjective ends in -ant** **Refers to action, state or quality**
	observant participant hesitant tolerant abundant distant dominant expectant pregnant buoyant	hesitance tolerance resistance brilliance attendance ignorance elegance arrogance alliance defiance distance guidance

-ent *depend, exist,* differ, solve	-ence *indulge, compete,* silent, reside
Adjective maker	Noun maker Used when related adjective ends in -ent Refers to action, state or quality
emergent, solvent, abhorrent, different, consistent, existent, strident, sufficient, resident, urgent, deficient	innocence, confidence, dependence, independence, indulgence, competence, existence, evidence, residence, interdependence, reference, difference, conference, excellence, convenience, silence
-ency *fluent, urgent* solvent	-ancy *hesitate, expect,* pregnant, infant
Noun maker Used when related adjective ends in -ent Refers to action, state or quality	Noun maker Used when related adjective ends in -ant Refers to action, state or quality
absorbency, emergency, solvency, consistency, fluency, urgency, sufficiency, deficiency	abundancy, flippancy, expectancy, hesitancy, pregnancy, buoyancy, infancy, truancy, redundancy
-able *Port (carry), enjoy, approach,* comfort, fix	-ible *struct (build), flex, sist (stand),*
Adjective maker Primarily used with Anglo-Saxon roots	Adjective maker Primarily used with Latin roots
readable, portable, reasonable, approachable, fixable, enjoyable, comfortable, explainable, understandable, teachable	accessible, illegible, flexible, destructible, visible, legible, credible, incredible, resistible, irresistible

	Add -ability to make a noun:	**Add -ibility to make a noun:**
	readability portability teachability	accessibility illegibility legibility destructibility flexibiliy credibility
	-able (drop e rule) ***Love, excite,* observe, desire**	**-ible (drop e rule)** **sense, force, *verse (turn),***
	Adjective maker **Primarily used with Anglo-Saxon roots**	**Adjective maker** **Primarily used with Latin roots**
	likable movable notable observable forgivable excitable desirable recognisable lovable	reversible irreversible forcible illegible legible collapsible sensible reducible resistible irresistible
	-ability ***Read***	**-ibility** ***cred (believe)***
	Noun maker	**Noun maker**
	likability reability notability excitability desirability portability	reversibility legibility collapsibility sensibility resistibility irresistibility
	-ably ***Reason, note,* forgive**	**-ibly** ***Leg (read)***
	Adverb	**Adverb**
	likably reasonably comfortably understandably notably desirably lovably forgivably observably	legibly sensibly incredibly flexibly forcibly irresistibly

End Note

1. You can also use the 2014 English Curriculum Appendix 1 Spelling word list to find examples of further words for each year group.

8. Lesson Plan Masters

With guidance

Photocopying these guidance sheets in colour is strongly recommended, and laminating them is desirable.

Day 1: Learning a new root (page 1 of 2)

Name:	**Year group/class:**	**Week no.:**	**Date:**
New word root: **Choose one – use planning**	**Word list:** Between 2–12 words containing this week's root depending on learner's speed and size of group. In the first few weeks there may only be 3 possible words		
Notes from previous lesson(s):	Write here anything that came up needing reinforcing or practice, any tricky words or morpheme		
Resources: Alphabet arc set out (set out before lesson using tactile letters), trigger cards, blank trigger card, Morpheme Cards (chosen in advance), book to write in, pencil/pen, ruler, highlighter pens (green, yellow, blue), **Word Agility** game & resources, text or book for **Word Espionage** (reading), Morph Mastercard			

Morphological Awareness (6 mins)	Targeted area:	Activity/game: This can be a few quick questions or a game. EG: Morph Match, Spinner Games for Morphological Awareness Development, Happy Families, Pairs Down Games may need adapting according to time
Notes: Choose a game from the appendix to match your targeted area directly from the assessment. Example: Targeted area: word relationships. Game: voice recorder game 1		

Test trigger cards (spell + meaning/function if relevant) (2 mins)

Any problems? Learners spell the **word** on the front of the trigger card. If forgotten or not correct, turn card over to use trigger on the back and make a note for future teaching.

Day 1: Learning a new root (page 2 of 2)

<table>
<tr>
<td>Word Root Work
(11 mins)

ROOT</td>
<td>Include previously taught affixes/root Use colour coding where possible. Reinforce with The Morph handshake to ensure this activity is kinaesthetic
• Introduce this week's root: Read it (use Morpheme Card or write it on whiteboard for pupil to read). What does it mean? Pupil makes it with tactile letters.
• What other words can you make with this root? Pupil uses Morpheme Cards (roots and affixes) to make them and say them each time using The Morph handshake.
• Learners make a portal in books for the root (keep Morpheme Cards in view). Include any other words learners can think of: limit this to words using today's root as long as they include known morphemes.
• Dictate the words for pupil to write. Highlight the root. Make a trigger card. The learners write the morpheme with a word on one side, and decide on a "trigger" to draw/ write on the back which will help them remember.
• Write the root on the Morph Mastercard (centre). On the centre page of the Mastercard, write it in the appropriate box for the initial letter of the root.</td>
<td>Word Agility: quick game – reading or spelling. Highlight one:
Morph Guess
Morph Match & Spell
Spin Words
Spin Words Trick
Spinner Match/ Dice Match
Spinner Match Trick
Voice Families (voice recorder)</td>
</tr>
</table>

<table>
<tr>
<td>Word Espionage (reading text)
(10 mins)</td>
<td>Learners read their individual reading books OR a text from a lesson - either previous or future lesson. They hunt morphemes and write them down in words on whiteboards, as well as any tricky words.</td>
<td>Morphemes found:
(If appropriate, adult picks a word for Word Mastery activity in Day 2.)
Choose one linked to current learning if possible. If no word from this text is appropriate, just choose a different word for Day 2.</td>
</tr>
<tr>
<td colspan="2">Any identified vocabulary? Note any interesting words containing taught or discussed morphemes.</td>
<td>Any tricky words identified?
Note any words the learners found difficult to read for future teaching.</td>
</tr>
</table>

<table>
<tr>
<td>Review with learner (1 min): What word root did you learn today? Which words are derived from this root? Which word did you find tricky to spell/understand? How will you remember it next time?</td>
</tr>
<tr>
<td>Adult Review</td>
</tr>
</table>

Day 2: Learning a new suffix/prefix (page 1 of 2)

Name:	**Year group/ class:**	**Week no.:**	**Date:**
Targeted Root (from Day 1): **New affix:** identified in planning	**Word list:** Choose 3–12 depending on pupil's ability and/or size of group (in early weeks fewer than this may be necessary). All the words should contain targeted affix and, if possible, include one or two using this week's root.		
Notes from previous lesson(s):	Write here anything that came up needing reinforcing or practice, any tricky words or morpheme.		
Resources: Alphabet arc set out (set out before lesson using tactile letters), trigger cards, Morpheme Cards (root and affix, chosen in advance), book to write in, pencil/pen, ruler, highlighter pens (green, yellow, blue), **Word Agility** game and resources, chosen word for **Word Mastery** (may have been chosen in **Word Espionage** section of Lesson 1), **Word Mastery** cards (choose a minimum of 2 cards), Morph Mastercard			

Morphological Awareness (8 mins)	**Targeted area:**	**Activity/game:** EG: Morph Match, Spinner games for Morphological Awareness Development, Happy Families, Pairs Down
Comment/notes: Choose a game from the appendix to match your targeted area directly from the assessment. For example: Targeted area decomposition of transparent morphemes. Game: spinner game 1		

Test trigger cards (read + meaning/function if relevant) (2 mins)
Any problems? Learners read the word on the front of the trigger card. If forgotten or not correct, turn card over to use trigger on the back and make a note for future teaching.

Day 2: Learning a new suffix/prefix (page 2 of 2)

Word Affix Work (14 mins)

Targeted affix:

Use colour coding where possible. Reinforce with The Morph handshake to ensure this activity is kinaesthetic.

- Introduce this week's affix. Read it (use Morpheme Cards or write it on the whiteboard for the pupil to read). What does it mean? Pupil makes it with tactile letters.
- What other words can you make with this affix? Aim to include this week's targeted root.
- Pupil uses Morpheme Cards (root and affix) to make them and say them each time using The Morph handshake.
- Pupils make a portal for the affix. Include any other words learner can think of.
- Dictate the words for pupil to write. Highlight the affix. Make a trigger card. The learners write the morpheme with a word on one side, and decide on a "trigger" to draw/write on the back which will help them remember.
- Write the affix on the Morph Mastercard (back page). Write the suffix or prefix in the relevant column along with the targeted root (Day 1).

Word Agility: spelling game Highlight one:

- Spinner Match
- Spinner Match Trick
- Spin Words
- Spin Words Trick
- Morph Guess
- Morph Connect
- Morph Match & Spell
- Stealth
- Voice Families

Word Mastery (5 mins)

Study a multi-morphemic word (at least 2 morphemes) linked to this week's root or affix, splitting it into its morphemes, considering its meaning and the meaning of its morphemes (if appropriate). The word may have been chosen in Lesson 1 from **Word Espionage** text. Use **Word Mastery** cards – choose 3 or more cards. Use word chosen from Lesson 1 **Word Espionage** activity (reading). Use word mastery cards – choose two or more depending on learners' ability. Learners ask the questions – prompt where necessary. Pupils may think of their own questions in addition.

Review with learner (1 min): What affix did you learn today? Which words can you make with this affix? Which word did you find tricky to spell/understand? How will you remember it next time?

Adult Review

Day 3: Word Agility Development (page 1 of 2)

Name:	**Year group/ class:**	**Week no.:**	**Date:**
Targeted Root (from day 1): Targeted Affix (from day 2):	**Word list:** Choose 6–12 words containing a combination of this week's root and affix.		
Notes from previous lesson(s):			
Resources: Alphabet arc set out (set out before lesson using tactile letters), trigger cards, Morpheme Cards (root and affix), **Word Agility** game and resources, prepared sentence and paper/computer for dictation, pen/pencil, highlighter pens (green, yellow, blue), a sample of pupils' writing for **Word Espionage**, Morph Mastercard			

Morphological Awareness (5 mins)	**Targeted area:**	**Activity/game:** e.g.: Morph Match, Spinner games for Morphological Awareness Development, Happy Families, Pairs Down
Comment/notes: Choose a game from the appendix to match your targeted area directly from the assessment. e.g.: Targeted area: production of words containing opaque morphemes. Game: Pairs Down game 1		

Test trigger cards (read or spell + meaning/function if relevant) (2 mins) Any problems? Learners spell the **word** on the front of the trigger card. If forgotten or not correct, turn card over to use trigger on the back and make a note for future teaching. **Morph Mastercard:** Any new words to add? Ask the learner to look for words in their class or home reading and writing that related to what they have been learning and interest them.

Word Agility: extended word building game (8 mins)	**Highlight 1:** Word Morph Word Craft Pairs Down Happy Families	**Notes:**

Day 3: Word Agility Development (page 2 of 2)

Writing (5 mins)	Sentence dictation. Sentence (prepared in advance):
The sentence should use words containing taught morphemes only – avoid using new or tricky words. Pupil must highlight all taught morphemes according to Morph Mastery colour coding (green = prefix, yellow = root, blue = suffix).	

Word Espionage (6 mins): Writing Check
Together, pupil and adult look through a piece of learner's class writing to search for morphemes. Look for what morphemes the pupil has used, and look for words/morphemes that have been taught. Point out any interesting patterns/rules/opaque morphemes (9 minutes) If there is time and opportunity, the learner and/or class teacher can choose the piece of writing together. Read it aloud and scan for taught morphemes or other morphemes that are interesting. Discuss and write down words that have been found. (Optional) Discuss which morphemes you could have used to make the words in the writing more interesting. Point out any spelling rules/interesting bits/opaque morphemes as appropriate to the pupil.
Comments/notes

Review with learner (4 min): What word root did you learn this week? What affix did you learn? Which words are derived from this root or affix? Which other morphemes have you learnt this week? What did you find tricky to spell and how will you remember it? Discuss the root and affix that you have learned this week. Write any related words of interest or tricky words in the appropriate box in the centre of the Morph Mastercard.
Adult Review

9. Lesson Plan Masters

Day 1: Learning a new root

Name:	Year group/class:	Week no.:	Date:
New word root:	Word list:		
Notes from previous lesson(s):			
Resources: Alphabet arc set out, trigger cards, blank trigger card, Morpheme Cards (chosen in advance), book to write in, pencil/pen, ruler, highlighter pens (green, yellow, blue), **Word Agility** game & resources, text or book for **Word Espionage** (reading), Morph Mastercard			

Morphological awareness (6 mins)	**Targeted area:**	**Activity/game:** e.g.: Morph Match, Spinner Games for Morphological Awareness Development, Happy Families, Pairs Down
Notes:		

Test trigger cards (spell + meaning/function if relevant) (2 mins) Any problems?

Word root work (11 mins) ROOT	Include previously taught affixes/root • Introduce this week's root: Read it (use Morpheme Card or write it on whiteboard for pupil to read). What does it mean? Pupil makes it with tactile letters. • What other words can you make with this root? Pupil uses Morpheme Cards (roots and affixes) to make them and say them each time using The Morph handshake. • Learners make a portal in books for the root (keep Morpheme Cards in view). Include any other words learners can think of. • Dictate the words for pupil to write. Highlight the root. Make a trigger card. • Write the root on the Morph Mastercard (centre).	Word Agility: quick game – reading or spelling. (Highlight one): Morph Guess Morph Match & Spell Spin Words Spin Words Trick Spinner Match/Dice Match Spinner Match Trick Voice Families (voice recorder)
Notes:		

Word espionage (reading text) (10 mins)	Book:	Morphemes found: (If appropriate, adult picks a word for Word Mastery activity in Day 2)
Any identified vocabulary?		Any tricky words identified?

Review with learner (1 min): What word root did you learn today? Which words are derived from this root? Which word did you find tricky to spell/understand? How will you remember it next time?
Adult review

Day 2: Learning a new suffix/prefix

Name:	**Year group/ class:**	**Week no.:**	**Date:**
Targeted root (from day 1): **New affix:**	**Word list:**		
Notes from previous lesson(s):			
Resources: Alphabet arc set out, trigger cards, Morpheme Cards (root and affix, chosen in advance), book to write in, pencil/pen, ruler, highlighter pens (green, yellow, blue), **Word Agility** game and resources, chosen word for **Word Mastery** (may have been chosen in **Word Espionage** section of lesson 1), **Word Mastery** cards, Morph Mastercard			

Morphological awareness (8 mins)	**Targeted area:**	**Activity/game:** e.g.: Morph Match, Spinner games for Morphological Awareness Development, Happy Families, Pairs Down
Comment/notes:		

Test trigger cards (read + meaning/function if relevant) (2 mins) Any problems?

Word affix work (14 mins) Targeted affix:	• Introduce this week's affix. Read it (use Morpheme cards or write it on the whiteboard for the pupil to read). What does it mean? Pupil makes it with tactile letters. • What other words can you make with this affix? Pupil uses Morpheme Cards (root and affix) to make them and say them each time using The Morph hand shake. • Pupils make a portal for the affix. Include any other words learner can think of. • Dictate the words for pupil to write. Highlight the affix. Make a trigger card. • Write the affix on the Morph Mastercard (back page).	**Word Agility**: spelling game. Highlight one: Spinner Match Spinner Match Trick Spin Words Spin Words Trick Morph Guess Morph Connect Morph Match & Spell Stealth Voice Families
Notes:		

Word mastery (5 mins) Targeted word:	Study a multi-morphemic word (at least 2 morphemes) linked to this week's root or affix, splitting it into its morphemes, considering its meaning and the meaning of its morphemes (if appropriate). The word may have been chosen in lesson 1 from **Word Espionage** text. Use **Word Mastery** cards – choose 2 or more cards.
Notes:	

Review with learner (1 min): What affix did you learn today? Which words can you make with this affix? Which word did you find tricky to spell/understand? How will you remember it next time?
Adult review

Day 3: Word Agility Development

Name:	Year group/class:	Week no.:	Date:
Targeted Root (from Day 1): Targeted Affix (from Day 2):	Word list:		
Notes from previous lesson(s):			
Resources: Trigger cards, **Word Agility** game and resources, prepared sentence and paper/computer for dictation, pen/pencil, highlighter pens (green, yellow, blue), a sample of pupils' writing for **Word Espionage**, Morph Mastercard			

Morphological awareness (5 mins)	**Targeted area:**	**Activity/game:** e.g.: Morph Match, Spinner games for Morphological Awareness Development, Happy Families, Pairs Down
Comment/notes:		

Test trigger cards (read or spell + meaning/function if relevant) (2 mins) Any problems? **Morph mastercard:** Any new words to add?

Word agility: extended word building game (8 mins)	**Highlight 1:** Word Morph Word Craft Pairs Down Happy Families	**Notes:**

Writing (5 mins)	Sentence dictation. Sentence (prepared in advance):
Notes:	

Word espionage (6 mins): Writing Check
Together, pupil and adult look through a piece of learner's class writing to search for morphemes. Look for what morphemes the pupil has used, and look for words/morphemes that have been taught. Point out any interesting patterns/rules/opaque morphemes (9 minutes).
Comments/notes:

Review with learner (4 min): What word root did you learn this week? What affix did you learn? Which words are derived from this root or affix? Which other morphemes have you learnt this week? What did you find tricky to spell and how will you remember it? Discuss the root and affix that you have learned this week. Write any related words of interest or tricky words in the appropriate box in the centre of the Morph Mastercard.
Adult Review

10. Meet the Masters

11. Morph Mastercard

These are the roots I already know and interesting derivatives

Aa	Bb	Cc
Gg	Hh	Ii
Mm	Nn	Oo
Ss	Tt	Uu V

Dd	Ee	Ff
Jj	Kk	Ll
Pp	Qq	Rr
Ww Xx	Yy	Z

Affixes I know with roots

Prefix	
Root	
Suffix	

Prefix	
Root	
Suffix	

Prefix	Root	Suffix

Morph Mastercard

Name: ________________

Class: ________________

12. Word Mastery Questions

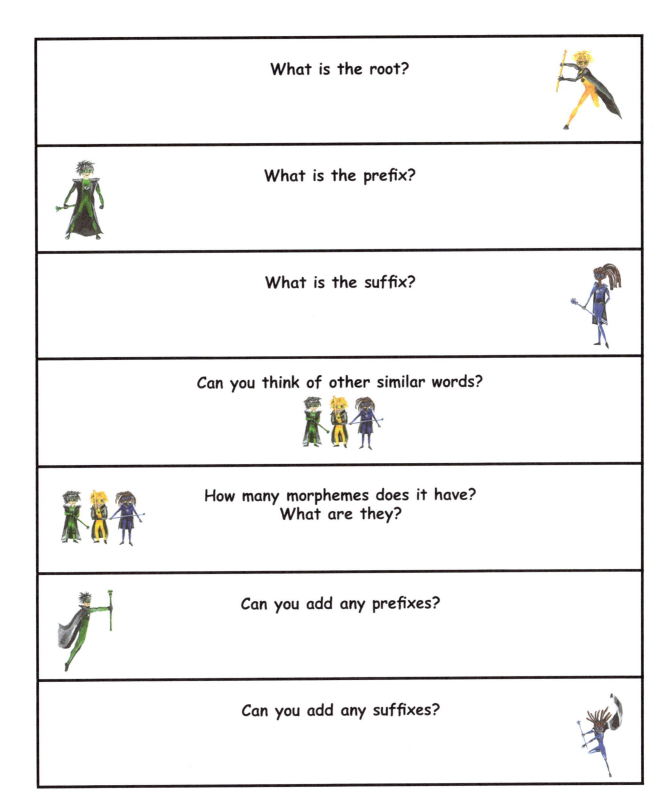

What is the root?
What is the prefix?
What is the suffix?
Can you think of other similar words?
How many morphemes does it have? What are they?
Can you add any prefixes?
Can you add any suffixes?

Word Mastery Questions
Can you change the root?
Can you change the prefix or suffix?
Has the root changed at all when the suffix was added?
What does the word mean?
What does the suffix mean/do?
What does the root mean?
What does the prefix mean?

13. Examples of phonologically opaque morphemes

When a phonologically opaque morpheme is added to a root, the root sounds different and cannot be easily detected by hearing. Sometimes, but not always, it is easier to detect the root visually, as the spelling is generally retained or only slightly changed.

Irregular plurals

calf – calves
child – children
foot – feet
goose – geese
half – halves
life – lives
loaf – loaves
man – men
person – people
sheep - sheep
tooth – teeth
woman - women

Changes in phoneme when affixing

Adding suffix does not add syllable but sound changes

five – fifth
heal – health
scribe – script

Changes in phoneme when affixing

Hard c becomes soft

elastic – elasticity
electric – electrician
magic – magician
music – musician
politics – politician

Changes in phoneme when affixing

Final sound changes with suffix

abuse – abusive
close – closure

Changes in phoneme when affixing

Changing t to c

accurate – accuracy
consistent – consistency
delicate – delicacy
evident – evidence
fluent – fluency
excellent – excellence
intelligent – intelligence
legitimate – legitimacy
literate – literacy
pirate – piracy
private – privacy
secret – secrecy
silent – silence
urgent – urgency
violent – violence

Changes in phoneme when affixing

-ion where end sound changes

admit – admission
collect – collection
compose – composition
compete – competition
comprehend – comprehension
concentrate – concentration
confess – confession
convert – conversion
create – creation
decide – decision
dictate – dictation
edit – edition
extend – extension
exclude – exclusion
expand – expansion
expel – expulsion
express – expression
hesitate – hesitation
include – inclusion
infect – infection
insert – insertion
intrude – intrusion
invite – invitation
perfect – perfection
permit – permission
present – presentation
produce – production
project – projection
success – succession
tense – tension
Relate – relation

Changes in phoneme when affixing

Suffix changes so stress is different

able – ability
advertise – advertisement
agile – agility
biology – biological
baptise - baptism
Catholic – Catholicism
Christ – Christmas
Christian – Christianity
combine – combination
company – companion
console – consolation
courage – courageous
criticise - criticism
divide – division, divisive
hero – heroism, heroic
hexagon – hexagonal
hostile – hostility
human – humanity
hypnotise – hypnotism

know – knowledge
library – librarian
mechanics – mechanism
miracle – miraculous
mobile – mobility
mystery – mysterious
national – nationality
octagon – octagonal
photograph – photography
please – pleasure
real - reality
resign – resignation
ridicule – ridiculous
sign – signature, signal
Spain – Spanish
super – superfluous, superlative
volcano – volcanic
wise – wisdom

Irregular verbs

build – built
buy – bought
creep – crept
draw – drew
drink – drank
eat – ate
forget – forgot
freeze – froze
go – went
grow – grew
hide – hid
learn – learnt
light – lit
make – made
pay – paid
rise – rose
run – ran
say – said
sell – sold
shine – shone
sink – sank
sleep – slept
slide – slid
sing – sang
speak – spoke
swim – swam
take – took
wake – woke

14. Morpheme Cards

Prefix and suffix

These should be photocopied onto double sided paper or card and laminated. Sample pages are printed in this appendix; all pages can be downloaded from www.routledge.com/cw/speechmark.

Morpheme Cards Prefix and suffix (sample pages): download all pages from companion website

un-	-s	-es
-ing	-ed	-er
-est	-ment	-ness

Y1 blue, Y2 orange, Y3/4 green, Y5/6 purple

Morpheme Cards Prefix and suffix (sample pages): download all pages from companion website

Morpheme Cards Prefix and suffix (sample pages): download all pages from companion website

-ful	-ly	-less
-ation	-ly	-ous
dis-	mis-	in-

Y1 blue, Y2 orange, Y3/4 green, Y5/6 purple

Appendix 14: Morpheme Cards prefix and suffix

Morpheme Cards Prefix and suffix (sample pages): download all pages from companion website

Morpheme Cards Prefix and suffix (sample pages): download all pages from companion website

il-	im-	ir-
re-	sub-	inter-
super-	anti-	auto-

Y1 blue, Y2 orange, Y3/4 green, Y5/6 purple

Morpheme Cards Prefix and suffix (sample pages): download all pages from companion website

-ant	-ance	-ancy
-ent	-ence	-ency
-able	-ably	-ible

Y1 blue, Y2 orange, Y3/4 green, Y5/6 purple

Morpheme Cards Prefix and suffix (sample pages): download all pages from companion website

Morpheme Cards Prefix and suffix (sample pages): download all pages from companion website

-ibly	-y	-es
-ed	-er	-est
-ing		

Y1 blue, Y2 orange, Y3/4 green, Y5/6 purple

Morpheme Cards Prefix and suffix (sample pages): download all pages from companion website

Morpheme Cards Roots Year 1

cat	day	school
friend	fix	wish
train	mark	cook

Morpheme Cards Roots Year 2

move	place	rude
fit	kind	great
care	harm	pain

Morpheme Cards Roots Year 2 (sample pages): download all pages from companion website

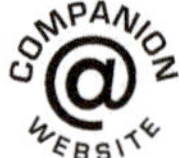

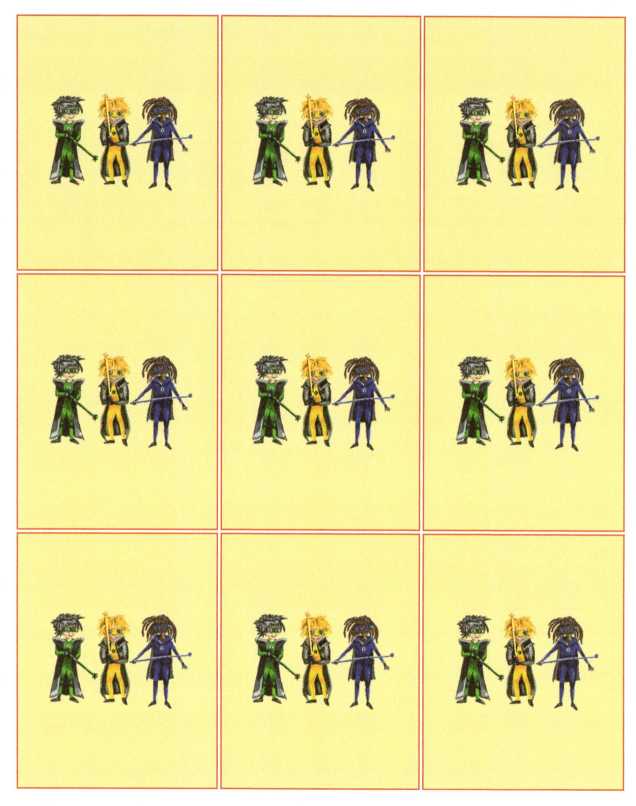

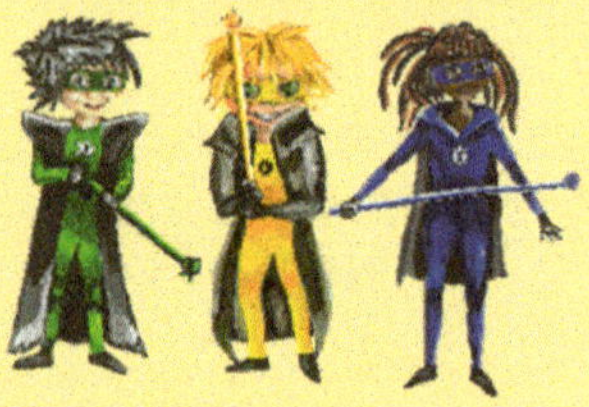

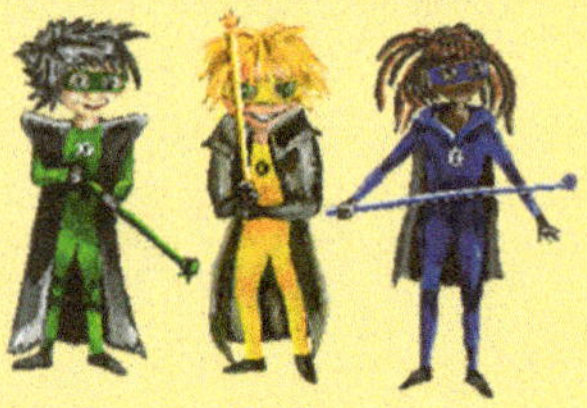

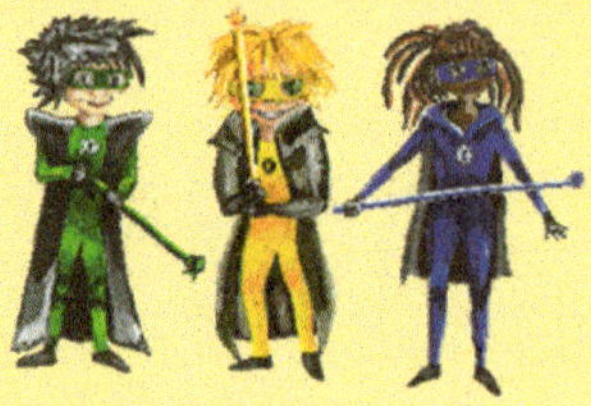

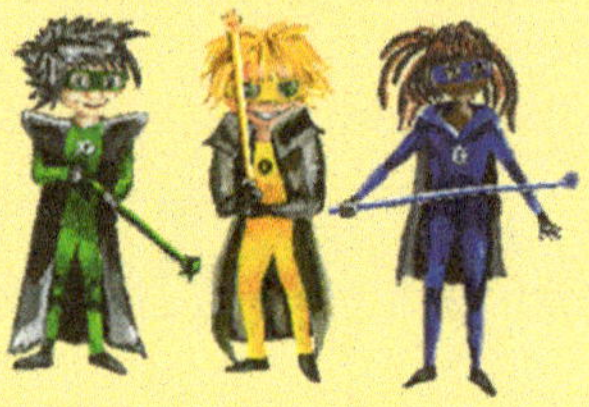

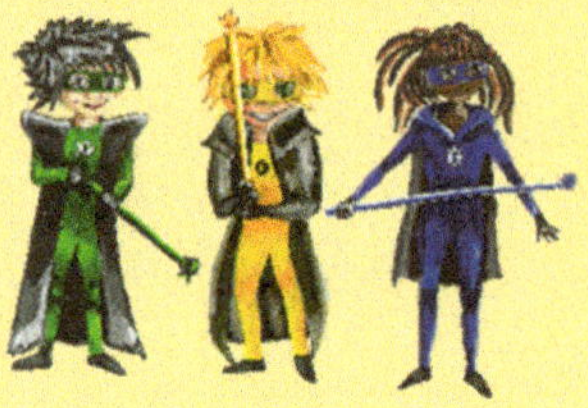

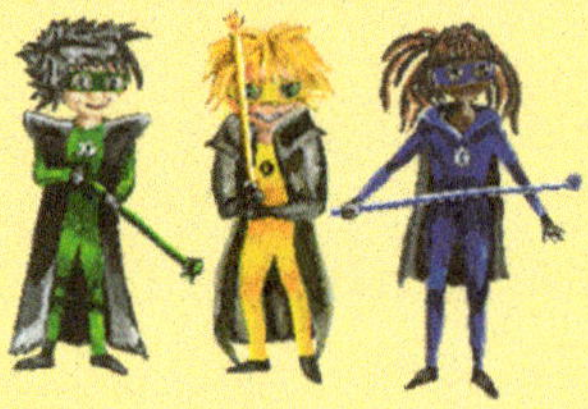

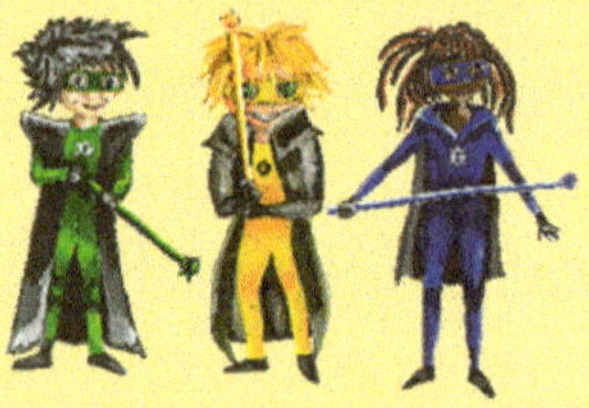

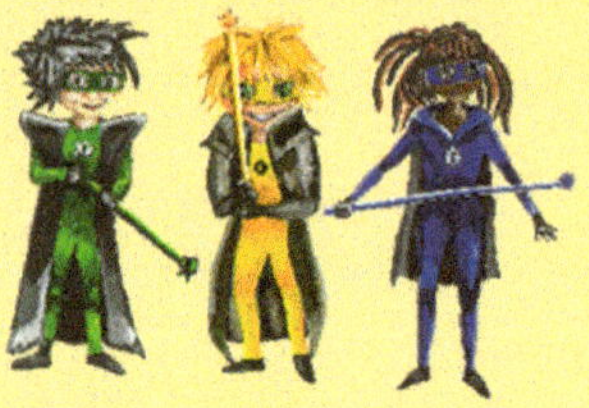

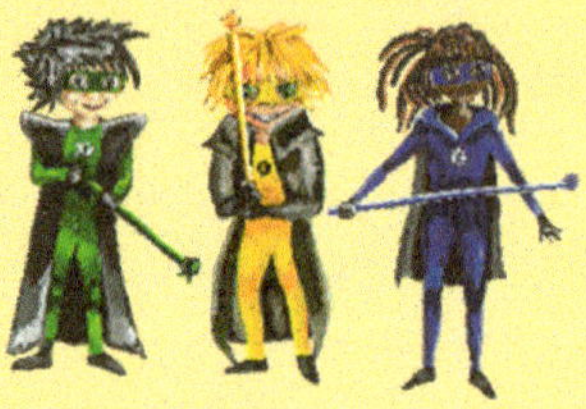

Morpheme Cards Roots Year 3 & 4

agree	obey	cover
like	honest	heart
lodge	own	please

Morpheme Cards Roots Year 5 & 6

vice	grace	space
sist	malice	rebel
repeat	stit	caution

COMPANION
@
WEBSITE

15. Latin and Greek

Meanings and derivatives

LATIN ROOTS		
Root	**Meaning**	**Derivatives**
anni, annu	year	annual, anniversary, biannual
aud	hear	audible, auditory, audio, audit, audition
cede, cess	to go or surrender	access, excess, precede, interceded, recede success, process
cise	cut	concise, decide, incisor, precise, scissors
conus	cone	conical, cone, conifer
cred	believe	credit, credible, creed, accredited, discredit
dict	say or tell	contradict, dictate, diction, dictionary, verdict
duct	lead	abduct, conduct, deduction, induction, reduction, production
fact, fect	do or make	affect, infect, defect, refectory, fact, factory, confectionery, artefact
fer	to bear or yield	confer, defer, differ, different, ferry, fertile, infer, offer, prefer, refer, suffer, transfer
fid, fide	trust or faith	confide, confident, fidelity, federal, infidelity, bona fide, diffident, perfidious, defy
fin	finish, end	final, infinity, define, refine, confine, finite
flect, flex	to bend or curve	flex, deflect, reflect, flexion, reflex, flexible
grat	a favour	grateful, gracious, grace, gratitude, graceful
form	shape	inform, formation, reform, deformed, unformed, uniform, conform, perform, formulate, formula, transform
fortis	strong	fort, comfort, fortune
fuse	pour	infuse, refuse, defuse, fusion
ject	throw	eject, abject, dejected, inject, interject, object, project, subject, trajectory

LATIN ROOTS		
Root	**Meaning**	**Derivatives**
judic	judge	judge, prejudice, judicial, judiciary
jur, jus	lay or right	jury, just, justice, adjust, conjure, justify
leg (al)	of the law	legal, illegal, legislate, legitimate, privilege
leg (ible), lect	to read or speak	legible, legend, dialect, lecture, lectern, elect
lit	letters	alliteration, literal, literature, literate, obliterate, literacy, literary
medic	to heal	medicine, medicinal, medical, paramedic
merge	to dip, immerse	submerge, emerge, emergency
mit, miss	to send	admit, dismiss, submit, omit, emit, permit, transmit, commit, mission
mob	to move	mobile, promote, demote, automobile, mobility, mobilize
pare	to make ready	prepare, parent, pare, compare
pati	to suffer	patient, compatible, sympathetic, pathetic
ped	foot	pedal, pedicure, pedestrian, pedestal, centipede, millipede, pedicure, pedometer
pend	hang or weigh	pend, depend, dependent, impending, expensive, pendant, pendulum, suspend, pension, pensive, appendix, compensate, dispense, indispensable. appendage,
plore	search	explore, implore
ply	fold	apply, comply, plywood, multiply, imply
pose	put, place, set	impose, compose, depose, deposit, dispose, expose, impose, oppose, position, positive, propose, purpose, suppose
port	carry	export, import, portable, port, airport, deport, portal, important, porter, reporter, support, transport, portfolio, teleport
scrib	write	scribe, script, scribble, inscribe, scripture, describe, transcribe, prescribe, subscribe
rotare	spin	rotate, rotary, rota, rotation
rupt	tear	interrupt, rupture, erupt, abrupt, corrupt, disrupt, bankrupt

LATIN ROOTS		
Root	**Meaning**	**Derivatives**
sanus	healthy	sane, insane, sanity, sanitary
sect	cut	section, dissect, insect, intersect, sector, segment
sens	feeling	sensation, sentiment, nonsense, sensitive
sist, stit, sta	stand	assist, consist, distant, insist, resist, subsistent, substitute, superstitious
solve	loosen or release	solve, solvent, dissolve, resolve, insolvent, solution, dissolution,
spect, spec	see or watch	aspect, respect, expect, inspect, perspective, prospect, specify, spectacle, spectator, suspect
spire	breathe	inspire, expire, perspire, conspire, respiration, aspire, spirit, transpire
struct	to build	construct, destruct, instruct, structure, reconstruct, instrument, obstruct
tend, tens	stretch or strain	tension, attend, extend, distend, contend, intent, intense, tent, pretend, intentional
tract	draw or pull	tractor, traction, retract, distract, abstract, extract, protractor, attract, detract, contract
vent	come	invent, advent, adventure, event, eventually, prevent, intervene, convenient, convent
viv, vit	life	survive, revive, vitamin, vivid, vivacious, vital, revitalise, vivarium
vid, vis	see	view, evident, divide, visible, provide, video, visit, visual, revise, supervise, television
voke	call	evoke, invoke, provoke, revoke, vocal, vociferous, advocate, vocation, vocabulary

LATIN PREFIXES		
Prefix	**Meaning**	**Derivatives**
a-	on or in	around, asleep, await, alive, across
ab-	from or away	abduct, abject, absent, abrupt, abuse
ad-	to, toward, near, in	adventure, adverb, advise, admit, adjust
anti-	opposite or against	antifreeze, antisocial, antibiotic, anticlimax,
bene-	well or good	benefit, benefactor, benediction
bi-	two	biannual, bicentenary, bicycle, biceps, biplane, binocular
cent-	hundred	cent, centigrade, centimetre, centipede, century
circum-	around or about	circumference, circumstance, circumnavigate
con-, com-	together, with	condense, conform, conscript, confer, concave, concise, compare, commit, compile, compose, compartment
contra-	against	contradict, contraband,
counter-	opposite, contrary	counterpart, counterculture, counterbalance
de-	down or away from	decamp, deformed, deport, debug, deflect
dec-	ten	decade, decagon, December, decathlon, decimal
dis-	not, apart	disconnect, discontinue, dislike, distend
ex-, e-	out	export, extract, extend, expire, express, eject, elect, erupt, evoke
in-, il-, im-	in, on or toward	infer, infect, illuminate, implore, impose,
in-, il-, im-, ir-	not	insensitive, indirect, insane, illegal, illegible, immobile, immoral, irregular, irrelevant
inter-	between	interact, interrupt, interject, interview
intro-	in or inward	introvert, introduce
mal-	bad, badly	malfunction, maladapted, malware, malpractice, malicious, malnutrition
mille	thousand	millennium, millennial, millipede, million
mis-	wrong, wrongly, bad, badly	misadventure, misspell, mislead, misuse
nona-, nove	nine	nonagenarian, nonagon, November
oct-	eight	octagon, octagonal, October, octogenarian, octopus

LATIN PREFIXES		
Prefix	**Meaning**	**Derivatives**
per-	through	perform, permit, persist, perfume, perspective
post-	after, behind	postscript, postmark, postdate
pre-	before, earlier	predict, predate, prepare, prejudge, prevent, prefer, preheat
pro-	forward, earlier	produce, promote, provide, provoke, production, process
re-	back or again	rebound, recall, reclaim, recount, reflect, revise, refresh, rejoice, reverse, revive
quad-	four	quadbike, quadrilateral, quarter, quadruple, quartet
quint-	five	quintet, quintuplet, quintuple
re-	back or again	reject, refer, recount, refresh, resist, revive
se-	apart, aside, without	secret, secure, sedate, select, sever
sept	seven	September, septet, septuagenarian
sex-	six	sextet, sextuple
sub-	under	subway, subscribe, submerge, submit, subtract, subject, subhuman
trans-	across, beyond	transfer, transcribe, transform, transport
tri-	three	triangle, triceratops, tricycle, tripod
un-	not, the opposite of or to undo	unfair, unformed, unsafe, unlearn, unlock, unhappy
uni-	one	unicycle, uniform, universe, unicorn

LATIN SUFFIXES
(most Latin suffixes have a grammatical function and can be found on the Word lists for planning in Appendix 7)

Suffix	**Meaning**	**Derivatives**
-age	collection, relationship	baggage, coinage, drainage, mileage, wreckage
-dom	quality, state of	boredom, kingdom, freedom, stardom, wisdom
-ess	feminine	actress, duchess, governess, lioness
-ette	small or diminutive	brunette, cigarette, statuette, rosette, maisonette
-hood	condition or state	boyhood, brotherhood, childhood, likelihood, manhood, neighbourhood
-ship	skill, office, quality	authorship, readership, friendship, partnership, leadership, citizenship, workmanship

GREEK COMBINING FORMS (These can be used as prefixes, suffixes or roots. Where marked with –, they are usually used as prefixes, e.g. auto-. Sometimes suffixes are added to these combining forms.)		
Morpheme	**Meaning**	**Derivatives**
ast	star	astrology, astronomy, asteroid, astronaut, asterix
auto-	self	autism, autobiography, automatic, autograph, autopsy, automatic, automobile
bio	life	antibiotic, biography, biology, bionic
cycl	wheel or circle	cycle, cyclist, bicycle, unicycle, cyclone, recycle, tricycle
di-	two	digraph, dioxide
dyn	power, force	dynamo, dynamic, dynamite, dynasty
dys-	bad or difficult	dyslexia, dyscalculia, dysfunctional, dysentery
eco	house or home	economy, ecology, economic, ecological
geo-	earth	geography, geology, geometry, geothermal
giga-	billion	gigabyte, gigahertz, gigametre
graph	written or drawn	autograph, choreography, graphic, graph, graphite, grapheme, bibliography
hemi-, demi-, semi-	half	hemisphere, semicircle, semi-final, semicolon, semiconscious
hect-	hundred	hectare
hept-	seven	heptagon, heptathlon
hex-	six	hexagon, hexameter
kilo-	thousand	kilogram, kilometre, kilowatt
kritikos	judge or decide	critic, critical, criticise, criteria, critique
mega-	million, large, great	megabyte, megawatt, megaphone
mono-	one	monocle, monochrome, monocycle, monopoly, monarch, monastery, monosyllabic, monotony
para-	beside, position	parallel, parachute, paralysed, paraphernalia, paradox, paralegal, paramedic
pent-	five	pentagon, pentathlon
photo	light	photograph, photogenic, photosensitive
poly-	many	monopoly, polygon, monopolize

GREEK COMBINING FORMS (These can be used as prefixes, suffixes or roots. Where marked with –, they are usually used as prefixes, e.g. auto-. Sometimes suffixes are added to these combining forms.)		
Morpheme	**Meaning**	**Derivatives**
scope	watch or see	periscope, stethoscope, scope, telescope, kaleidoscope, horoscope
syn-	together or with	synagogue, syndicate, syndrome, synergie
tele-	distant	telegraph, telephone, television, telescope, telepathy, teleport, telegram
tetra-	four	tetragon, tetrahedron
ter-	three	tertiary, tercentenary
therm	heat, hot	thermal, thermometer, thermostat

16. Morpheme Cards

Additional Latin and Greek

These should be photocopied onto double sided paper or card and laminated. Sample pages are printed in this appendix; all pages can be downloaded from www.routledge.com/cw/speechmark.

Prefix and suffix additional Latin and Greek

a-	ab-	ad-
bene-	circum-	con-
contra-	counter-	de-

Morpheme cards prefix and suffix - additional Latin and Greek (sample pages)

Roots Year 3 & 4 additional Latin and Greek

agree	obey	cover
like	honest	heart
lodge	own	please

Words in black type originate from Old English, French or Italian.

Words in red type originate from Latin

Words which are underlined originate from Greek

COMPANION
@
WEBSITE

Roots Year 5 & 6 additional Greek and Latin

vice	grace	space
sist	malice	rebel
repeat	stit	caution

Words in black type originate from Old English, French or Italian.
Words in red type originate from Latin.

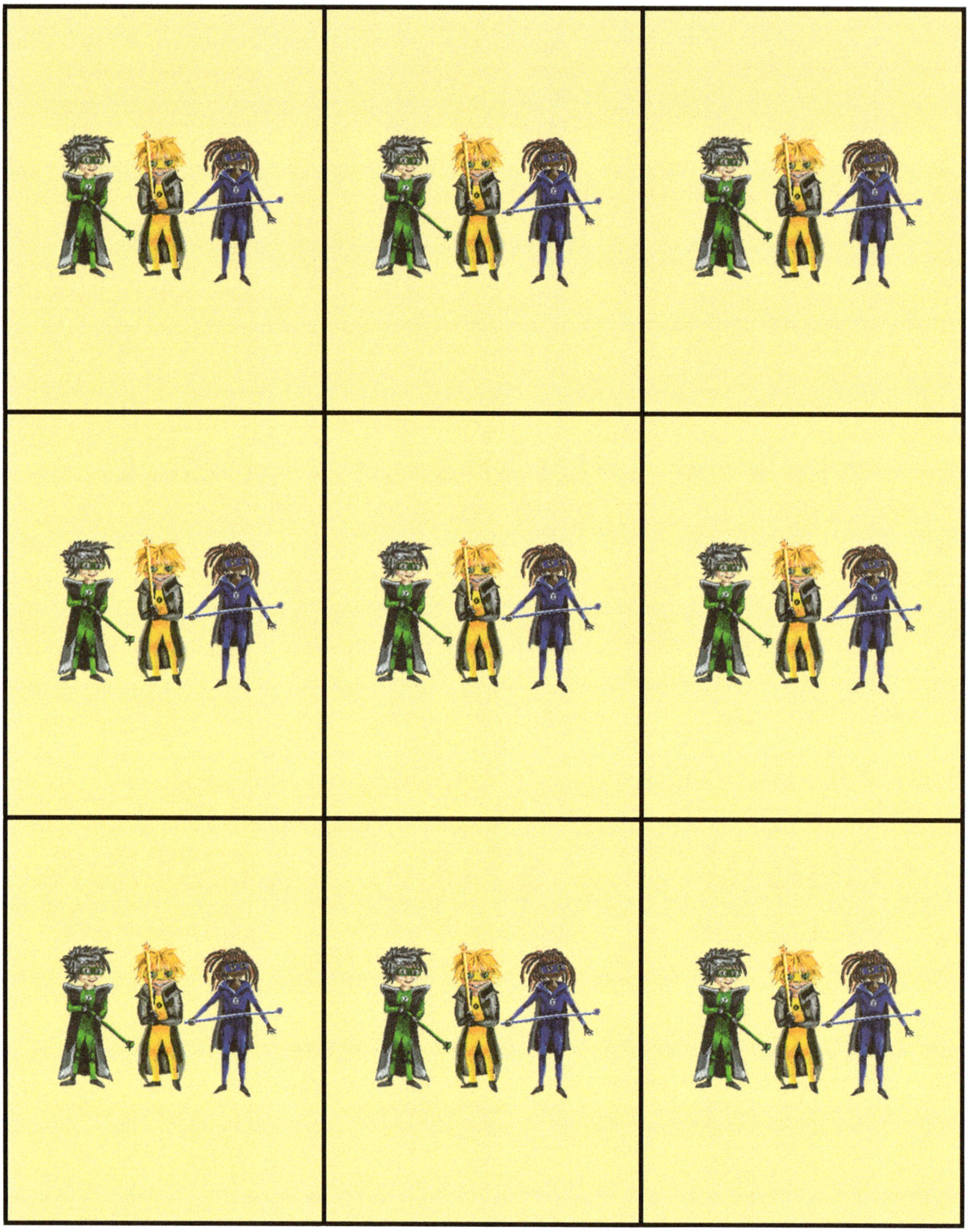

Morpheme cards roots Year 5 & 6 - additional Latin and Greek (sample pages)

17. Impact data

About the Wechsler Individual Achievement Test 3rd Edition for Teachers

This test battery consists of subtests in **Reading Comprehension, Word Reading, Oral Reading Fluency** and **Spelling**. All the scores achieved by the pupils in the pilot are presented on the table in Figure A16.1. In the **Reading Comprehension** test, which measures an individual's ability to understand text, the learner is required to read three passages either aloud or silently. After each passage, s/he is asked questions about it. In the **Word Reading** test, which measures a learner's ability to read words in isolation, s/he reads a list of words out of context. The **Oral Reading Fluency** test measures a combination of speed and accuracy when reading passages. The learner reads two passages, and the reading is timed, with errors recorded. Three scores are obtained for this test. **Reading Speed** and **Reading Accuracy** are measured, and these are combined to make an **Oral Reading Fluency** score. The **Spelling** test measures an individual's ability to spell words out of context.

Three types of score are provided, along with descriptors, for each sub-test. These are:

- **Standard score:** this measures the learner's performance against other learners of the same age. A standard score of 100 is the mean, or average, and a score between 85 and 115 is within the average range, representing 68% of the population. Learners making expected progress would hold the same standard score – it is not expected to improve over time.
- A **percentile:** this offers a form of "ranking". A percentile score of 40 would indicate that the individual performed better than 39% of other individuals of the same age. 60% would have scored higher. Percentiles are linked to standard scores, and as such would not be expected to improve over time.
- **Reading age or spelling age:** the age equivalent represents the age at which a particular score is obtained by the average pupil. For example, if the average raw score of a pupil aged 10 years and 0 months on a spelling test is 40, any pupil with a raw score of 40 will have a spelling age of 10 years and 0 months. In contrast with standard scores and percentiles, reading and spelling ages are expected to improve over time, as the individual gets older.

Individual test results and progress (WIAT 3T)

			Reading Comprehension						Word Reading					
Pupil name	**Year group**	**Weeks of intervention**	**Reading age: entry**	**Reading age: final**	**SS / %ile: entry**	**SS / %ile: final**	**Descriptive band: entry**	**Descriptive band: final**	**Reading age: entry**	**Reading age: final**	**SS / %ile: entry**	**SS & %ile: final**	**Descriptive band: entry**	**Descriptive band: final**
Elsie	5	12	9:0	19:1	99/47	117/87	Mid Average	Above Average	8:0	8:8	91/27	93/32	Mid Average	Mid Average
Mary	6	9	10:0	17.0	100/50	111/77	Mid Average	High Average	9:4	9:4	95/37	91/27	Mid Average	Mid Average
Matty	5	11	6:8	13:8	79/8	107/68	Well Below Average	Mid Average	9:8	10:4	105/63	106/66	Mid Average	Mid Average
Tamsin	6	9	8:4	15:0	89/23	105/63	Low Average	Mid Average	6:8	7:0	70/2	70/2	Well below average	Well Below Average
Ivan	6	9	7:0	8:8	78/7	92/ 30	Well below Average	Mid Average	6:8	10:0	70/2	92/30	Well Below Average	Mid Average
Nathan	5	9	8:4	15:0	94/34	109/73	Mid Average	Mid Average	6:8	7:0	77/6	75/5	Well Below Average	Well Below Average

Oral Reading Fluency						Spelling					
Reading age: entry	**Reading age: final**	**SS & %ile: entry**	**SS & %ile: final**	**Descriptive band: entry**	**Descriptive band: final**	**Spelling age: entry**	**Spelling age: final**	**SS & %ile: entry**	**SS & %ile: final**	**Descriptive band: entry**	**Descriptive band: final**
7.8	8:8	89/23	95/37	Low Average	Mid Average	8:0	8:8	90/25	93/32	Mid Average	Mid Average
8:4	9:4	89/23	92/30	Low Average	Mid Average	7:8	8:4	83/13	85/16	Below Average	Low Average
9:8	10:4	104/61	106/66	Mid Average	Mid Average	8:8	9:8	96/39	101/53	Mid Average	Mid Average
6:8	7:0	66/1	68/2	Very Low	Very Low	7:4	9:0	76/5	86/18	Well Below Average	Low Average
7:8	8:8	76 5	80/9	Well Below Average	Below Average	6:4	7:8	67/1	74/4	Very Low	Well Below Average
9:8	10:8	104/61	107/68	Mid Average	Mid Average	7:4	7:8	82/12	83/13	Below Average	Below Average

Scores show progress during the 6-month period between initial and final testing. Reading ages are represented as years: months. SS refers to standard score. %ile refers to percentile. Scores which are highlighted indicate where more than expected progress has been made (accelerated progress).

Individual test results and progress (non-standardised Morph Mastery tests)

This table shows individual test results using the non-standardised tests within Morph Mastery: **Morphological Awareness, and Knowledge of Morphemes** for reading and spelling.

			Morphological Awareness			Knowledge of Morphemes (Reading)			Knowledge of Morphemes (Spelling)			Total Score		
Pupil name	Year Group	Weeks of Intervention	Entry Score /50	Final Score /50	Progress	Entry Score /50	Final Score /50	Progress	Entry Score /50	Final Score /50	Progress	Entry Total score /150	Entry Final Score	Progress
Elsie	5	12	31	45	14	45	47	2	21	42	21	97	134	37
Mary	6	9	41	47	6	47	49	2	31	46	15	119	142	23
Matty	5	11	34	43	9	44	50	6	37	49	12	115	142	27
Tamsin	6	9	47	48	1	36	47	11	19	45	26	102	140	38
Ivan (group)	6	9	16	28	12	48	48	0	13	32	19	77	108	31
Nathan (group)	5	9	28	40	12	41	44	3	10	43	33	79	127	48

Combined test results: combined test results: average progress

Figure A16.3 shows average progress in each of the subtests of the WIAT 3T.

	Average increase in age equivalent (shown in months)	Average increase in standard score (shown in SS points)	Average increase in percentile
Reading Comprehension	80	17	38
Word Reading	10	3	4
Oral Reading Fluency	10	4	6
Spelling	11	5	7

Combined accelerated progress

Test	Targeted Area	% of learners who made accelerated progress in age equivalent*
WIAT3 T	Reading Comprehension	100
	Word Reading	50
	Oral Reading Fluency	83
	Spelling	83
		% of learners who made accelerated progress compared with 6 months prior to intervention**
Teacher Assessment	Reading	67%
	Writing	50%

*Age equivalents were considered to indicate accelerated progress if they increased in more months than the number of months that had passed chronologically.

** According to teacher assessment, the progress made in the six months following the initial Morph Mastery assessments was compared with the progress each learner made in the six months prior to the initial Morph Mastery assessments. If the rate of progress, according to teacher assessment, had increased, the learner was considered to have made accelerated progress.

18. Useful resources

Essential

1. **Voice recorders:** you will need **either:**

    - Two voice recorders with at least six easily accessible buttons, for example Chatterbox Recordable Cube (TTS) or Talking Photo Album (TTS)
    - **Or** at least 12 recordable sound buttons/individual voice recorders, for example Talking Point Recordable Sound Buttons (TTS), Clever Tiles (TTS), Voice Pads (Talking Products) or Talking Tins (Talking Products)

2. **Spinners:** widely available but Clear Spinners from Crossbow Education have been used for the Morph Mastery templates. You will need two of these for the intervention.
   For larger groups or whole classes, there are a variety of online spinners available as an alternative.
3. **Trigger cards:** it's recommended to have these in green, yellow and blue. Make your own or purchase from Partners in Education, who also supply rings to hold them together.
4. **Tactile letters:** you'll need several sets of the alphabet. There are many suppliers of these, but Smart-kids supply magnetic foam letters in a dyslexia friendly font
5. **Alphabet arc:** these are available from Smartkids or LDA.
6. **Whiteboards and pens**
7. **Green, yellow and glue highlighters**
8. **Storage for morpheme cards:** either use a rectangular prism shaped chocolate tin (After Eights are the perfect size) or a collector's album for trading cards (e.g. Match Attax or Pokemon) – available on Amazon. You'll need to sort them into alphabetical order.
9. **Optional resources:** Word Building Dominoes by Learning Resources, also available on Amazon, Cross-bow Education, Partners in Education
   Sand and/or glitter & tray, playdough, plasticine, play putty, and other tactile resources.
10. **Websites:**

    www.crossboweducation.com
    www.ldalearning.com
    www.partnersineducation.co.uk
    www.smartkids.co.uk
    www.talkingproducts.com
    www.tts-group.co.uk

19. Glossary

Term	Meaning
Affix	The umbrella term for all prefixes and suffixes (Chapter 5)
Assess-Plan-Do-Review	The cycle of intervention identified in the UK SEND Code of Practice: 0 – 25 Years (2015)
Common Exception Word	Words which do not follow the usual spelling rules, e.g. phonics, or words which are spelled in rare ways
Decoding	Using your knowledge of written letters and the sounds they make to read words
Encoding	Using your knowledge of sounds and how they are written to spell words
Metacognition	Thinking and talking about learning
Metalinguistic skills	Thinking and talking about words and language
Morpheme	A term for any single unit of meaning within a word. It can be a root, prefix or suffix (Chapter 1, 5)
Morpheme Cards	Cards used in every lesson representing morphemes
Morphological Awareness	The awareness of, and ability to manipulate, morphemes within words (Chapter 5)
Morphological skills	The ability to recognise and manipulate morphemes within words
Morphology	The system of language by which words can be broken up into morphemes (Chapter 1)
Multi-sensory	Say it, make it, hear it, do it, move it, see it (Chapter 4)
Opaque morpheme (phonologically opaque)	Morphemes which cannot be easily detected within a spoken word. For example, the /z/ sound at the end of ***close*** (as in close the school) changes to a different sound in ***closure***. The hard c in ***politics, magic***, and ***music*** becomes soft in ***politician***, ***magician*** and ***musician*** (Chapter 5)

Overlearning	Practice, practice and more practice! In Morph Mastery this is targeted specifically to practise what has been taught and what is not yet mastered (Chapter 4)
Percentile	A type of standardised score which offers a form of "ranking". A percentile score of 40 would indicate that the individual performed better than 39% of other individuals of the same age. 60% would have scored higher (Appendix 17)
Phoneme	A spoken unit of sound
Phonics	A method of teaching reading and spelling by linking spoken sounds with letters systematically
Phonological Awareness	The ability to discriminate and manipulate speech sounds. It involves hearing, identifying and playing with them (Chapter 1)
Phonologically Opaque Morphemes	See Opaque Morphemes
Phonology	The system of language by which words are broken up into units of sound called phonemes (Chapter 1)
Planning Precisely	2 options: 1. Planning that follows the principle that if something is not known, it needs to be explicitly taught. Precision planning uses specific assessments to decide what to teach 2. Planning that follows the principle of sticking to what the pupils know, ***except*** the thing you are teaching. In other words, the only challenge is the targeted piece of learning; nothing else should be new or difficult (Chapter 4)
Portal	A three columned table representing the morphemes in a word. The concept is that morphemes can be "inputted" with multiple possibilities of their "output"
Prefix	A single unit of meaning (morpheme) which is placed in front of a root. For example, the prefix ***re-*** can be added to the root ***take*** to create the word ***retake***. Prefixes are not words in themselves (Chapter 1, 5)

Root	The purest unit of meaning within a word, once prefixes and suffixes are removed. It is the most basic form of a word. Roots can be words that we know and use in their own right, e.g. help. They can also derive from Greek or Latin (Chapter 1, 5)
SMART targets	Specific, Measurable, Achievable, Realistic and Time Limited targets
Specific Learning Difficulties	An umbrella term to describe difficulties in certain skills, for example spelling, reading, writing, number calculations. Dyslexia is a specific learning difficulty
Standard Score	A type of standardised score which measures an individual's performance against other learners of the same age. A standard score of 100 is the mean, or average, and a score between 85 and 115 is within the average range, representing 68% of the population (Appendix 17)
Suffix	Suffixes, like prefixes, are not words in their own right, but units of meaning (morphemes) which are placed at the end of the word (Chapter 1, 5)
The M Factor	A phrase used to describe the meaningful craft of words in Morph Mastery (Chapter 1)
The Morph	A secret 3 step handshake designed for use only by Morph Masters and Morph Masters in training (Chapter 1 & 9). Each step of The Morph represents one of the morphemes in a word
The Morph Mastercard	A card used to aid transference of learning into class and to support recall of previous learning Prefix | Root | Suffix Morph Mastercard Name: ________ Class: ________
Transparent Morpheme (phonologically transparent)	Morphemes which can be easily detected within a spoken word. For example, if you hear the word ***unhelpful*** you can hear all three morphemes ***un-***, ***help*** and ***-ful***. (Chapter 5)

Trigger Cards	Flashcards used in every lesson to support overlearning – 1 trigger card is made for every morpheme taught 
Word Agility	Playing games and conducting experiments with word structures and meanings. Word agility involves constructing, deconstructing, comparing and transforming words (Chapter 3). In Morph Mastery, Word Agility games are spelling and reading games (Chapter 10)
Word Espionage	The act of being a spy when reading and writing text, done on Day 1 in reading texts and Day 3 in writing. See Chapter 9 for more information (Chapter 3)
Word Mastery	The study of words and their parts, done on Day 2 (Chapter 3)
Word Mastery Question Cards	The cards used for Word Mastery 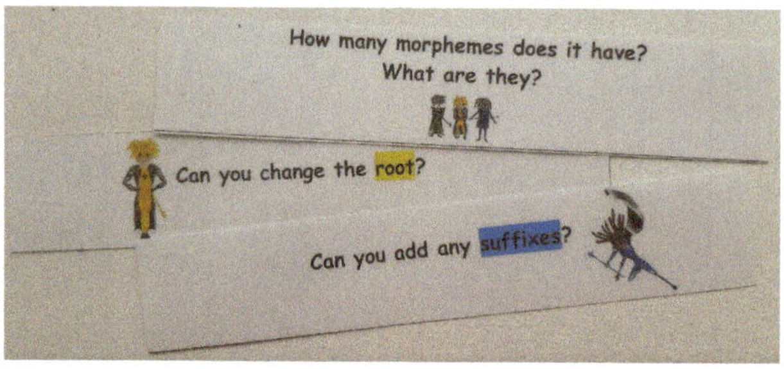
Working Memory	The ability to store information whilst working on it (Chapter 2)

Index